FLORIDA'S HISTORY THROUGH ITS PLACES
Properties in the National Register of Historic Places

COMPILED BY

Morton D. Winsberg
Department of Geography
Florida State University

PREPARED BY

Florida Resources and Environmental Analysis Center
Institute of Science and Public Affairs
Florida State University

IN COOPERATION WITH

Bureau of Historic Preservation
Division of Historical Resources
Florida Department of State
Sandra B. Mortham, Secretary of State

August 1995

Library of Congress Catalog Card Number: 87-083334

Distributed by the
University Press of Florida

University Press of Florida
15 Northwest 15th Street
Gainesville, FL 32611

Cover by Bill Celander

ii

STAFF

Elizabeth D. Purdum
Managing and Manuscript Editor

Peter A. Krafft
Production Director

Christopher D. Wilkes
Production Specialist

Iris Kahrmann
Map and Layout Preparation

Tanya McKay
Research Assistant

Shell Kimble
Production Assistant

James R. Anderson, Jr.
Director
Florida Resources and Environmental Analysis Center

ACKNOWLEDGMENTS

Elizabeth Kirby, formerly with the Florida Department of State, Division of Historical Resources, proposed the first edition of this catalog published in 1988 and from its inception worked hard to facilitate its completion. Edward A. Fernald, Associate Vice President for Academic Affairs and Director of the Institute of Science and Public Affairs at Florida State University, provided staff and was instrumental in obtaining funding for this edition. Funds for printing the catalog were provided by the Florida Department of State, Division of Historical Resources. Many persons from the Department of State helped make this second edition a reality. Special thanks are extended to George Percy, Jim Miller, Scott Edwards, Barbara Mattick, and Bill Celander.

PHOTOGRAPHIC CREDITS

Below are credits for photographs and drawings. All illustrations used may be found in the site files maintained by the Division of Historical Resources in Tallahassee. Those without specific attribution may also be found in the site files. Credits are given by page number and position on page: (U)pper, (M)iddle, and (L)ower.

Melanie Barr, 123U.
William C. Bauer, 78L.
Phil Brodatz, 25L.
Richard Brunck, 11U, 11L.
Ann Bynre, 2U.
E.W. Carswell, 133L.
David Cleveland, 112U.
Glenna Dame, 115U.
Judy Davis/D. Vedas, 37, 40L.
DeFuniak Springs Chamber of Commerce, 132L.
Dan G. Deibler, 32L, 64L.
Lewis Ellsworth, 54L.
Mary K . Evans, 7U, 21M, 26L .
J. Walter Fewkes, Preliminary Archeological Explorations at Weeden Island, Florida (Smithsonian Miscellaneous Collections 76, 1924), 101U.
Florida Department of Commerce, 81U.
Florida Department of Commerce, Florida News Bureau, 25U, 82U, 106L, 131U.
Florida Department of State, Division of Historical Resources, Bureau of Archaeological Research, 72U (photo), 72L, 121U.
Florida Department of Natural Resources, Division of Recreation and Parks, 21U.
Florida Park Service, 128L.
Florida Photographic Archives, 23U, 23M, 28U, 34M, 36M, 40M, 43U, 44L, 47M, 48U, 49L, 59M, 59L, 67L, 109M, 129L.
Florida Trust for Historic Preservation, 20M.
Dan Forer, 29.
Mildred L. Fryman, 62L.
Alan Gantzhorn, 115.
A. Green, 95U.
Stephen Hale, based on photo, University of Florida Map Library, 91M.
Howard Hansen, 97L.
Harper's Weekly, February 9, 1861, 47M.

Karl Holland, Florida Department of Commerce, Florida News Bureau, 85M.
Lynn M. Homan, 98.
Indian Temple Mound Museum, 86U.
Diana Jarvis, 43L.
Ken Johns, 75M.
Johnny Johnson, Florida Department of Commerce, 69U.
B. Calvin Jones, 65U, 72U (drawing).
Ron Jones, 70U.
Jim Kern, 27U.
Kurt T. Kivyk, 8L.
David Knox, 56.
Janet Kodras, 84L.
Lakeside Inn, 66L.
Mary F McCahon, 55M.
John McCarthy, 117U, 117M, 117L, 118M, 118L, 119U.
John L. Markham, 102M.
Elizabeth B. Monroe, 76U.
Clarence B. Moore, Certain Aboriginal Mounds of the Florida Central West Coast (Academy of Natural Sciences of Philadelphia, 1903), 15L.
NASA, 8M.
Jane Plante, 87M.
James Quine, 110L.
Rock Gate, 24L.
Ivan A. Rodriguez, 31U, 33U.
Gary Shapiro, 73L.
Bruce Sherwood, 88.
Carl Shiver, 97U.
Stan Smith, 1L.
Ray Stanyard, 71L.
Robert Steinbach, 111M.
Robert Taylor, National Park Service, Southeast Archeological Center, 19L.
Thomas W. Taylor, 125U.
U.S. Coast Guard, 13.
U.S. Navy, 82L.
Virginia Vanneman, 58L.
Paul L. Weaver, 7L, 38U, 41L,111U.
C. Randolph Wedding, 100L.
Phillip A. Werndli, 96M.
Phillip Whitley, National Park Service, 108L.
Morton D. Winsberg, 31M, 34L, 35L, 42L, 55U, 57L, 58U, 59U, 74L, 90L, 95U, 100U, 104L, 109U.
Michael Zimny, 18L.

CONTENTS

The National Register of Historic Places vi
Use of the Catalog vii
The Settlement of Florida ix
The Properties xv
The Counties xvi
Alachua County 1
Baker County 6
Bay County 7
Bradford County 7
Brevard County 8
Broward County 11
Calhoun County 13
Charlotte County 14
Citrus County 15
Clay County 16
Collier County 18
Columbia County 19
Dade County 20
De Soto County 34
Dixie County 35
Duval County 35
Escambia County 43
Flagler County 47
Franklin County 48
Gadsden County 49
Hamilton County 51
Hardee County 51
Hendry County 52
Highlands County 52
Hillsborough County 54
Indian River County 61
Jackson County 62
Jefferson County 63
Lake County 65

Lee County 67
Leon County 69
Levy County 75
Liberty County 75
Madison County 76
Manatee County 76
Marion County 78
Martin County 80
Monroe County 80
Nassau County 84
Okaloosa County 86
Okeechobee County 86
Orange County 86
Osceola County 89
Palm Beach County 90
Pinellas County 95
Polk County 102
Putnam County 106
St. Johns County 108
St. Lucie County 112
Santa Rosa County 113
Sarasota County 115
Seminole County 121
Sumter County 122
Suwannee County 123
Taylor County 123
Union County 124
Volusia County 124
Wakulla County 131
Walton County 132
Washington County 133

Appendix: Properties Categorized by
Function and Listed Chronologically 134

THE NATIONAL REGISTER OF HISTORIC PLACES

The National Register of Historic Places is an outgrowth of the National Historic Preservation Act of 1966, which sought to protect the nation's cultural heritage. The register is the nation's comprehensive list of historic properties. In Florida the Bureau of Historic Preservation, which is in the Division of Historical Resources, within the Department of State, in coordination with various federal and state agencies, initiates field surveys and research to identify properties and determine their eligibility for entry in the register. The bureau processes nomination proposals received from local preservation agencies and organizations and interested individuals, and prepares nominations recommended by the Florida National Register Review Board. Nominations are submitted to the Keeper of the National Register in Washington, D.C., for final decision and official listing of the historic resource. As of November 15, 1994, there were 1020 listings within Florida in the National Register (740 buildings, 95 archeological sites, 126 historic districts, and 59 miscellaneous). In all there are 96,000 sites of historical or archaeological significance for which reports have been filed within the state. Local governments, nonprofit organizations, businesses, and academic institutions, as well as concerned individuals participate both in the survey work and the nomination of properties to the register. Owners of National Register properties are eligible for various economic incentives to encourage preservation of structures of historical interest. The National Register program also gives recognition to local governments for their participation in National Register-related activities, gives special attention to archaeological sites and to federally owned historic properties, and supports nonprofit preservation groups through the National Trust for Historic Preservation.

In order to be designated to the register properties must normally have achieved historical significance at least 50 years before and must have maintained their historical integrity in respect to design, setting, material, and workmanship. Properties may qualify by one or more of these criteria: (1) association with events in the nation's history; (2) association with the lives of persons who have played significant roles in the nation's past; (3) embodiment of the distinctive characteristics of a type, period, or method of construction, or representation of the work of a master, or possession of high artistic value, or existence as a significant and distinguishable entity whose components may lack individual distinction; and/or (4) they have yielded, or may be likely to yield, archaeological information important in prehistory or history.

For further information on the nomination of properties to the National Register write

State Historic Preservation Officer
Division of Historical Resources
Florida Department of State
R.A. Gray Building
Tallahassee, FL 32399-0250

USE OF THE CATALOG

Descriptions of the properties and sites have been standardized with information given in an established order. Properties are first grouped alphabetically by place within the county. The property is followed by the address and the year the major structure or structures on the property were built, or in the case of sites and districts, their periods of importance. For archaeological sites these dates are often rough approximations. For a building, the description includes its architectural style and, if known, the architect. For earlier buildings the person who designed the structure may not have been a professional architect. Height of the building, material, and outstanding details follow. Where appropriate a statement of the historical and/or architectural significance is given. Whether the property is within the private or public domain is included. It should be remembered that most properties are not open to the public and to be visited will require permission from their owners or, in the case of public properties, the responsible agency. The year the property was placed on the National Register (N.R.) concludes the description.

Information for this catalog was taken from the National Register nomination forms on file within Florida's Bureau of Historic Preservation as of November 15, 1994. Some properties have now been on the register for more than 20 years. Since their nomination, an undetermined number of structures on these properties have been greatly altered or through fire or demolition destroyed and the Bureau of Historic Preservation never notified. The compiler visited approximately one-third of the sites in December 1987. Through visits as well as contact with regional and county preservation boards and local historical societies, efforts have been made to provide a contemporary description. Some structures within the catalog, however, may no longer exist or may have been moved to another site. Most photographs used as illustrations in this catalog are found in the site's nomination file kept in the Bureau of Historic Preservation in Tallahassee.

This catalog can provide information for interesting self-guided field trips, whereby the state's past is revealed through its places. In addition, visiting a number of sites within a large metropolitan area will illuminate changes in the city's neighborhoods, since many of the older buildings are in sections of the city which have experienced severe economic decline. If the reader chooses to look at a number of sites within a large metropolitan area, it is suggested that the reconnaissance be made on a Sunday or holiday, when there is less likely to be traffic congestion.

THE SETTLEMENT OF FLORIDA

A brief account of the settlement of Florida follows. To illustrate aspects of that settlement, properties placed in the National Register for their historical or architectural significance have been cited, with the counties in which they are situated. These properties are only representative, and through use of the catalog and thematic appendix that follow, other examples of settlement for most periods can be found that are near the reader and can be conveniently visited. It must be emphasized, however, that many properties are privately owned and to be visited will require permission of their owners.

Florida's First People

The first among the many millions of people who have moved to Florida were the Indians, who migrated into the peninsula more than 12,000 years ago. At this time the peninsula was larger and drier than it is today and its plants and animals much different. Mastodons, camels, mammoths, saber cats, giant sloths, bisons, and horses roamed vast grasslands. Florida's first inhabitants were highly nomadic, moving, probably in small family groups, in search of big game. Hundreds of stone projectile points similar to Clovis and other Paleo-lndian points from elsewhere in the U.S. have been found in north Florida river beds. Springs (Warm Mineral Springs and Little Salt Spring, Sarasota) have also yielded, and continue to yield, valuable information.

As large game animals became extinct, the Indians began to depend more on smaller game and shellfish. Gradually the climate became more humid and the sea level rose. Indians began making pottery, often an indicator of at least a partially sedentary way of life. From the Archaic period (6500 B.C.– 1000 B.C.) a greater number of archaeological sites are found (Windover, Brevard; Kimball Island Midden and Bowers Bluff Midden, Lake). The sites are considerably larger and their materials more varied than sites from the earlier Paleo-lndian period; for instance the Kimball Island Midden in Ocala National Forest is 700 feet by 390 feet and 17 feet high, and the Windover site has yielded fabric, jewelry, tools, and utilitarian items as well as human brain tissue and bones.

The Formative period (1000 B.C.– A.D. 1300) in Florida was characterized by much more regional diversity than previous periods. Archaeologists have used various styles and types of pottery as ways of distinguishing the various cultures. Indians began burying their dead in mounds along with elaborate goods (Crystal River Mound, Citrus; Ft. Walton Mound, Walton; Weeden Island, Pinellas). Agriculture was developed during this time although Indians in the southern part of Florida continued a fishing-hunting-gathering economy until European contact.

By A.D. 1000 changes began to occur in some parts of present-day Florida as the influence of the Mississippian tradition—which encompassed much of the Southeast—spread south. Cultivation of beans, corn, and squash intensified in the north, and population increased in in-land areas. During this period Florida's Indians established trade and cultural relations with Indians as far away as the lower Mississippi Valley and the Midwest. Some villages featured ceremonial mounds and plazas (Lake Jackson Mounds, Leon) similar to those raised in the same period in the Mississippi and the Ohio river valleys. On the coasts remains of man-made canals and levees may be seen (Pineland Site, Lee).

At least 100,000 Indians, perhaps several times more, were living in Florida in 1500. The most densely populated area was in the vicinity of present-day Tallahassee where the Apalachee numbered at least 25,000. The various tribes of the Timucua numbered at least 40,000. Indians had no resistance to European diseases and many died in the early years of contact.

The Europeans

The most immediate concern of the Spanish when they first reached Florida in 1513 was to find things of value. Although Juan Ponce de León, leader of the first expedition, is popularly believed to have been in search of the Fountain of Youth, in reality he was much more interested in finding precious metals and Indians who could be carried off as slaves to mine gold on the Caribbean islands. In 1539 the huge Hernando de Soto expedition, commissioned to explore North America, landed in Tampa Bay (De Soto National Memorial, Manatee). From there the group began its long and fruitless search for riches in North America. In 1539, at a site within today's Tallahassee, the expedition is believed to have celebrated the first Christmas Mass on the North American continent (Governor John W. Martin House, Leon).

Spain's interest in the New World focused on its most promising regions for valuable minerals or for raising profitable export crops. Florida had neither, nor were the Indians tractable enough to be used as peasants on large haciendas, like those established in Mexico, Central America, and the Andes. But for its

Florida Milestones

14,000 B.C. Big game hunters from the north settle Florida

1000 B.C.– A.D. 1500 Flourishing Native American cultures

1513, April 2 Ponce de León lands on east coast and names "La Florida"—land of flowers

1528 Pánfilo de Narváez expedition

1539 Hernando de Soto expedition

1559 Tristan de Luna establishes Pensacola; abandoned 2 years later

1564 Frenchman René de Laudonnière establishes colony at mouth of St. Johns River

1565 Spaniard Pedro Menéndez de Avilés destroys French settlement and founds St. Augustine

1600s Spanish missions established in Indian lands across north Florida

1704 Last of missions destroyed by Colonel James Moore from Carolina

1700s Indians from South—later known as Seminoles—begin to settle in Florida

1763 Britain acquires Florida from Spain

1783 Britain returns Florida to Spain for the Bahamas

1816–1818 First Seminole War; Andrew Jackson invades Florida

1819 Spain cedes Florida to the U.S.

1821 U.S. acquisition of Florida completed; Andrew Jackson becomes 1st territorial governor

1824 Tallahassee chosen as capital; cotton plantations thrive between the Apalachicola and Suwannee rivers

1835–42 2nd Seminole War

1845, March 3 Florida becomes state

1848 Dr. John Gorrie of Apalachicola invents 1st ice-making machine

1860 Railroad completed between Fernandina and Cedar Key

1860–80 Population grows from 140,000–270,000

1861, January 10 Florida secedes from Union

1875 Publication of Sidney Lanier's *Florida: Its Scenery, Climate, and History*

1880s Vincente Martinez Ybor brings cigar industry to Tampa

1894 Flagler's railroad reaches Palm Beach

1894–95 Frosts force citrus industry south from north central Florida

1901 Great Fire nearly destroys Jacksonville, Florida's largest city

1925 481 hotels and apartment buildings rose on Miami Beach

1928 Marjorie Kinnan Rawlings arrives in Cross Creek; Ernest Hemingway arrives in Key West; hurricane kills thousands when dike around Lake Okeechobee collapses

1969 July 16, Apollo 11 lifts off Pad A at Cape Kennedy on journey to moon

strategic significance to Spain, Florida would have been totally ignored. Spain's presence on the Florida Peninsula was vital in order to protect its ships from pirates. French Huguenots reached the area in 1562 and quickly established a settlement (Fort Caroline National Memorial, Duval). The Spanish reaction was to send an expedition led by Pedro Menéndez de Avilés, which in 1565 intercepted the French and massacred over 300 (Fort Matanzas National Monument, St. Johns). Menéndez then founded St. Augustine, which became the first permanent settlement on the North American continent (St. Augustine Historic District, St. Johns). Eventually a large stone fort was built to protect this small outpost of the Spanish Empire (Castillo de San Marcos National Monument, St. Johns). Although most concerned with Florida's northeast coast, Spain, to keep other European nations out, established its presence elsewhere. In the interior, from St. Augustine to where Tallahassee is today, Franciscan missionaries founded a number of missions to serve the Indians (San Luis de Apalache, Leon). A small fort was raised at the mouth of the St. Marks River (San Marcos de Apalache, Wakulla), and later a military garrison was posted at Pensacola (Fort Barrancas Historic District, Escambia).

Spain's power in Europe greatly weakened during the 18th century. At the beginning of the 18th century British colonists to the north with their Indian allies attacked and destroyed the Franciscan missions and even laid an unsuccessful siege to the then new stone fort at St. Augustine. By 1710 Florida's native Indian population was almost completely destroyed. During the 1700s Indians from other parts of the Southeast— who would later become known as Seminoles—began to move into Florida. The British actually gained control of Florida between 1763 and 1783, and in that short period did more to develop it than in the almost two centuries of Spanish occupation (Fish Island Site, St. Johns). The Spanish, however, regained Florida in 1783, an indirect consequence of the winning of independence by the United States. After Spain regained Florida, it made a number of large land grants to Americans, in the mostly unfulfilled hope that they would become loyal Spanish subjects (Kingsley Plantation, Duval). Throughout the Second Spanish Period, the increasingly more powerful Americans raided Florida for escaped slaves and to subdue the Indians, whom they considered a threat to their Alabama and Georgia settlements. One of the most spectacular confrontations was in 1816, when an American military force engaged a large group of blacks and Indians who, armed by British traders, were defending the Negro Fort (Fort Gadsden Historic Memorial, Franklin). When the fort's powder magazine exploded, several hundred of its defenders were killed.

Territory and Statehood

In 1821 Spain finally faced the inevitable and relinquished sovereignty of Florida to the United States (Plaza Ferdinand II, Escambia). Initially far better land was available in the nation's Midwest and comparatively few who wished to farm chose to migrate to Florida. Nonetheless, some did come to engage in agriculture. Tallahassee, midway between, Pensacola and St. Augustine, was established as the territorial capital (Florida State Capitol, Leon). The site of Tallahassee was within the territory's most promising agricultural area, located between the Apalachicola and Suwannee rivers. Here planters from other states arrived with their slaves and began to cultivate cotton. Classical Revival architectural styles have become synonymous with southern plantation homes, and this part of Florida has many rural and urban antebellum residences of that style (Lyndhurst Plantation, Jefferson; the Columns, Leon; and Judge P.W. White House, Gadsden). Poor whites, who could not afford to own slaves also arrived, and built more modest residences (Burnsed Blockhouse, Baker; and Lavalle House, Escambia).

Efforts to settle peninsular Florida were complicated by the presence of Seminole Indians, who vigorously resisted incursion into their territory. Three wars were fought with the Indians. By their conclusion Indians had burned a number of sugar plantations near the St. Johns River (Bulow Plantation Ruins, Flagler; New Smyrna Sugar Mill Ruins, Volusia; and Dunlawton Plantation-Sugar Mill Ruins, Volusia), and battles between the U.S. Army and the Indians had been fought (Dade Battlefield Historic Memorial, Sumter; Fort Cooper, Citrus; Fort Foster, Hillsborough; and Okeechobee Battlefield, Okeechobee). In 1845, three years after the end of the Second Seminole War, Florida became a state. By the end of the Third Seminole War in 1858 the Indian population was reduced to 100 to 300 individuals living in the Everglades. Gradually, with the Indians removed American settlement of the peninsula advanced (Newnansville Town Site, Alachua; and Micanopy Historic District, Alachua). The environment, however, was so uninviting that, except for a handful of intrepid frontier cattlemen who settled in the Kissimmee River Valley and a small group of Leon County cotton planters who established sugar plantations in Manatee County (Robert Gamble House, Manatee; and Braden Castle, Manatee), few participated in this frontier movement .

Even before the Civil War, Key West had emerged as Florida's largest city (Key West Historic District, Monroe), and throughout the 19th century only lost the lead once, to Pensacola in 1860. Its strategic significance was recognized early, and the United States government invested heavily in its defense

Llambias House, St. Augustine, St. Johns County, late 18th century, excellent example of local architectual style.

(Fort Zachary Taylor, Monroe; and Fort Jefferson National Monument, Monroe). Florida's Atlantic coast as well as its keys had acquired a reputation since colonial times as being dangerous for shipping, and many ships had foundered on their reefs and bars (Spanish Fleet Survivors and Salvors Camp Site, Indian River; San Jose Shipwreck Site, Monroe; and Indian Key, Monroe). At great expense lighthouses were built to protect shipping (Cape Florida Lighthouse, Dade; Carysfort Lighthouse, Monroe).

Florida entered the Civil War with only about 140,000 inhabitants, approximately half of whom were black. The vast majority of people still lived in its northern counties. The state's major contributions to the war effort, aside from a large share of its young white male population who went off to fight, were beef cattle and salt. To prevent trade the Union immediately blockaded Florida's coast and seized Key West, which it held throughout the war. Other Florida ports were intermittently occupied by Union troops, and on occasion the Confederates would resist these incursions (Yellow Bluff Fort, Duval). When Union forces tried to penetrate the interior to cut off the state's supply lines to Georgia, the Confederates inflicted severe damage. In 1864 they defeated a large Union force attempting to enter the state's interior from Jacksonville (Olustee Battlefield, Baker), and in 1865 a Union force which landed near St. Marks (St. Marks Lighthouse, Wakulla) was defeated on its march toward Tallahassee (Natural Bridge Battlefield, Leon).

Following the war Union occupation of Florida awakened the nation to its economic opportunities, and many who came from the north with the armed forces, or who later arrived to govern it, chose to remain. By the latter half of the 19th century technology was beginning to make the state's peninsular resources of much greater significance. Railways penetrated down the peninsula after the Civil War, and riverboats began to more intensively utilize the St. Johns River system. At the beginning of the Civil War, only 6 percent of Florida's inhabitants lived south of Gainesville, but by the end of the century, the share of the population south of Gainesville had risen to 28 percent.

Turn of the Century

Towns throughout Florida began to reflect the prosperity brought by the new economic connections with other states. Those Floridians who prospered after the Civil War usually chose to display their wealth in the manner of their peers elsewhere in the nation. Neighborhoods with large and stately Classical and later Victorian style homes grew throughout the state (Ocala Historic District, Marion; Quincy Historic District, Gadsden; Hyde Park Historic District, Hillsborough; and Fernandina Beach Historic District, Nassau). As elsewhere the most popular Victorian style in Florida was the Queen Anne. Of all the Queen Anne homes in the state on the National Register, over half were built between 1890 and 1900. Classical architectural styles, so popular among the wealthy of North Florida before the Civil War, also were prized throughout the state well into the 20th century. Of all the classical homes built in Florida in the National Register, 40 percent were antebellum, but the popularity of this style was revived in the 20th Century when another 40 percent were built. Even in South Florida classical styles were common, often with clever adoption of local building materials and modifications to meet the near tropical conditions (Halissee Hall, Dade; and Sample Estate, Broward).

Many homes of less affluent Floridians also have survived. They are of interest for their use of design elements to accommodate the severity of the state's long and hot summers (Moseley Homestead, Hillsborough; Marjorie Kinnan Rawlings House, Alachua; West Tampa Historic District, Hillsborough; South Lake Morton Historic District, Polk; and North Hill Preservation District, Escambia). Also, scattered throughout Florida there remain many simple frame churches, commonly built in the Gothic style (All Saints' Episcopal Church, Volusia).

Florida's improved economic environment can be seen in the styles chosen for governmental and commercial buildings. The state's capitol had been transformed from a small vernacular building to an imposing classical style structure (Florida State Capitol, Leon). Courthouses were often regarded by county elected officials as symbols of local prosperity. On the National Register are courthouses in Bradford, Clay, Hendry, and Osceola counties, and a jail in Hamilton County. In Key West the post office was built in Richardsonian Revival style and is regarded as the finest example of that popular Victorian design within the state (Old Post Office and Customhouse, Monroe). The spirit of the times can be seen today in Arcadia (Arcadia Historic District, De Soto), as well as

in many buildings scattered throughout the state (Rogers Building, Orange).

Vernacular governmental and commercial buildings far outnumbered those built using Classical or Victorian design. Few remain today, since in their simplicity they were commonly regarded as expendable and demolished to make room for newer structures. Nonetheless, in Wakulla County an old frame courthouse survives (Old Wakulla Courthouse, Wakulla) and elsewhere are frame rural stores (L.S. Pender General Store, Jackson; Bradley's Country Store, Leon; William Anderson General Store, Dade; and Ted Smallwood Store, Collier).

In the last quarter of the 19th century tourism grew rapidly. Even before the Civil War St. Augustine and later Jacksonville began to attract winter visitors, but only after the war did the wealth of enough Americans rise sufficiently so that it was profitable for Floridians to invest in tourist facilities to attract them. The two great railroad men of Florida, Henry Flagler (Henry Morrison Flagler House, Palm Beach) and Henry Plant began to construct hotels. The most ambitious project was that of Flagler, who endeavored to turn St. Augustine into the "Riviera of America" (St. Augustine Historic District, St. Johns; Model Land Company Historic District, St. Johns). Employing imaginative young architects and new building techniques, he built several outstanding hotels within the city (Hotel Ponce de Leon, St. Johns), and as his railway advanced down the east coast, others as well (Breakers Hotel Complex, Palm Beach). Plant

Old Hendry County Courthouse, La Belle, Hendry County, 1927, weather and market reports vital to the county agricultural economy are still placed on a blackboard on the front veranda.

American National Bank Building, Pensacola, Escambia County, 1908+, a product of a boom period in the city's history and the tallest building in Florida when completed.

followed a similar plan for the Gulf coast, and although he built others, his two outstanding hotels must be mentioned (Tampa Bay Hotel, Hillsbrough; Belleview-Biltmore, Pinellas).

Manufacturing never has been of great importance within Florida's economy. During the antebellum period there were only a handful of cotton and saw mills (Arcadia Mill Site, Santa Rosa) and milltowns (Bagdad Village Historical District, Santa Rosa). After the War, in large part as a result of the rise in the national demand for cigars and deteriorating political conditions in Cuba, Cuban cigar manufacturers began to move their factories to Key West (Eduardo H. Gato House, Monroe). Later, labor costs became so high within that city that the manufacturers moved to Tampa, where they attracted cheap Hispanic and Italian labor (Ybor Factory Building, Hillsborough; Ybor City Historic District, Hillsborough; El Centro Español of West Tampa, Hillsborough), and to St. Augustine (Solla Cacaba Cigar Factory, St. Johns).

Modern Florida

Florida's cities began to assume a more modern appearance after the turn of the century. By then Jacksonville had become the "gateway" to the state, as reflected in its impressive train station (Jacksonville Terminal Complex, Duval), and had overtaken Key West as the state's largest city. The city's downtown, which had largely been burnt during a fire in 1901, was undergoing reconstruction, the architect Henry J. Klutho playing a major role (Dyal-Upchurch Building,

Duval; St. James Building, Duval). The construction of modern office and store buildings was reshaping other downtowns as well as that of Jacksonville (American National Bank Building, Escambia; and Tampa City Hall, Hillsborough).

Enthusiasm for Florida as a place to live, but more importantly as a place to visit, escalated in the early 20th century, and in the pre-World War II period peaked between 1920 and 1926, a time which has come to be known as the "Florida Land Boom." In those six years approximately 30 percent of the 741 buildings within Florida presently listed in the National Register were built. Enthusiasm to build was found throughout the state, but it was greatest on the southeastern and southwestern coasts .

During the Florida Land Boom Mediterranean Revival was the most popular architectural style among the affluent. Spanish Mission, Pueblo Indian, and Moorish motifs often were incorporated into the design of less expensive homes. Enthusiasm for these styles did not originate as a consequence of Florida's colonial heritage, but was nationwide. No Florida architect contributed more to the popularity of Mediterranean Revival within the state than Addison Mizner, most of whose buildings are located in Palm Beach County, the site of his planned community of Boca Raton (Administration Buildings, Palm Beach; Via Mizner, Palm Beach County).

Mediterranean Revival homes of the wealthy may be seen throughout the state (Caples'-Ringlings' Historic District, Sarasota; Casa de Muchas Flores, Pinellas; and Mar-A-Lago National Historic Landmark, Palm Beach). Pueblo Revival became a common architectural style in South Florida (Country Club Estates Thematic Resource Area, Dade), and in Jacksonville during the 1920s one development corporation chose Spanish Mission style (San Jose Estates Thematic Resource Area, Duval). Without question the most bizarre variant on the Mediterranean theme was used in the planned community of Opa-locka, where the motif was Moorish Revival, and buildings were designed based on visual fantasies from the book *1001 Tales from the Arabian Nights* (Opa-locka Thematic Resource Area, Dade).

Mediterranean Revival was chosen as the design for hotels and theaters as well as residences. Although since World War II many of the hotels and theaters built during the 1920s have suffered severe neglect and a good many have been demolished, a number remain for Floridians and visitors to admire (Miami-Biltmore Hotel, Dade; Vinoy Park Hotel, Pinellas; El Vernona-Broadway Apartments, Sarasota; Vineta Hotel, Palm Beach; Don Ce Sar Hotel, Pinellas; Saenger Theater, Escambia; Tampa Theatre, Hillsborough; Olympia Theatre, Dade; Alladin Theater, Brevard; and Florida Theatre, Duval). Some of these buildings have been greatly altered, others are empty and in advanced stages of disrepair, while a few have been carefully restored to their earlier grandeur.

During the Great Depression of the 1930s population within Florida grew relatively slowly. In several places, however, construction did greatly alter the landscape. Undoubtedly the most radical change was on the southern end of Miami Beach. Here, influenced by a Parisian decorative arts exposition held in 1925, the Century of Progress World's Fair of Chicago, which began in 1933, and the New York World's Fair, which opened in 1939, developers chose Art Deco or Moderne designs for their buildings (Miami Beach Architectural District, Dade). In Lakeland, despite the constraints imposed by poor economic conditions, an outstanding educational complex was built designed by the famous architect Frank Lloyd Wright. Here is the nation's largest concentration of buildings of his design (Florida Southern College Architectural District, Polk).

Many Floridians are relative newcomers whose history is elsewhere. It is hoped that this catalog will introduce them to the richness of Florida's past.

Morton D. Winsberg, Department of Geography, Florida State University, Tallahassee, Florida 32306

SELECTED READINGS

This list of general works on Florida or specific places is not complete. The books, however, are widely available in public libraries.

BLOODWORTH, BERTHA E. AND ALTON C. MORRIS. *Places in the Sun: The History and Romance of Florida Place Names.* Gainesville, Fla.: University Presses of Florida, 1978.

BOYD, MARK F., HALE G. SMITH, AND JOHN W. GRIFFIN. *Here They Once Stood: The Tragic End of the Apalachee Missions.* Gainesville, Fla.: University of Florida Press, 1951.

BROWARD, ROBERT C. *The Architecture of Henry John Klutho: The Prairie School in Jacksonville.* Jacksonville, Fla.: University of North Florida Press, 1983.

CERWINSKE, LAURA. *Tropical Deco: The Architecture and Design of Old Miami Beach.* New York: Rizzoli, 1981.

CURL, DONALD W. *Mizner's Florida: American Resort Architecture.* Cambridge, Mass.: MIT Press, 1984.

DUNLOP, BETH. *Florida's Vanishing Architecture.* Englewood, Fla.: Pineapple Press, 1987.

DUNN, HAMPTON. *Florida: A Pictorial History.* Norfolk, Va.: The Donning Co., 1987.

FEDERAL WRITERS' PROJECT OF THE WORK PROGRESS ADMINISTRATION FOR THE STATE OF FLORIDA. *The WPA Guide to Florida : The Federal Writers' Project Guide to 1930s Florida.* Reprint. New York: Pantheon, 1984.

FERNALD EDWARD A. AND ELIZABETH PURDUM (EDS.). *Atlas of Florida.* Gainesville, Fla.:University Press of Florida, 1992.

GILL, JOAN AND BETH READ (EDS.). *Born of the Sun: The Official Florida Bicentennial Commemorative Book.* Hollywood, Fla.: Bicentennial Commemorative Journal, Inc., 1975.

HATTON, HAP. *Tropical Splendor: An Architectural History of Florida.* New York: Knopf, 1987.

JAHODA, GLORIA. *Florida: A Bicentennial History.* New York: Norton, 1976.

MANUCY, ALBERT. *The Houses of St. Augustine: Notes on the Architecture from 1565-1821.* St. Augustine, Fla.: St. Augustine Historical Society, 1962.

MILANICH, JERALD T. AND CHARLES H. FAIRBANKS. *Florida Archaeology.* New York: Academic Press, 1980.

MORMINO, GARY R. AND GEORGE E. POZZETTA. *The Immigrant World of Ybor City: Italians and Their Latin Neighbors in Tampa, 1885-1985.* Urbana, Ill.: University of Illinois Press, 1987.

MORRIS, ALLEN. *Florida Place Names.* Coral Gables, Fla.: University of Miami Press, 1974.

PAISLEY, CLIFTON. *From Cotton to Quail: An Agricultural History of Leon County, Fla., 1860-1967.* Gainesville, Fla.: University of Florida Press, 1981.

PATRICK, REMBERT W. AND ALLEN MORRIS. *Florida Under Five Flags.* Gainesville, Fla.: University of Florida Press, 1967.

RODRIGUEZ, IVAN A. AND MARGOT AMMIDOWN. *Wilderness to Metropolis: The History and Architecture of Dade County (1825-1940).* Miami, Fla.: County Office of Community and Economic Development, Historic Preservation Division, 1982.

TEBEAU, CHARLTON W. *A History of Florida.* Miami, Fla.: University of Miami Press, 1980.

WARNKE, JAMES R. *Balustrades and Gingerbread: Key West's Handicraft Homes and Buildings.* Miami, Fla.: Banyan Books, 1978.

WRIGHT, JAMES LEITCH. *Florida in the American Revolution.* Gainesville, Fla.: University of Florida Press 1975.

THE PROPERTIES

THE COUNTIES

Escambia, Santa Rosa, Okaloosa, Walton, Holmes, Washington, Jackson, Bay, Calhoun, Gadsden, Leon, Jefferson, Madison, Hamilton, Liberty, Wakulla, Taylor, Suwannee, Columbia, Baker, Nassau, Gulf, Franklin, Lafayette, Union, Bradford, Clay, Duval, Dixie, Gilchrist, Alachua, Putnam, St. Johns, Levy, Marion, Flagler, Citrus, Lake, Volusia, Sumter, Seminole, Brevard, Hernando, Orange, Pasco, Osceola, Pinellas, Hillsborough, Polk, Indian River, Manatee, Hardee, Okeechobee, St. Lucie, Sarasota, De Soto, Highlands, Martin, Charlotte, Glades, Palm Beach, Lee, Hendry, Broward, Collier, Dade, Monroe

ALACHUA COUNTY

Vicinity of Alachua. NEWNANSVILLE TOWN SITE. 1.5 mi. NE of Alachua on Fl. 235. 1824–1890. Site of well-developed 19th-century rural community. Contains remains of road, 2 cemeteries, 2 wooden structures. First county seat, but decline began when county seat moved to Gainesville in 1854 and accelerated when the railroad bypassed it in 1884. Public-Private. N.R. 1974.

Cross Creek. MARJORIE KINNAN RAWLINGS HOUSE. Fl. 325 S of Cross Creek. c. 1890. Frame Vernacular. 1 story, board-and-batten, built in 3 sections, connected by breezeways. Typical 19th-century Cracker house of Central Florida. Purchased by the novelist Marjorie Kinnan Rawlings in 1928 and owned by her until her death in 1953. Several of her novels, including *The Yearling,* were set in the locale. State Park. House museum. Public. N.R. 1970.

Evinston. EVINSTON COMMUNITY STORE AND POST OFFICE. CR 225 north of CR SE 10. 1883–84. Frame Vernacular. 1 story. Served as warehouse since 1884 and general store since 1896. Moved 25 yards to its present site in 1957, but little changed. Private. N.R. 1989.

Gainesville. MAJ. JAMES B. BAILEY HOUSE (Bailey Retirement Center). 1121 NW 6th St. 1854. Frame Vernacular with Greek Revival elements. 1$^{1}/_{2}$ stories, clapboarding, double-pitch gabled roof, front veranda. Builder was one of the city's pioneer settlers and a major civic figure in the city's formative years. Presently a retirement center. Private. N.R. 1972.

Marjorie Kinnan Rawlings House

Gainesville. BAIRD HARDWARE COMPANY WAREHOUSE. 619 S. Main St. c. 1910. Masonry Vernacular. 1 story, brick. Baird Hardware Company was a major commercial enterprise in the Gainesville area for over 90 years. This at one time was its main warehouse. Presently divided into commercial establishments. Private. N.R. 1985.

Gainesville. BAIRD THEATER (Simmonson Opera House). 19 SE 1st Ave. 1887. Masonry Vernacular. 3 stories. Gainesville's most important legitimate theater until the 1920s. Later named the Baird Theater and after 1939 occupied by the Cox Furniture Store. Private. N.R. 1994.

Gainesville. BOULWARE SPRING WATERWORKS. 3400 SE 15th St. 1895–1908. Eclectic. 2 stories, masonry, metal roof. Gainesville's first municipal waterworks. The site is historically significant since it was here in 1853 that an assembly chose Gainesville as the county seat. Under restoration to be a site museum. Public. N.R. 1985.

Boulware Spring Waterworks

Gainesville. **COX FURNITURE WAREHOUSE**. 602 S. Main St. 1914. Romanesque Revival. 1¹/₂ stories. The central "nave" of the building is raised to allow clerestory lighting. For many years occupied by a wholesale grocery concern. Later used as a warehouse and retail firm by Cox Furniture Company. Private. N.R. 1994.

Gainesville. **DIXIE HOTEL** (Seagle Building). 408 W. University Ave. 1926+. Mediterranean Revival. G. Lloyd Preacher, architect. 11 stories, brick, upper floors stuccoed, lower 2 floors sheathed in stone. The city's most ambitious commercial building project in the 1920s. Never used as a hotel. Used by the University of Florida between 1937 and 1979. Remodeled for residential, retail, and office use in 1982–83. Private. N.R. 1982.

Cox Furniture Warehouse

Gainesville. **EPWORTH HALL**. 419 NE 1st St. 1884. Eclectic. 2 stories, brick. At the time of its construction it served as a classroom for the state-operated East Florida Seminary. The seminary was abolished in 1905 and in 1906 the new University of Florida held its first class there. When the new campus was built, the structure was sold (1911) to the First Methodist Church. Private. N.R. 1973.

Gainesville. **HOTEL THOMAS**. NE 2nd and 5th Sts. and NE 6th and 7th Aves. 1906–1910, 1928. French Classical with Mediterranean elements. 2¹/₂ stories, U-shaped, masonry, stuccoed, tile roof. Private residence of Major William Reuben Thomas, who was instrumental in the development of the city's social and cultural life. Between 1926 and 1928 converted into a luxury resort hotel, the first of its kind in the city. Renovated in 1976–78 for city government office space and use as a cultural center. Public. N.R. 1973.

Hotel Thomas

Gainesville. MARY PHIFER McKENZIE HOUSE. 617 E. University Ave. 1895+. Queen Anne. 2½ stories, frame, patterned shingling, 3½-story octagonal tower, 1-story veranda. Built by John Lamberth, native of Georgia. It has since been the home of several influential Gainesville families and reflects the tastes of the affluent at the turn of the century. Private. N.R. 1982.

Gainesville. MATHESON HOUSE. 528 SE 1st Ave. 1867. Frame Vernacular with Greek Revival elements. 2 stories, clapboarding, full-width porch, gambrel roof. Home of Chris Matheson, mayor of the city for 8 terms and state legislator. Believed to be the second oldest house in the city. Private. N.R. 1973.

Gainesville. NORTHEAST GAINESVILLE RESIDENTIAL DISTRICT. 1875–1920. 160 acres. Predominant styles: Masonry and Frame Vernacular, Classical Revival, Victorian, and Bungalow. Houses in this district represent a spectrum of architectural styles used in the late 19th and early 20th centuries. Although conservative, the homes are nonetheless good examples of their time and clearly reflect the area's continuing evolution as an important residential neighborhood. N.R. 1980.

Gainesville. OLD P.K. YONGE LABORATORY SCHOOL. SW 13th St. 1934. Collegiate Gothic. Rudolph Weaver, architect. 2½ stories. Red brick exterior, terra-cotta roof tiles. Formerly the university demonstration school. Included grades K–12. Presently used for other university functions. Public. N.R. 1990.

Gainesville. OLD WRUF RADIO STATION. Museum Rd. and Newell Dr. 1928. Tudor Revival. Rudolph Weaver, architect. The only building of its style on the University of Florida campus. Public. N.R. 1989.

Gainesville. PLEASANT STREET HISTORIC DISTRICT. 1875–1935. 271 buildings, 259 of historical interest. Mainly Frame Vernacular, but some are Revival style. Gainesville's oldest black neighborhood. Several churches are located within the district. Private. N.R. 1989.

Gainesville. SOUTHEAST GAINESVILLE RESIDENTIAL DISTRICT. 1867–1934. 103 buildings, 96 of historical interest. Frame Vernacular predominates, many with metal roofs. A neighborhood considered highly representative of the early period of the community's history. Public and Private. N.R. 1988.

Gainesville. STAR GARAGE. 119 SE 1st Ave. 1931. Masonry Vernacular. 1 story, brick, large painted parapet facade. One of the earliest automobile agencies in the city. Present building contains elements of earlier livery stable. Renovated in 1986–87 and now used for offices. Private. N.R. 1985.

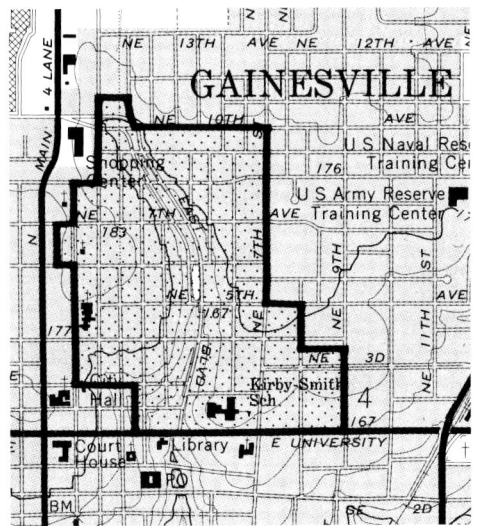

Northeast Gainesville Residential District

3

Gainesville. 313 NW 7th Ave. c. 1913. Frame Vernacular bungalow. 1 story. Selected because it is highly representative of homes in its neighborhood. Private. N.R. 1989.

Gainesville. U.S. POST OFFICE. 25 SE 2nd Pl. 1909. Beaux-Arts Classical. James Knox Taylor, architect. 3¹/₂ stories, yellow brick. North facade dominated by monumental portico with 6 Corinthian columns. Exterior walls have richly detailed panels. One of the finest examples of Beaux-Arts Classical style in Florida. Elegantly trimmed with carved limestone and granite exterior details. Renovated as a theater in 1980. Public. N.R. 1979.

Gainesville. UNIVERSITY OF FLORIDA CAMPUS HISTORIC DISTRICT. 1905–1925. Collegiate Gothic. William A. Edwards and Rudolph Weaver, architects. Predominant architectural elements are red brick, high-pitched tile roofs, widespread use of crenelated parapets interrupted by stepped gables. Elaborate arched main entrances and much stone trim. Anderson Hall (1913), Bryan Hall (1914), Buckman Hall (1907), Flint Hall (1910), Floyd Hall (1912), Library East (1925), Newell Hall (1910), Peabody Hall (1913), Rolf Hall (1927), Thomas Hall (1905), and Woman's Gymnasium (1919) are the important early buildings of the new University of Florida, which had been moved to Gainesville in 1905. Style was chosen as a logical response to a need for a sense of dignity and timelessness on the campus. Public. N.R. 1989.

Peabody Hall, University of Florida

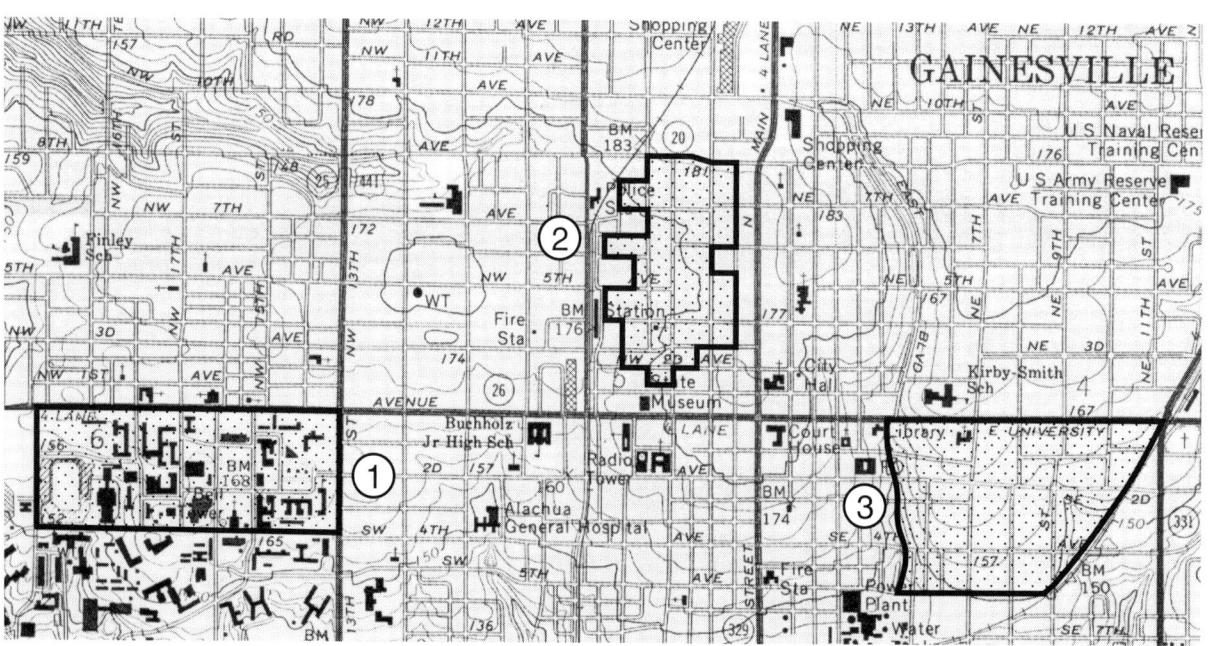

① University of Florida Campus Historic District, ② Pleasant Street Historic District, ③ Southeast Gainesville Residential District.

Vicinity of Gainesville. KANAPAHA (Haile Plantation). 8 mi. SW of Gainesville and ¼ mi. N of Fl. 24. c. 1850. Frame Vernacular. 1 story, frame, full-width front porch, rests on 3-foot piers. Representative of the antebellum plantation houses of north central Florida. Private. N.R. 1986.

High Springs. HIGH SPRINGS HISTORIC DISTRICT. 1885–1940. 266 buildings, 218 of historical interest. Mainly Frame Vernacular residences. A few Victorian and Revival-style homes, including Queen Anne and Gothic. Several residential neighborhoods and a small central business district. The development of the district coincides with the period when the town was an important railroad center. Public and Private. N.R. 1991.

Melrose. MELROSE HISTORIC DISTRICT. 1877–1929. 87 buildings, 66 of historical interest. Predominant style is Frame Vernacular, but several are Folk Victorian. A small, primarily residential neighborhood whose period of significance coincided with Melrose's years as a center of citrus production and a winter resort. Few buildings constructed after the devastating freezes of 1894–95, which destroyed the surrounding groves. Public and Private. N.R. 1990.

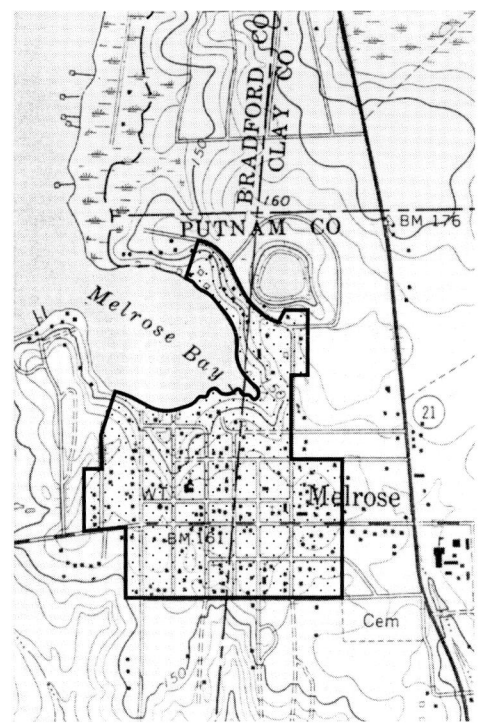

Melrose Historic District

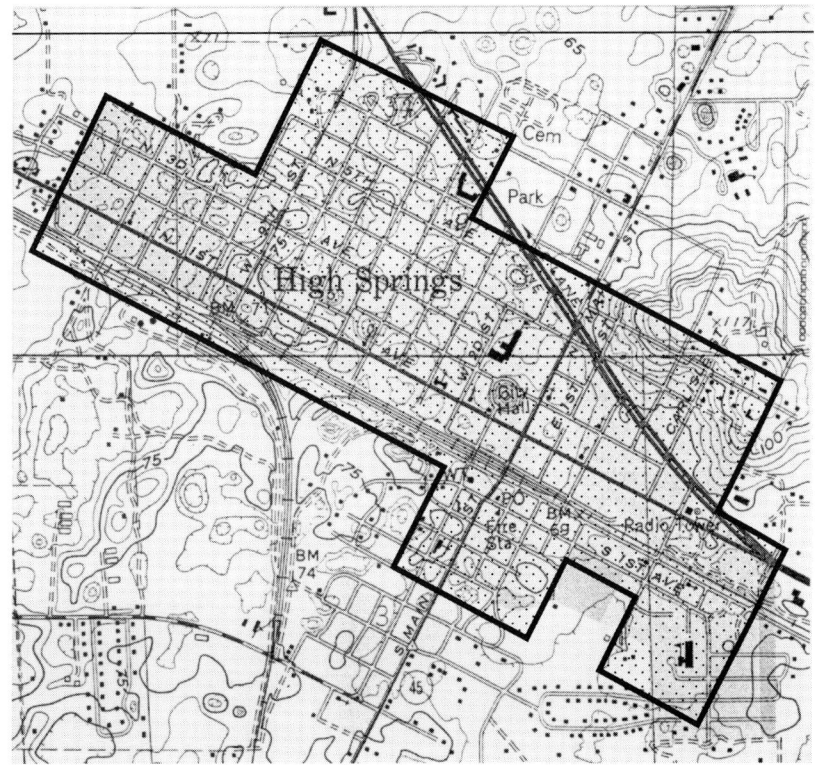

High Springs Historic District

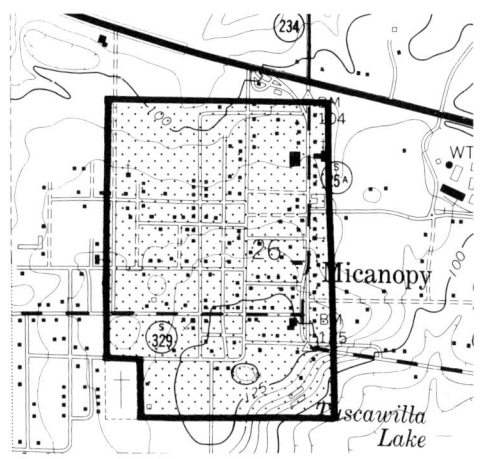

Micanopy Historic District

Micanopy. MICANOPY HISTORIC DISTRICT. 1776–1930. 16 blocks. Predominant styles: Frame Vernacular, Classical, Victorian, and Bungalow. The site of the town contains evidence of aboriginal occupation. The town has been continuously settled since 1821. It was once a thriving market town, but by the late 19th century it began to decline as it fell under the social, political, and economic shadow of Gainesville. N.R. 1983.

Newberry. CITY OF NEWBERRY HISTORIC DISTRICT. 1894–1938. 87 buildings, 48 of historical interest. Predominantly Frame Vernacular as well as Commercial style. Most homes are frame, some with Victorian-style elements. Craftsman and other styles represented. The most substantial building is the Municipal Building, a WPA (Works Progress Administration) project built during the Depression and made from local limestone. Public and Private. N.R. 1987.

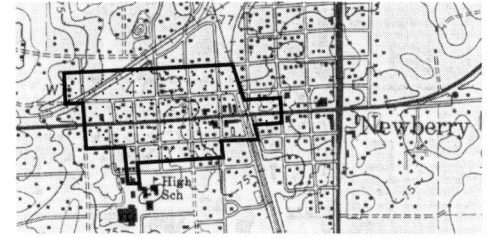

City of Newberry Historic District

Rochelle. ROCHELLE SCHOOL. Off Fl. 234. c. 1885. Frame Vernacular with Italianate elements. 2 stories, clapboarding, center bell tower. One of the few remaining buildings of a once thriving community. Rochelle is one of the oldest settlements in the county. Presently used as a community center. Private. N.R. 1973.

Windsor. NEILSON HOUSE. Fl. 325. 1890. Stick style. 1$^1/_2$ stories, frame, clapboarding, decorative wall shingling, center 2-story gabled entrance tower, 2nd-floor porch. Stick work used on tower. One of the few Stick-style houses in Florida. Private. N.R. 1973.

BAKER COUNTY

Neilson House

Macclenny. OLD BAKER COUNTY COURTHOUSE. 14 W. McIver St. 1908. Colonial Revival. Edward C. Hosford, architect. 2 stories, red brick, pyramidal roof surmounted by a cupola with 4 clocks. Architect designed a number of courthouses in Georgia and Florida. Built during the time the county's agriculture became commercially valuable and prosperity had increased. Public. N.R. 1986.

Vicinity of Olustee. OLUSTEE BATTLEFIELD (Battle of Ocean Pond). 2 mi. E of Olustee on U.S. 90. 1864. On February 18, 1864, a Union force of approximately 5000 met a Confederate force of roughly the same number defending positions around Ocean Pond. Union forces withdrew after sustaining an estimated 1900 casualties. Confederate losses were 946. The major Civil War battle fought in Florida. Museum. Public. N.R. 1970.

Burnsed Blockhouse

Vicinity of Sanderson. BURNSED BLOCKHOUSE. FL. 127, 15 mi. N of Sanderson. 1837. Frame Vernacular. 2 stories, kitchen detached, peepholes and openings in wall to fire rifles from. An example of an early frontier Florida home. One of the finest examples of a hand-hewn structure in the state. Public. N.R. 1973.

BAY COUNTY

Panama City. ROBERT L. McKENZIE HOUSE (Belle Booth House). 17 E. 3rd Ct. 1909. Frame Vernacular. 1¹/₂ stories, gabled roof, full-width screen porch in front. Home of Robert L. McKenzie, Georgian, who settled in the city and was active in the wood products industry. A civic leader, he did much to improve transportation within the area. Private. N.R. 1986.

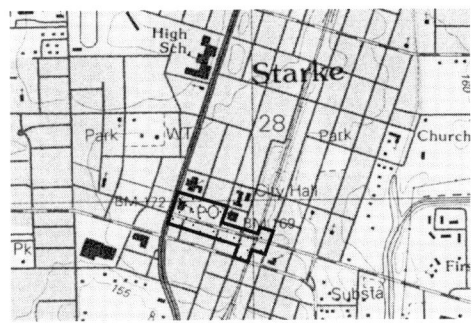

Call Street Historic District

BRADFORD COUNTY

Starke. CALL STREET HISTORIC DISTRICT. 1857–1931, 41 buildings of historical significance in a 10-block area. Predominant style is Masonry Vernacular 1- and 2-story detached commercial buildings. The district reflects the physical development of the town between 1859 and 1931. N.R. 1985.

Starke. OLD BRADFORD COUNTY COURTHOUSE. 209 W. Call St. 1902. Romanesque Revival. 2 stories, tall central tower with elaborate roof details. The building was built following a bitter contest between Starke and Lake Butler for the county seat. In 1898 Starke decided to build a courthouse. In 1921 the county was divided, and Lake Butler became the county seat of the new Union County. Public. N.R. 1974.

Old Bradford County Courthouse

Old St. Luke's Episcopal Church

BREVARD COUNTY

Cocoa. ALADDIN THEATER BUILDING. 300 Brevard Ave. 1924. Italian Renaissance. P. Thornton Marye, architect. 4 stories. Concrete slab foundation. Flat ceramic roof. Restored in the 1980s to its original appearance. Building displays fine decorative brickwork. Focal point of community's civic and cultural activities during the late 1920s and 1930s. Public. N.R. 1991.

Cocoa. CAPE CANAVERAL AIR FORCE STATION LAUNCH PADS NOS. 5,6,13,14,19,26,34 AND CONTROL. Cape Canaveral Air Force Station. 1950+ . Launch pads, hangars, administrative buildings, and other facilities related to the nation's space programs. The nation's first unmanned probes into space and near space, followed by manned space flights, were launched from Cape Canaveral. Public. N.R. 1984.

Cocoa. PORCHER HOUSE. 434 Delannoy Ave. 1916. Classical Revival. 2¹/₂ stories, coquina limestone, 2-story semicircular portico with 4 fluted Ionic columns. Built for Edward Postel Porcher, pioneer citrus grower. It is an example of the Classical Revival style adapted to the Florida environment. Restored in 1987. Public. N.R. 1986.

Launch Pads 34 and 37 (background), Cape Canaveral Air Force Station

Courtenay. OLD ST. LUKE'S EPISCOPAL CHURCH AND CEMETERY. 5555 N. Tropical Trail. 1888. Late Gothic Revival. 1 story. Vertical board-and-batten exterior. Interior walls completely unfinished and are the inner side of the board-and-batten exterior. One of the earliest surviving buildings in the community. Private. N.R. 1990.

Indianola. DR. GEORGE E. HILL HOUSE. 870 Indianola Dr. 1890. Frame Vernacular. 2 stories. Exterior of weatherboard. Built as a winter hunting refuge for Dr. Hill, a Scranton, Pennsylvania, dentist. A 937-foot dock, now in ruin, associated with the house. Private. N.R. 1993.

Melbourne. FLORIDA POWER AND LIGHT COMPANY ICE PLANT. 1604 S. Harbor City Blvd. 1927. 2 stories, masonry, decorative stucco detailing. Of great commercial importance to the community, serving households and commercial establishments as well as local commercial fishermen. During the pre-World War II period utility companies throughout Florida commonly produced and sold ice, since home refrigerators were rare. Private. H.R. 1982.

Melbourne Beach. COMMUNITY CHAPEL OF MELBOURNE BEACH. 501 Ocean Ave. 1892, 1942. Frame Vernacular. Rufus Beaujean, architect. 1 story. Front gabled roof, stained glass windows over alter installed in 1942. One of the earliest existing nonresidential structures in the community. Private. N.R. 1992.

Florida Power and Light Company Ice Plant

Melbourne Beach. MELBOURNE BEACH PIER. Ocean Ave. and Riverside Dr. 1888–1889. 650 feet long, 12 feet wide. Vital to the establishment and initial growth of the town, the oldest beach community in the county. Used for docking of passenger and freight vessels. Since 1920s primarily used for recreation. Public. N.R. 1984.

Vicinity of Merritt Island. OLD HAULOVER CANAL. N of Merritt Island. 1843. 725 feet long. Situated on the narrowest part of Merritt Island. Used by Indians and traders as a portage for their canoes until the canal was dug. Private/Public. N.R. 1978.

Palm Bay. ST. JOSEPH'S CATHOLIC CHURCH. Miller St. NE. 1914. Frame Vernacular with elements of Stick style. Rectangular with gabled roof and board-and-batten siding. One of the earliest churches in community. Private. N.R. 1987.

Rockledge. BARTON AVENUE RESIDENTIAL DISTRICT. 1884–1926. 44 buildings, 41 of historical interest. Mainly Frame Vernacular and a few of various Revival styles. District reflects the early period of settlement of Rockledge and many of the buildings are representative of the city's beginnings as a tourist resort during the late 19th century. Public and Private. N.R. 1992.

Rockledge. ROCKLEDGE DRIVE RESIDENTIAL DISTRICT. 1880–1926. 124 buildings, 100 of historical interest. Mainly Frame Vernacular, with some Revival style buildings. Rockledge Drive, which follows the Indian River, is among the most scenic historic roads in Florida. District contains a former city hall and fine boat houses. Public and Private. N.R. 1992.

Rockledge. VALENCIA SUBDIVISION RESIDENTIAL DISTRICT. 1924–1926. 71 buildings, 56 of historical interest. Mediterranean Revival. Comprised entirely of single-family residences, all executed in the Mediterranean Revival style. The majority of the buildings are masonry with exterior stucco walls. Private. N.R. 1992.

Vicinity of Rockledge. MOCCASIN ISLAND. On the SE shore of Lake Winder approximately 8 miles SW of Rockledge. 4000 B.C.–2000 B.C., 500 B.C.–A.D. 800, A.D. 800–A.D. 1565. Archaic and St. Johns periods . A midden 740 feet by 100 feet. Highest elevation is 6 feet. Abundant material, including food remains and pottery fragments. Private. N.R. 1994.

Vicinity of Rockledge. PERSIMMONS MOUND. On the E bank of a former channel of the St. Johns River approximately 10 miles SW of Rockledge. 4000 B.C.–2000 B.C., 500 B.C.–A.D. 800, A.D. 800–A.D. 1565. A midden 165 feet by 100 feet. Highest elevation 4.2 feet. Within it have been found animal bones, pottery fragments, tools, and shell. Public. N.R. 1994.

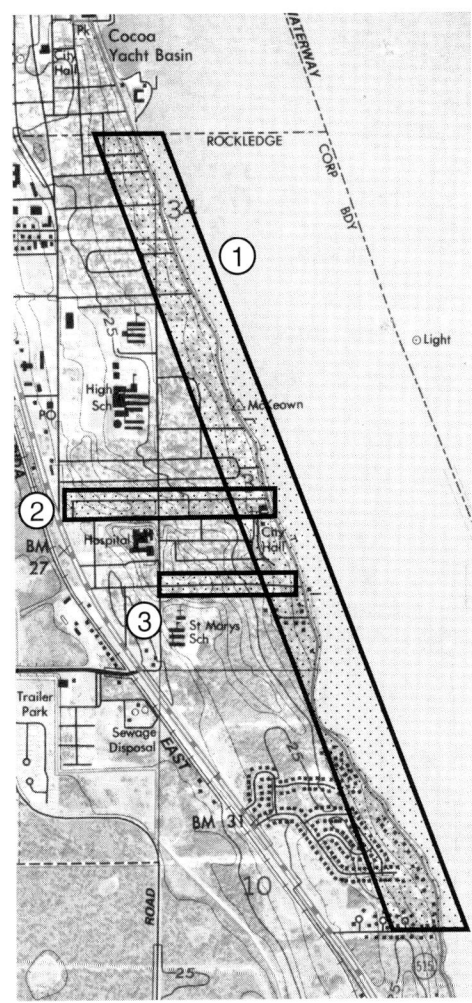

① Rockledge Drive Residential District, ② Valencia Subdivision Residential District, ③ Barton Avenue Residential District.

Vicinity of Rockledge. TURTLE MOUND (Duda Ranch Mound). On the E bank of the St. Johns River floodplain approximately 11 miles SW of Rockledge. 4000 B.C.–2000 B.C., 500 B.C.–A.D. 800, A.D. 800–A.D. 1565. Midden 320 feet by 205 feet. Highest elevation 11 feet. Midden contains a wide variety of cultural material. Private. N.R. 1994.

Titusville. PRITCHARD HOUSE. 424 S. Washington Ave. c. 1891. Queen Anne. 2 stories. frame. Includes ogee-shaped bargeboard with encased scroll work on front facade. James Pritchard, born in New York, came to Titusville in 1876 and became a banker. He operated the city's first electric generator on the grounds of his home. Private. N.R. 1990.

Titusville. JUDGE GEORGE ROBBINS HOUSE. 703 Indian River Ave. c. 1892. Dutch Colonial Revival. 2 story. George Robbins, born in Maine, was a lawyer who moved to Florida in 1886. He worked for Henry Flagler, who built the railroad along Florida's east coast. Private. N.R. 1990.

Judge George Robbins House

Titusville. ST. GABRIEL'S EPISCOPAL CHURCH. 414 Palm Ave. 1887. Gothic Revival. Edwin G. Weed, architect. 1 story, frame, gabled roof, pointed arched windows with stained glass, tall steeple at southeast corner. Church is noted for its fine collection of Victorian stained glass. Private. N.R. 1972.

Titusville. SPELL HOUSE. 1200 Riverside Dr. c. 1911. Queen Anne. 2¹/₂ stories. Queen Anne. One of the best remaining examples of Queen Anne style in Titusville. James Spell was the first licensed pharmacist in the town. Home remains in the Spell family. Private. N.R. 1990.

Titusville. TITUSVILLE COMMERCIAL DISTRICT. 1890–1930. 24 buildings, 21 of historical interest. Mediterranean Revival. All buildings are 1 and 2 story. Area was mostly developed in the 1920s land boom when the Mediterranean Revival architectural style was very popular in Florida. Private. N.R. 1990.

Titusville. WAGER HOUSE. 621 Indian River Ave. c. 1895. Frame Vernacular. 2¹/₂ stories. Associated with Ellis Wager, son of the builder, who published the *Florida Star*, the county's first newspaper. Often used for community social events. Private. N.R. 1990.

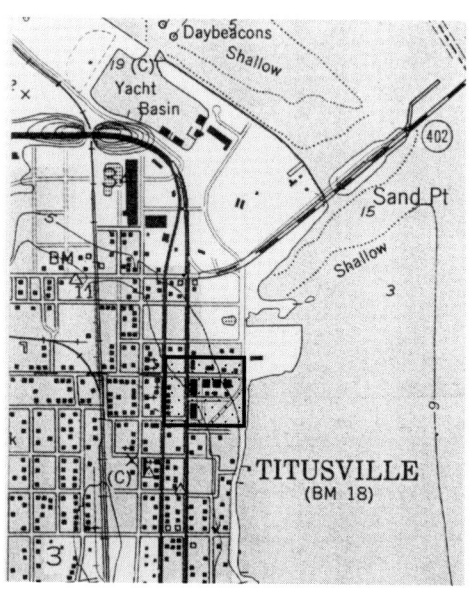

Titusville Commercial District

Vicinity of Titusville. INDIAN FIELDS. On the SE bank of Ruth Lake, approximately 8 miles west of Titusville. 4000 B.C.–2000 B.C., 500 B.C.–A.D. 800, A.D. 800–A.D. 1565. Archaic and St. Johns periods. A 540-feet-by-400-feet midden, 11 feet at highest elevation. Contains abundant food remains as well as pottery fragments. Private. N.R. 1994.

Vicinity of Titusville. LAUNCH COMPLEX 39. Kennedy Space Center. 1968. Launch site of many space voyages including first U.S. unmanned earth orbital (1967), first lunar landing (1969), Apollo-Soyuz (1975) and all shuttle missions (1981-present). Public. N.R. 1973.

Vicinity of Titusville. WINDOVER ARCHAEOLOGICAL SITE. 5000 B.C. A small isolated peat deposit containing human burials and artifacts dating from the Early Archaic period. One of the largest collections of human skeletal material in the New World, made famous by the discovery of human skulls with brain tissue containing DNA. Private. N.R. 1987.

Hand-woven textile, Windover. Made from plant fibers, these specimens (found in 37 burial mounds) are probably the largest, most complex set of fabrics of this antiquity from the southeastern United States.

BROWARD COUNTY

Davie. DAVIE SCHOOL. 6650 Griffin Rd. 1918. Masonry Vernacular. August Geiger, architect. 2 stories. Geiger was one of South Florida's best-known early architects. One of the least altered elementary school buildings in South Florida and the oldest school in continuous use in the district. Public. N.R. 1988.

Deerfield Beach. DEERFIELD SCHOOL. 651 NE 1st St. 1927. Mediterranean Revival. Thomas McLaughlin, architect. 2 stories. Barrel-tile roof and arcaded walkways. Oldest operative school in Deerfield Beach and second oldest in the county. Public. N.R. 1990.

Davie School

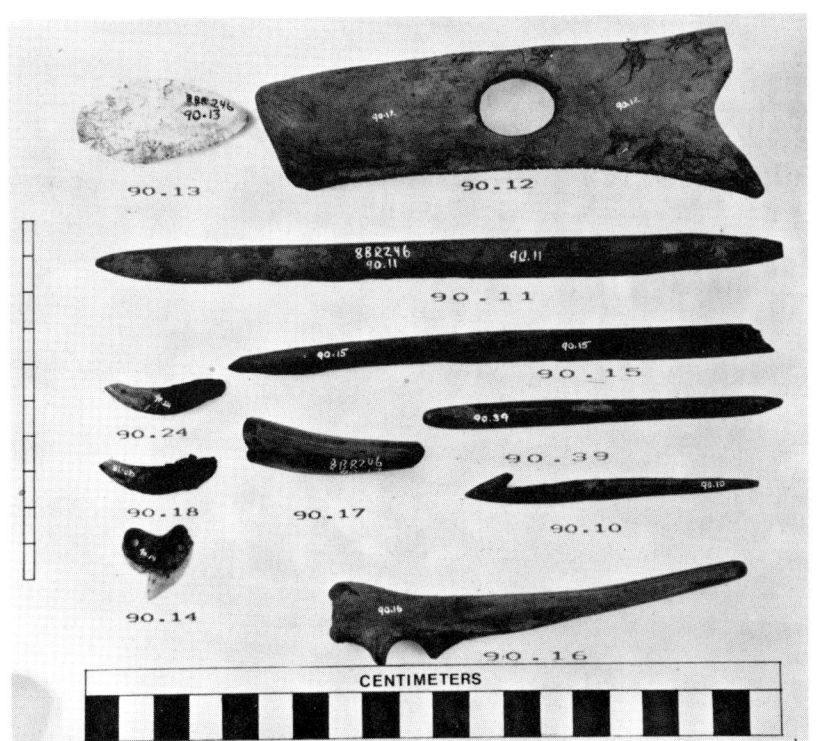

Windover Archaeological Site, projectile point, canine and shark's teeth, feline bone, and barbed point found in burial mound.

11

Deerfield Beach. OLD SEABOARD AIR LINE RAILROAD STATION. 1300 W. Hillsboro Blvd. 1926. Mediterranean Revival. Gustave Maas, architect. 1 story. Representative of an architectural style closely associated with South Florida. Significant because of the role it played in the early economic development of the town. Public. N.R. 1990.

Fort Lauderdale. BONNET HOUSE. 900 Birch Rd. 1920. Eclectic. Frederick Clay Bartlett, architect. 2 stories, cinder block, wide 2nd-story gallery. House designed by owner, an artist, in a highly unusual manner. One of a rapidly dwindling number of ocean-front estates in South Florida. Set in extensive grounds. Private. N.R. 1984.

Bonnet House

Fort Lauderdale. NEW RIVER INN (City Hall Annex). 229 SW 2nd Ave. 1905. Masonry Vernacular. 2¹/₂ stories, concrete, 2-tier veranda around 2 sides. Large early hotel. Served railroad and ship travelers. Public. N.R. 1972.

Fort Lauderdale. OLD DILLARD HIGH SCHOOL OR COLORED SCHOOL. 1001 NW 4th St. 1924. Masonry Vernacular with Mission-style elements. John M. Peterman, architect. 2 stories. First black high school in Broward County. Important center of Afro-American life in Ft. Lauderdale and Broward County. Represents the struggle in area for equal education. Public. N.R. 1991.

Fort Lauderdale. STRANAHAN HOUSE (The Pioneer House). 335 SE 6th Ave. (on New River). 1902. Frame Vernacular. 2 stories, steep hipped roof, prominent 2-story porch. Site of trading post and travelers' lodging built by Frank Stranahan, Fort Lauderdale's first white permanent settler. Present home built on site for wife. Now a house museum. Private. N.R. 1973.

Joseph Wesley Young House

Hollywood. JOSEPH WESLEY YOUNG HOUSE. 1055 Hollywood Blvd. 1925. Mediterranean Revival. Preston C. Rubich and Edgar Otis Hunter architects. 2¹/₂ stories. Fenestration includes French doors and various kinds of casement windows. Bell tower. Residence of Joseph Young, the founder and designer of Hollywood. Private. N.R. 1989.

Lighthouse Point. CAP'S PLACE (Club Unique). 2980 NE 31st Ave. 1928. Frame Vernacular. 1 story. A group of 5 buildings of which 4 are of historical interest. An early Broward County restaurant. The first restaurant building was constructed on a beached dredging barge in 1928. Other extant structures include the bar, fish house, dock and walkways. Private. N.R. 1990.

Oakland Park. OAKLAND PARK ELEMENTARY SCHOOL. 936 NE 33rd St. 1926. Mediterranean Revival. Thomas D. McLaughlin, architect. 2-story auditorium, 1-story main classroom building. Distinguished by arcaded walkways and open courtyard. Oldest school in Broward County still in use as a school. Public. N.R. 1988.

Plantation. LOCK NO. 1, NORTH NEW RIVER CANAL. 6521 W. Fl. 84. 1911–1912. Single lock, 149 feet long, entry controlled by wooden gates. Ocean entrance lock of the North New River Canal that connects the Atlantic with Lake Okeechobee. First to be built on the canal. Remains the best preserved of all the surviving South Florida locks. Public. N.R. 1978.

Pompano Beach. SAMPLE ESTATE (McDougald House). 3161 N. Dixie Highway. 1916. Colonial Revival. 2 stories, frame of local pine and cypress, colonnaded porch in Tuscan style. Built by Albert Neal Sample (1868–1941), early Broward County resident. In 1943 acquired by the McDougald family. Private. N.R. 1984.

Vicinity of Pompano Beach. HILLSBORO INLET LIGHT STATION. Hillsboro Inlet. 1907. Open iron frame. 132 feet high, octagonal. Built at the entrance of Hillsboro Inlet. Light automated in 1974. Public. N.R. 1979.

Hillsboro Inlet Light Station

CALHOUN COUNTY

Blountstown. OLD CALHOUN COUNTY COURTHOUSE. 314 E. Central Ave. 1904+. Romanesque Revival. Frank Lockwood and Benjamin Bosworth, architects. 2 to 2¹/₂ stories, brick, hipped main roof, 3 1-story porches. One of only two extant Romanesque Revival courthouse buildings in Florida. Both architects, Alabamians, had outstanding regional reputations for the design of public buildings. Public. N.R. 1980.

Vicinity of Blountstown. CAYSON MOUND AND VILLAGE SITE. 3 mi. SE of Blountstown on the Apalachicola River. A.D. 900–A.D. 1500. Fort Walton period. Flat-topped pyramidal temple mound of local clay, 20 feet high, 75 feet long and, 60 feet wide. Village complex, including plaza, nearby. Private. N.R. 1976.

CHARLOTTE COUNTY

Willis Fish Cabin and Icing Station

Bull Key. WEST COAST FISHING COMPANY RESIDENTIAL CABIN, WILLIS FISH CABIN AND ICING STATION. In Charlotte Harbor. 1920–1930. Frame Vernacular with metal roofs. 1 story. Buildings to house fishermen and process fish when fishing was a very important activity in Charlotte Harbor. Buildings were portable and have been in several places in the harbor. Private. N.R. 1991.

Vicinity of Placida. BIG MOUND KEY/BOGGESS RIDGE ARCHAEOLOGICAL DISTRICT. CR 771. A.D. 400–A.D. 1748. Weeden Island and Safety Harbor periods. 4 shell mounds on Big Mound Key and 3 linear sand ridges, each 20 meters wide and 35 to 100 meters long, 400 meters to the N on Boggess Ridge. Private. N.R. 1990.

Punta Gorda. CHARLOTTE HIGH SCHOOL. 1250 Cooper St. 1926. Masonry Vernacular with Neo-Classical elements. 3 stories. For over 60 years the school has been Punta Gorda's chief educational facility. Public. N.R. 1990.

Charlotte High School

Punta Gorda. A. C. FREEMAN HOUSE. 639 E. Hargraves Ave. (moved). 1903. Carpenter Queen Anne. 2 stories, frame. County pine with exterior trim of pine, cypress, and some oak. Square tower on northeast corner. One of the best-preserved buildings in Punta Gorda from the turn of the century. N.R. 1987.

Punta Gorda. OLD FIRST NATIONAL BANK OF PUNTA GORDA (Old Merchants Bank). 133 W. Marion Ave. 1912. Masonry Vernacular with Neo-Classical elements. 2 stories. Marble facing used liberally in the interior. Oldest extant bank building in Charlotte County. Played major role in the development of commerce in the city. Private. N.R. 1991.

Old First National Bank of Punta Gorda

Punta Gorda. PUNTA GORDA ATLANTIC COAST LINE DEPOT. 1009 Taylor Rd. 1928. Mediterranean Revival. 1 story. Excellent example of the use of Mediterranean Revival in commercial transportation. Largely a freight depot. Played a major role in linking town's fish catch to northern markets. Only structure left in town related to railroad period. Private. N.R. 1990.

Punta Gorda. PUNTA GORDA ICE PLANT. 408 Tamiami Trail. 1913, expanded in 1926. Masonry Vernacular. 2 stories. Played a significant role in both the fishing and railroad industry in the community between 1913 and 1933. Served the fishing industry as far south as Fort Myers. Private. N.R. 1990.

Punta Gorda. **PUNTA GORDA RESIDENTIAL DISTRICT**. 1880–1910. 163 buildings, 125 or historical interest. Masonry and Frame Vernacular, some Neo-Classical style and Craftsman. The houses reflect a prosperous and well-planned community, which based its economy on several different industries—fishing, phosphate, railroad transportation, and tourism. Lack of a large number of masonry buildings indicates little participation in the state's 1920s land boom. Private. N.R. 1991.

Punta Gorda. **PUNTA GORDA WOMAN'S CLUB**. 118 Sullivan St. 1925. Mediterranean Revival. 1 story. Gabled roof on front with built-up parapet. Club formed from merger of 3 woman's clubs. Still in use as a woman's club. Site of first community library. Private. N.R. 1991.

Punta Gorda. **H.W. SMITH BUILDING** (Smith Arcade). 121 E. Marion Ave. 1926. Mission and Mediterranean Revival. 1 story. Designed as an arcade, it has a central hallway with commercial space on both sides. Important commercial building in the center of the city. Post Office occupied space in the building for 30 years. Private. N.R. 1991.

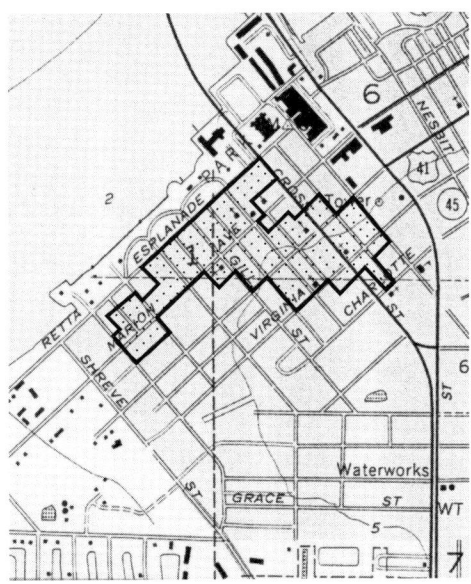

Punta Gorda Residential District

Punta Gorda. **VILLA BIANCA**. 2330 Shore Dr. 1926. Mediterranean Revival. Maxwell Charles Price, architect. 2½ stories. Stucco exterior. Excellent example of a residence built for an affluent town resident. Building and grounds retain much of the character they had in the 1920s. Original owner was a Virginia doctor who came to Florida in 1920. Private. N.R. 1990.

CITRUS COUNTY

Crystal River. **CRYSTAL RIVER INDIAN MOUNDS**. 2 mi. NW of Crystal River on U.S. 19–98. A.D. 1000–A.D. 1500. Swift Creek, Weeden Island, Safety Harbor periods. 2 large truncated mounds, 1 conical burial mound, a large irregular-shaped shell-midden ridge, and a small oval-shaped shell-midden mound. Museum. Private-public. N.R. 1970.

Vicinity of Crystal River. **MULLET KEY**. 3 mi. S of the main mouth of the Crystal River. A.D. 500–A.D. 1500. Deptford through Safety Harbor periods. Oyster-shell midden situated on a key. Private. N.R. 1986.

Homasassa. **YULEE SUGAR MILL RUIN**. Fl. 490 W off U.S. 19. c. 1860. Once the site of a thriving sugar plantation owned by David Levy Yulee, who became a U.S. senator from Florida. Yulee mansion burned by Union troops (1864) and the mill ceased operation. Public. N.R. 1970.

Sherd from cylindrical vessel, Crystal River Mound

15

Old Citrus County Courthouse

Inverness. OLD CITRUS COUNTY COURTHOUSE. 1 Courthouse Square. 1912. Eclectic, with elements of Neo-Classical, Italian Renaissance, Prairie School and Mission styles. 2 stories. Buff-colored brick exterior, a copper cupola with a clock face on each of the 4 sides is topped with a belvedere with miniature columns. Oldest and most important public building in Citrus County. Public. N.R. 1992.

Vicinity of Inverness. FORT COOPER. 3 mi. NE of Inverness on U.S. 41 on W bank of Fort Cooper Lake. 1836. The fort was built and operated between April 2 and April 18, 1836. The 1st Georgia Battalion of Volunteers held off an attack of several hundred Indians throughout that period. Park. Public. N.R. 1972.

CLAY COUNTY

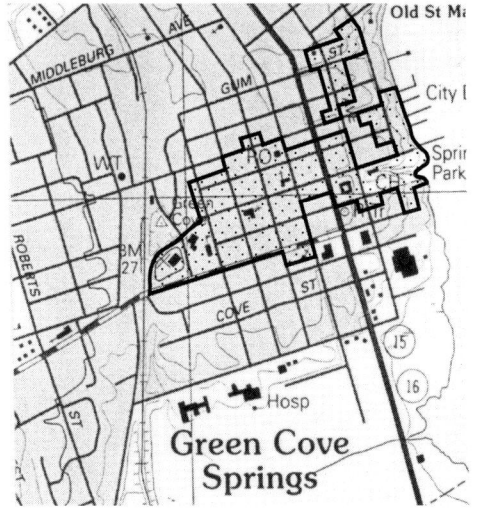
Green Cove Springs Historic District

Green Cove Springs. CLAY COUNTY COURTHOUSE. Brabantio Ave. 1890. Italianate and Second Renaissance elements. A.E. McClure, architect. 2 stories, brick, stuccoed, round arched entrance and small arcaded porch. 1 of only 4 pre-1900 county courthouses extant in the state. Public. N.R. 1975.

Green Cove Springs. GREEN COVE SPRINGS HISTORIC DISTRICT. 1869–1938. 113 buildings, 85 of historical interest. Frame and Masonry Vernacular the most common architectural style, with some Revival residences. The business district of a major port on the St. Johns River during the steamboat period. A number of buildings reflect the relative prosperity of the town during the period. Public and Private. N.R. 1991.

Green Cove Springs. ST. MARY'S CHURCH. St. Johns Ave. 1878. Carpenter Gothic. Lewis, Lawrence and Adams, architects. 1 story, frame, board-and-batten siding, square steeple with octagonal spire. One of the best examples of Carpenter Gothic style in Florida. The church was heavily supported by winter residents of the community. Private. N.R. 1978.

Vicinity of Green Cove Springs. PRINCESS MOUND. Fleming Island. 800 B.C.–A.D. 1300. St. Johns period. Aboriginal sand mound on upland hammock. Hematite nodules, lithics and ceramics found in a mound measuring 33 feet by 17 feet with a maximum height of 5 feet. Function was probably ceremonial. Private. N.R. 1990.

Hibernia. ST. MARGARET'S EPISCOPAL CHURCH. Old Church Rd. 1875. Gothic Revival. 1 story, board-and-batten siding. One of the smallest chapels in the state. The interior is beautifully paneled and wainscoted with local pine. Fine stained-glass windows. Private. N.R. 1973.

St. Mary's Church

Vicinity of Hibernia. BUBBA MIDDEN. E. bank of Black Creek, 2 miles N of its confluence with St. Johns River. 500 B.C.–A.D. 800. St. Johns period. Small refuge midden with aboriginal lithic and ceramic artifacts present. Private. N.R. 1990.

Frosard W. Budington House

Middleburg. FROSARD W. BUDINGTON HOUSE. 3916 Main St. 1910. Queen Anne. 1 story. This is the only example of this style in the community. Budington was a prominent realtor during town's most prosperous period, when it was a major port on the St. Johns River. Private. N.R. 1990.

Middleburg. GEORGE A. CHALKER HOUSE. 2160 Wharf St. 1897. Classical Revival. 2 stories. Wood frame with a flat-roof porch with crowning balustrades. Chalker ran a ferry service on Black Creek and later owned a general store. Private. N.R. 1990.

Middleburg. CLARK-CHALKER HOUSE. 3891 Main St. c. 1850s. Masonry Vernacular with French Colonial elements. 2¹/₂ stories. Tongue-and-groove boards cover the facade. One of the original houses built in the town and associated with 2 of the pioneer families of the town for almost a century. Home was plundered of its furnishings following the Civil War. Private. N.R. 1988.

George A. Chalker House

Middleburg. GEORGE RANDOLPH FRISBEE JR. HOUSE. 2125 Palmetto St. 1889. Frame Vernacular. 2 stories. Steep-pitched side gabled roof. 2-story hip-roof porch. Built at the height of Middleburg's development when the town had many more residents than today. Frisbee ran a grocery store. Private. N.R. 1990.

Middleburg. HASKELL-LONG HOUSE. 3890 Main St. 1890. Frame Vernacular. 2 stories. Metal-roof porch, fieldstone fireplace. Built largely of local materials. Representative of the steamboat era of town's development. Private. N.R. 1990.

Middleburg. METHODIST EPISCOPAL CHURCH AT BLACK CREEK. 3925 Main St. 1847. Frame Vernacular. Charles F. Barthlow, architect. 1 story. 3-part bell tower dominates the main facade. Built during town's first significant period of expansion. One of only 2 surviving antebellum buildings in community. Built by slaves. Private. N.R. 1990.

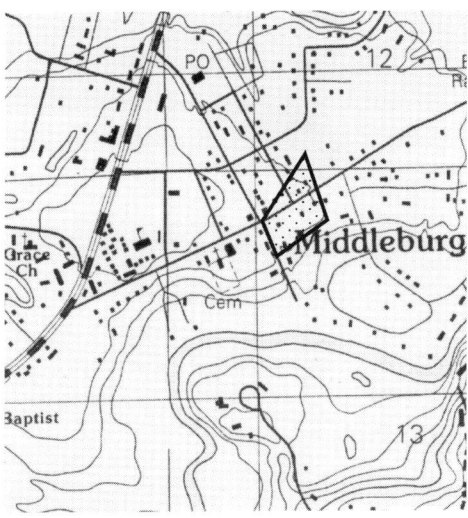

Middleburg Historic District

Middleburg. MIDDLEBURG HISTORIC DISTRICT. 1835–1912. 9 buildings, 6 of historical interest. Frame Vernacular, with Victorian and Italianate elements. Middleburg was a town of much greater relative importance in the area during the 19th century than today. Oldest house is the Clark-Chalker House on 3891 Main St. (c. 1835). N.R. 1990.

Ted Smallwood Store

COLLIER COUNTY

Big Cypress National Preserve. THE PLAZA SITE. Near Ochopee. 500 B.C.–A.D. 1700. Glades period. 4 distinct black-earth midden mounds. Major prehistoric village site. Cultural deposits at the site contained well-preserved materials reflecting subsistence and settlement patterns of early occupants. Public. N.R. 1986.

Vicinity of Carnestown. HALFWAY CREEK SITE. A.D. 800–A.D. 1400. Glades and Seminole periods. Black-dirt midden on 0.5 acres. An excellent example of a prehistoric midden within a mangrove estuarine environment. Site includes evidence of 19th-century Seminole occupation. Public. N.R. 1980.

Chokoloskee Island. TED SMALLWOOD STORE. Fl. 29 in Everglades National Park. 1917. Frame Vernacular. 1 story, board-and-batten, raised on 6-foot pilings. C.S. "Ted" Smallwood came to the island in 1897 and became a large landowner. He ran a general store and the post office. Private. N.R. 1974.

Key Island. KEEWAYDIN CLUB. 1935–. A complex of 20 buildings and 8 supporting structures. The major structure is the lodge, a 1-story irregular shaped building built of local yellow pine. Cottages nearby are 1-story Vernacular. One of a series of camps associated with the Keewaydin Movement, which began in 1849 to promote education through contact with the physical environment. Presently a retreat. Private. N.R. 1987.

Keewaydin Club

Vicinity of Miles City. HINSON MOUNDS. 3 mi. NE of Miles City. A.D. 400–A.D. 900. Glades period. Mounds on a hardwood hammock island which have produced evidence of Native American occupation. Public. N.R. 1978.

Vicinity of Miles City. PLATT ISLAND. N of Miles City off Fl. 29. A.D. 400–A.D. 900. Glades period. A hardwood hammock within a cypress slough containing mounds with materials reflecting subsistence and settlement patterns. Public. N.R. 1978.

Vicinity of Monroe Station. C. J. OSTL SITE. Off U.S. 41 near 50-Mile Bend. A.D. 800–A.D. 1200. Glades period. Black-dirt midden on a hammock island. Due to isolation one of the best-preserved midden sites in area. Public. N.R. 1978.

Naples. NAPLES HISTORIC DISTRICT. 1887–1937. 102 buildings, 78 of historical interest. Vernacular Victorian cottages and simple board-and-batten bungalows. Naples was first developed in 1887 by a group of Kentucky investors. Many homes were built by Midwest families for winter occupancy. Local materials commonly used in construction, including oyster tabby and oolitic limestone. Private. N.R. 1987.

Naples. PALM COTTAGE. 137 12th Ave. S. 1890+. Masonry Vernacular. 1½ stories, tabby exterior walls, stuccoed, 1-story screen porch on front. Built as winter home of Henry Watterson, editor of the *Louisville Courier-Journal*. One of the few remaining tabby-built buildings in Florida. Tabby is a primitive form of concrete made from local materials. Private. N.R. 1982.

Naples. SEABOARD COAST LINE RAILROAD DEPOT. 1051 5th Ave. S. 1926. Mediterranean Revival. L. Philips Clarke, architect. 1 story, concrete, stuccoed. Open arcade on 3 sides with 5 semicircular arches and 4 Corinthian columns. One of the oldest structures in Naples. Typical example of early railroad terminal buildings constructed in the state in 1920s. Now used as community art center and railroad museum. Private. N.R. 1974.

Naples Historic District

Vicinity of Ochopee. BURNS LAKE SITE. 3 mi. W of Ochopee on U.S. 41. A.D. 500–A.D. 1400. Glades period. 3 oval midden mounds covering approximately 1 acre. Prehistoric village area containing well-preserved materials reflecting subsistence and settlement patterns of occupants. Public. N.R. 1986.

Vicinity of Ochopee. SUGAR POT SITE. Big Cypress Swamp. A.D. 1000–A.D. 1400, A.D. 1800–A.D. 1900. Glades, Seminole, Historic periods. Hardwood hammock with 4 black oval mounds clustered around a plaza. Public. N.R. 1978.

Seaboard Coast Line Railroad Depot

Vicinity of Ochopee. TURNER RIVER SITE. 3 mi. S of Ochopee. A.D. 400–A.D. 1400 Glades period. Site includes 4 black-dirt mounds. Public. N.R. 1978.

COLUMBIA COUNTY

Fort White. FORT WHITE PUBLIC SCHOOL HISTORIC DISTRICT. E. Dorch at N. Bryant St. 1915–1940. 5 buildings, 3 of historical interest. Masonry Vernacular buildings. High school building has Italianate tower. High school building built in 1915, auditorium in 1936, and elementary classroom buildings in 1938. Public. N.R. 1989.

Turner River Site, mounds are located around stand of Australian pines

Columbia County High School

Lake City. COLUMBIA COUNTY HIGH SCHOOL. 528 W. Duval St. 1921, 1926. Masonry Vernacular with some Italianate elements. 2 stories. Was of major importance to the education of white high school students for many years. Served later as a junior high school, but was closed in 1989. Public. N.R. 1993.

Lake City. HORACE DUNCAN HOUSE. 202 W. Duval St. 1907. Queen Anne. 2^1/$_2$ stories. Hipped roof, 3 cross gables. House clad in stucco and brick. Associated with the development of Lake City's residential area during the late 19th century, when the area was one of the most important in Florida. Private. N.R. 1993.

T.G. Henderson House

Lake City. T. G. HENDERSON HOUSE. 207 S. Marion St. 1894. Queen Anne. George W. Barber, architect. 2^1/$_2$ stories, frame, complex grouping of porch, balconies, and a hexagonal turret. Much exterior ornamentation. One of the area's finest Victorian-style residences. Private. N.R. 1973.

Lake City. HOTEL BLANCHE (The Blanche). 212 N. Marion St. 1902. Masonry Eclectic. Frank Pierce Milburn, architect. Main facade has three bays. Building occupies a city block. For years Lake City's major hotel and its primary social facility. Presently hotel not in use. Private. N.R. 1990.

Lake City. LAKE ISABELLA HISTORIC RESIDENTIAL DISTRICT. 1866–1940. 183 buildings, 146 of historical interest. Primarily Frame Vernacular buildings, but a number of Classical Revival, Victorian, Craftsman, and Bungalow style. Private. N.R. 1993.

DADE COUNTY

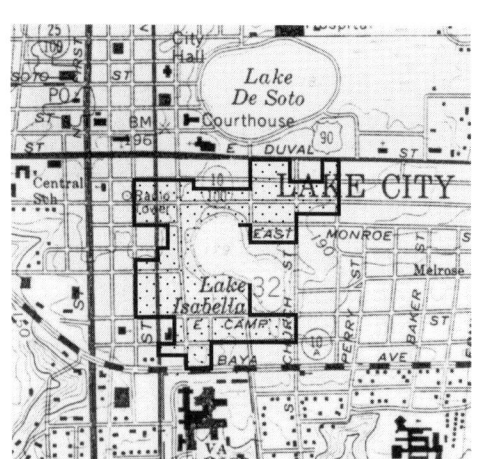

Lake Isabella Historic Residential District

Coconut Grove. EL JARDIN. 3747 Main Highway. 1918. Mediterranean Revival. Richard Kiehnel, architect. 2 stories, rectangular with stucco-finished walls and tile roof. Outstanding example of the Mediterranean Revival style. Richly detailed entrances of Spanish Churrigueresque origin. Built for John Bindley, an executive of Pittsburgh Steel Co. Today a private girls' school. Private. N.R. 1974.

Coconut Grove. FIRST COCONUT GROVE SCHOOL HOUSE. 3429 Devon Rd. 1894 (moved in 1969). 1 story, board-and-batten. 1-room school built by pioneers of Coconut Grove to serve their educational and religious needs. Private. N.R. 1975.

Coconut Grove. **THE KAMPONG.** 4013 Douglas Rd. c. 1890. An estate of 10 acres. Home of Dr. David Fairchild (1869–1954), world famous horticulturist. Here many exotic plants were acclimatized to South Florida. Spanish-style main building (c. 1890). Extensive gardens. Private. N.R. 1984.

Coconut Grove. **THE RALPH M. MUNROE HOUSE** (The Barnacle). 3485 Main Highway. 1891. Frame Vernacular. 2 stories, original 1-story frame structure with central octagonal room, raised above concrete-block ground floor about 1908. Example of regional building adapted to climatic conditions of South Florida. Considered one of the finest examples of Frame Vernacular architecture in area. Under restoration for a museum. Public. N.R. 1973.

Ralph M. Munroe House (The Barnacle)

Coconut Grove. **PAN AMERICAN SEAPLANE BASE AND TERMINAL BUILDING.** 3500 Pan American Dr. 1930–1938. Moderne. Fred J. Gelhaus and B.W. Reeser, architects. 2 stories, rectangular with 2 groups of steel-frame hangars. U.S. terminus for Pan American Airline Clipper Service to South America. Use declined in 1940s when air fields were built in South America. Today Miami's City Hall. Public. N.R. 1975.

Coconut Grove. **PLYMOUTH CONGREGATIONAL CHURCH.** 3429 Devon Rd. 1917. Mission style. Clinton MacKenzie, architect. 1 story, stone, gabled tile roof, 2 bell towers; main entry has 300-year-old carved door with original hardware. The church, organized in 1897, played a major role in the early settlement of the town. Private. N.R. 1974.

Pan American Seaplane Base and Terminal Building (Miami City Hall)

Coconut Grove. **RANSOM SCHOOL** (Pagoda). 3575 Main Highway. 1895–1902. Frame Vernacular with Chinese influence. 2 stories, board-and-batten siding. The core building of the nation's first 2-campus migratory boarding school, the other half being in New York State. Structure is of architectural significance. Private. N.R. 1973.

Coconut Grove. **WOMAN'S CLUB OF COCONUT GROVE.** 2985 S. Bayshore Dr. 1921. Mission style with Spanish Colonial elements. Walter C. de Garmo, architect. 1¹/₂ stories, coral-rock block walls. Interior auditorium with truss ceiling. Built to accommodate one of the earliest woman's clubs in South Florida. An excellent example of the use of local materials. Private. N.R. 1975.

Coral Gables. **CORAL GABLES CITY HALL.** 405 Biltmore Way. 1927–28. Mediterranean Revival. Phineas Paist and Denman Fink, architects. 3 stories, local limestone, stuccoed exterior, tile roof, central 3-stage clock tower, Corinthian colonnade. A major element in the plan of George E. Merrick, founder of Coral Gables, to create a Spanish-Mediterranean city. Public. N.R. 1974.

Coral Gables City Hall

Coral Gables Congregational Church

Coral Gables. CORAL GABLES CONGREGATIONAL CHURCH. 3010 De Soto Blvd. 1924. Mediterranean Revival. Kiehnel and Elliott, architects. Rectangular masonry with stucco finish and tile roof. The Baroque belfry is its most prominent feature; sculptural program over main entrance. One of the earliest religious structures in city. Designed as a replica of a church in Costa Rica. Private. N.R. 1978.

Coral Gables. CORAL GABLES ELEMENTARY SCHOOL. 105 Minorca Ave. 1923–1926. Mediterranean Revival. Richard Kiehnel, architect. 2 stories. A complex of 5 2-story buildings begun in 1923 and completed in 1926. Concrete block with smooth stucco finish. Encloses 2 courtyards connected by shed-roof loggias. School is still in use. Public. N.R. 1988.

Coral Gables. CORAL GABLES HOUSE. 907 Coral Way. 1899, 1906. Masonry Vernacular with Classical Revival details. 1¹/₂ stories, gabled tile roof, walls of local limestone and pine. The childhood home of George E. Merrick, founder of Coral Gables. House museum. Private. N.R. 1973.

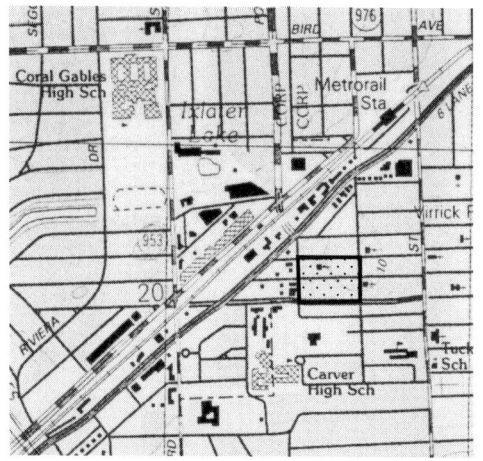

MacFarlane Homestead Historic District

Coral Gables. CORAL GABLES POLICE AND FIRE STATION. 2325 Salzedo St. 1939. Mediterranean Revival. Phineas Paist, architect. 2 stories, limestone exterior obtained from Florida Keys. Depression Moderne sculpture on the facade. Built by the Works Progress Administration to replace an earlier police and fire station. Presently houses city offices. Public. N.R. 1984.

Coral Gables. CORAL GABLES WOMAN'S CLUB. 1001 E. Ponce de Leon Blvd. 1936. Moderne. William Merriam and George Fink, architects. 1 story. Built by the Works Progress Administration (WPA) during the Depression. Constructed with local oolitic limestone. Terra-cotta panels. Rare example of Depression Moderne style. Woman's club was responsible for the city's first library. Private. N.R. 1990.

Coral Gables. DOUGLAS ENTRANCE (La Puerta del Sol). 800 Douglas Rd. 1925. Mediterranean Revival. Walter de Garmo, Denman Fink, and Phineas E. Paist, architects. 3 stories, stone, stuccoed, tile hipped roof, 90-foot belfry tower, 40-foot curved arch across road. Built at a cost of a million dollars as the main entrance to the city from Miami. Included a commercial and residential complex. Presently architects' offices. Private. N.R. 1972.

Coral Gables. MacFARLANE HOMESTEAD HISTORIC DISTRICT. 1930–1940. 38 buildings, 32 of historical interest. Masonry Vernacular. Small black neighborhood established shortly after the town was developed. Dominant structure in the district is St. Mary's First Missionary Baptist Church, built in 1926. Private. N.R. 1994.

Coral Gables. MIAMI-BILTMORE HOTEL. 1200 Anastasia Ave. 1926. Mediterranean Revival. Schultze and Weaver, architects. 10-story main block, 7-story wings, 15-story central tower, hipped roof. Tower inspired by Giralda Tower, Seville, Spain. Resort hotel built by George Merrick as the centerpiece of his planned city. Grounds originally featured canals with gondolas and extensive gardens. Later served as Veterans' Hospital, rehabilitated as a hotel at a cost of 47 million dollars and opened in 1986. Private. N.R. 1972.

Miami-Biltmore Hotel, 1926

Coral Gables. VENETIAN POOL. 2701 De Soto Blvd. 1924. Mediterranean Revival. Phineas E. Paist, architect. Swimming pool designed to resemble a natural lagoon in a Venetian setting. Part of the George Merrick plan to create a Spanish-Mediterranean-style city. Pool originally was a rock quarry. Public. N.R. 1981.

Cutler. CHARLES DEERING ESTATE. SW 167th St. and Old Cutler Rd. 1896, 1922. Frame Vernacular (1896), Mediterranean Revival (1922). This 368-acre site contains two significant architectural structures, one of the earliest remaining Vernacular buildings in the county and a large Mediterranean Revival house. Evidence of Pre-Columbian human occupation on site. Estate was owned by the Deering Family, which made its fortune in farm machinery. Public. N.R. 1986.

Venetian Pool, 1924

Florida City. FLORIDA PIONEER MUSEUM. 900 Krome Ave. 1904 (moved 1964). Frame Vernacular. 1¹/₂ stories, clapboard siding. Built as a residence for employees of the Florida East Coast Railroad. Private. N.R. 1973.

Goulds. WILLIAM ANDERSON GENERAL MERCHANDISE STORE. 15700 SW 232nd St. 1912. Frame Vernacular. 2 stories. The only known general store in Dade County that has survived from the early part of the century when general stores were of great importance. Private. N.R. 1977.

Charles Deering Estate

Goulds. SILVER PALM SCHOOL. 15655 SW 232nd St. 1904. Frame Vernacular. 2 stories, hip roof, and 2-story porch on south elevation. The first of several rural schools built during the early 1900s in south Dade County. School contributed significantly to the community's educational and cultural growth. One of the two surviving rural school houses in south Dade County. Now a private residence. Private. N.R. 1987.

Hialeah. HIALEAH RACE TRACK. E. 4th Ave. between E. 22nd St. and E. 31 St. 1925. Masonry Vernacular with Classical elements. First named the Miami Jockey Club, it became one of the most famous race tracks in the nation. Originally contained a Greyhound track and amusement park. Great efforts have been made to enhance its beauty, including extensive plantings and a famous flock of pink flamingoes. Private. N.R. 1979.

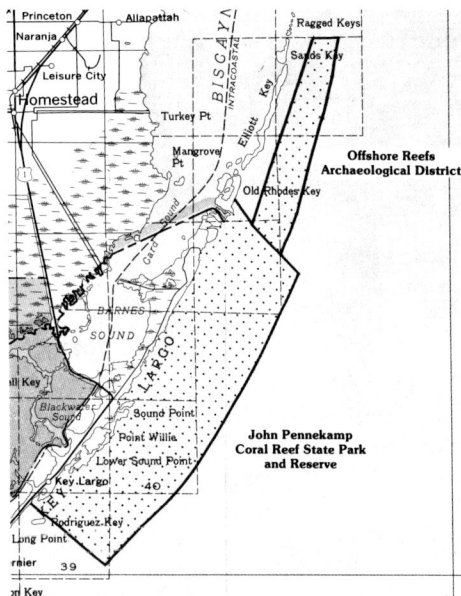

Offshore Reefs Archaeological District

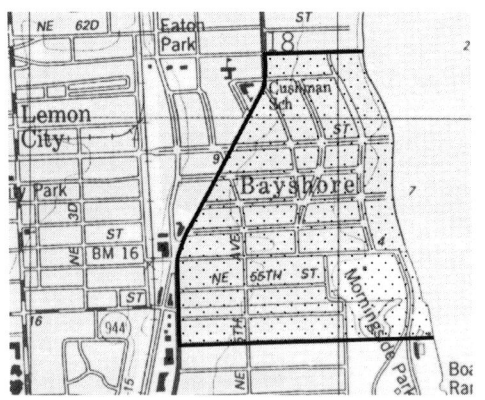

Bay Shore Historic District

Rock Gate and Edward Leedskalnin, c. 1950

Homestead. NEVA KING COOPER ELEMENTARY SCHOOL (Homestead Public School). 520 NW 1st Ave. 1913+. Mediterranean Revival. August Geiger, architect. 1 story, stucco exterior walls, red tile roof, colonnaded garden courtyard. One of the first multiroom schools in the county and one of South Florida's earliest examples of the popular Mediterranean Revival style. Public. N.R. 1985.

Vicinity of Homestead. OFFSHORE REEFS ARCHAEOLOGICAL DISTRICT. Biscayne National Park. Spanish Colonial period to late 19th century. Offshore reef of hard and soft coral which extends 30.1 miles north and south and 4.6 miles east and 7.7 miles west of the eastern boundary of Biscayne National Monument. Possibly as many as 42 ship-wrecks in this district from all periods of American history. Public. N.R. 1984.

Vicinity of Homestead. ROCK GATE (Coral Castle). 28655 S. Federal Highway. 1923 (moved to present site in 1937). Unique open-air sculpture garden with pieces made from local limestone. The creation of Edward Leedskalnin, Latvian immigrant. His works represented his interest in science as well as his yearning for a lost love who rejected him while a youth in Latvia. Private. N.R. 1984.

Miami. ALGONQUIN APARTMENTS. 1819–1825 Biscayne Blvd. 1924, addition in 1927. Mediterranean Revival. 3 stories. Stucco-sheathed building is divided into three bays. The apartments were built during a period when Biscayne Boulevard was being developed as a "modern" shopping street to compete with the older downtown. Private. N.R. 1989.

Miami. ATLANTIC GAS STATION. 668 NW 5th Ave. 1937. Mediterranean Revival. E. A. Ehmann, architect. 1 story. An excellent example of Mediterranean Revival applied to a utilitarian structure. The building's design was commissioned by Atlantic Petroleum Company before gas station design was standardized. Private. N.R. 1988.

Miami. BAY SHORE HISTORIC DISTRICT. 1922–1941. 235 buildings, all of historical interest. Mediterranean and Mission Revivals, Art Deco, and Vernacular styles. Encompasses approximately 100 acres. District is noted for its wide, tree-lined boulevards and its plentiful, flowering trees. Private. N.R. 1944.

Miami. BRICKELL MAUSOLEUM. 501 Brickell Ave. 1921. Masonry Classical Revival. 1 story. Granite with 4 Ionic columns. The mausoleum for the Brickells, one of Miami's most notable pioneer families. Today it stands empty. Public. N.R. 1989.

Miami. CAPE FLORIDA LIGHTHOUSE. Key Biscayne. 1825+ . Conical. Brick, originally 65 feet high, but in 1855 raised to 95 feet. One of a series of lighthouses built after Florida was incorporated into the U.S. The light indicated a dangerous reef. Lighthouse attacked and destroyed by Indians in 1836. Rebuilt in 1846. Became inactive in 1878. Believed to be the oldest structure in the county. Museum. Public. N.R. 1970.

Miami. CENTRAL BAPTIST CHURCH. 500 NE 1st Ave. 1926. Neo-Classical with elements of Renaissance Revival. Dougherty and Gardner, architects. 4 stories. Building is capped by a polygonal rotunda extending above the 4-story height. 2 projected porticos. Seating capacity of 2,500. One of the last 3 active churches to hold regular services within downtown Miami. Private. N.R. 1989.

Miami. CITY NATIONAL BANK BUILDING. 121 SE 1st Ave. 1925. Commercial style, 11 stories, embellished with Classical elements. Hampton and Ehmann, architects. A good example of commercial architecture. Open loggia and classical ornamentation. Private. N.R. 1989.

Miami. CITY OF MIAMI CEMETERY. 1800 NE 2nd Ave. 1897–1920. 10-acre site sold to city in 1897 by Brickell family for a public cemetery. Enclosed by a masonry wall with iron gate entrance. Julia Tuttle ,"mother of Miami," buried here. Jewish section. Small Mediterranean building in cemetery used as office. Public. N.R. 1989.

Cape Florida Lighthouse

Miami. CONGRESS BUILDING. 111 NE 2nd Ave. 1923, 1925. Commercial style with Classical elements. Martin L. Hampton, architect. 21 stories, beige, glazed terra-cotta exterior, 2nd floor has 5 arched bays. An excellent example of "boom time" architectural style. The building is also noteworthy because it was originally 5 stories, but designed to support additional floors which were built later (1925). Private. N.R. 1985.

Miami. DADE COUNTY COURTHOUSE. 73 W. Flagler St. 1925–28. Neo-Classical style. A. Ten Eyck Brown and August Geiger, architects. 28 stories. A broad base and central tower. The base of the building is faced with Stone Mountain granite, while the other floors are sheathed in terra-cotta tinted to match the granite slabs. Originally served the county and city governments, including the jail. Now entirely occupied by the judiciary. Public. N.R. 1989.

Miami. D.A. DORSEY HOUSE. 250 NW 9th St. c. 1914. Frame Vernacular. 2 stories. Home of one of Miami's most prominent black businessmen. An early developer of Overtown, Dorsey purchased Fisher Island and Elliot Key with the idea of setting up a resort for blacks. Private. N.R. 1989.

Congress Building

Miami. ALFRED I. DUPONT BUILDING. 169 E. Flagler St. 1937. Moderne, with Art Deco elements. Marsh and Saxelbye, architects. 17 stories. Steel frame skeleton and exterior walls clad in stone. Black granite wrapping around 1st floor. Very ornate lobby. The first Miami skyscraper since the Dade County Courthouse was built. First major downtown project following the collapse of the 1920s land boom. Private. N.R. 1989.

Miami. ENTRANCE TO CENTRAL MIAMI. Red Rd. at SW 34th St. and SW 35th St. 1925. Mediterranean Revival. 8 towers and a park at the western entrance to Coral Gables. Coral Gables Waterway passes through park. A pair of 13-foot square towers form the entrance. Smaller towers flank SW 34th and 35th streets. Public. N.R. 1989.

Entrance To Central Miami

Miami. FIRE STATION NO. 2. 1401 N. Miami Ave. 1926. Mediterranean Revival. August C. Geiger, architect. 2 stories. Square tower flanked by lower wings which contain arched entrance for vehicles. Barrel-tile roof. Once one of the city's principal stations, but now vacant. Public. N.R. 1989.

Miami. FIRE STATION NO. 4. 1000 S. Miami Ave. 1922. Mediterranean Revival. H. Hasting Mundy, architect. 2 stories, stucco exterior, hipped tile roof, arcaded porch, balconies, and decorative detail. The oldest and most outstanding fire station within the city. No longer used for this function. Public. N.R. 1984.

Miami. FLORIDA EAST COAST RAILWAY LOCOMOTIVE NO. 153. 12450 SW 152nd St. 1922. Pacific-type, 4-6-2, oil-burning locomotive. Originally constructed for the Flagler System's East Coast Railway, it was used for passengers and freight until 1937 when it was sold to the United States Sugar Corporation to haul cane from the fields to its Clewiston mill. Located now at the Gold Coast Railroad Museum. Private. N.R. 1985.

Freedom Tower

Miami. FREEDOM TOWER. 600 Biscayne Blvd. 1925. Spanish Renaissance Revival. Schutze and Weaver, architects. 14-story building surmounted by an octagonal tower with Spanish Plateresque detail. Formerly the home of the *Miami News,* the city's oldest newspaper. From 1962 until 1974 a reception center for Cuban refugees. Design was inspired by the Giralda Tower in Seville, Spain. Private. N.R. 1979.

Miami. GESU CHURCH. 140 NE 2nd St. 1922. Spanish Colonial Revival. 4 stories, brick, stucco; stepped belfry and tower complex over narthex. One of Miami's oldest Catholic churches. Situated in an area of the city which has greatly changed. Private. N.R. 1974.

Miami. GREATER BETHEL A.M.E. CHURCH. 245 NW 8th St. 1927, completed in 1942. Mediterranean Revival. John Sculthorpe, architect. 2 stories. Square towers flanked by a shed roof. Home of Miami's oldest black congregation, organized in 1896. Building that proceeded the "Greater" church was named "Little Bethel." The pay-as-you-go policy accounts for long construction period. Private. N.R. 1992.

Miami. I. AND E. GREENWALD STEAM ENGINE NO. 1058. 1906. 3898 Shipping Ave. Built in Cincinnati, Ohio, in 1906, the engine has an unusual power transmission system utilizing a rope drive. It is believed to be the only surviving engine of its type. Engine was relocated in 1984 from Beaumont, Texas, where for many years it was used in rice irrigation. Reconditioned. Private. N.R. 1987.

Miami. HÄHN BUILDING. 140 NE 1st Ave. 1921. Commercial style with Classical detail. George L. Pfeiffer and Gerald J. O'Reilly, architects. 2 stories. Represents an attempt to adopt a commercial building with Classical detail within local stylistic trends. Private. N.R. 1989.

Miami. HALISSEE HALL. 1700 NW 10th Ave. 1912. Masonry Vernacular with Classical Revival details. 2^{1}/$_{2}$ stories, walls of local limestone. 2-story portico with 6 fluted columns. Home of John Sewell, Miami pioneer merchant. Excellent example of the application of Classical Revival style to the South Florida environment. Presently part of University of Miami's medical center. Private. N.R. 1974.

I. and E. Greenwald Steam Engine No. 1058

Miami. HUNTINGTON BUILDING (Consolidated Bank Building). 168 SE 1st St. 1925. Commercial style. Louis Kamper, George L. Pfeiffer, and Gerald J. O'Reilly, architects. 13 stories. Exterior is clad in stucco. A wide belt course separates the first and second stories. Articulated roof line contains 11 knight figures sitting atop an extension of the vertical piers. Private. N.R. 1989.

Miami. INGRAHAM BUILDING. 25 SE 2nd Ave. 1926. Renaissance Revival. Schultze and Weaver, architects. 12 stories. Clad in Indiana limestone. Roof is hipped and sheathed in Spanish tiles. Interior of the building is very ornate. The same architectural firm designed New York's Waldorf Astoria Hotel. Private. N.R. 1989.

Miami. J & S BUILDING (Cola-Nip Building). 221-233 NW 9th St. 1925. Masonry Vernacular. 2 stories. Concrete block. First floor has a number of store fronts, most now boarded-up. Closely associated with the early commercial life of the Overtown community, one of the city's oldest black neighborhoods. Private. N.R. 1989.

Halissee Hall

Miami. DR. JAMES M. JACKSON OFFICE. 190 SE 12th Ter. 1905. Frame Vernacular with Classical Revival details. 1 story, over stone piers, Tuscan porch. Office and surgery of Dr. James M. Jackson, Miami's first resident physician. Presently the offices of the Dade Heritage Trust. Private. N.R. 1975.

Miami. KENTUCKY HOME (Anderson Hotel). 1221 and 1227 NE 1st Ave. 1918, 1924. Masonry Vernacular. 3 stories. 2 buildings linked by an arch at entrance to courtyard. Design adopted to local environment through 3-story open porches. An excellent example of a downtown rooming house, a dwelling common in the early history of Miami. Private. N.R. 1989.

Miami. LYRIC THEATER. 819 NW 2nd Ave. c. 1914. Masonry Vernacular. 2 stories. Concrete block sheathed in stucco. Arched parapet and elaborate bays. Was important as the center of Overtown's early social life. Overtown was one of the city's earliest black neighborhoods. Owned and operated by blacks, and primarily featured black entertainers. Popular among white Miamians as well. Private. N.R. 1989.

Miami. MARTINA APARTMENTS. 1023 S. Miami Ave. 1922. Mediterranean Revival elements. 3 stories. 3 blocks of apartments connected together along the S. Miami Ave. front. Private. N.R. 1989.

Miami Edison Senior High School, 1930s

Miami. MEYER-KISER BUILDING. 139 NE 1st St. 1925, 1926. Commercial style. Martin L. Hampton, architect. 17 stories (now 10). Originally the building was 17 stories, but the September hurricane of 1926 forced the removal of the upper 10 floors. Built to be hurricane resistant, it sustained severe hurricane damage only 1 year after it was completed. One of the few downtown buildings insured. Private. N.R. 1989.

Miami. MIAMI CITY HOSPITAL, BUILDING 1. 1611 NW 12th Ave. 1918 (moved in 1979). Mediterranean Revival with Beaux-Arts influence. August Geiger, architect. 1 story, 7-bay arcade on south facade; decorative stucco frieze. Miami's first hospital. Public. N.R. 1979.

Miami. MIAMI EDISON SENIOR HIGH SCHOOL. 6101 NW 2nd Ave. 1928–1931. Masonry Vernacular with Art Deco auditorium. Mundy, Pfieffer and Robertson, architects. 3 stories, masonry, stuccoed. The main classroom building is Vernacular, while the auditorium is Art Deco with extensive interior detail. Public. N.R. 1986.

Miami Senior High School

Miami. MIAMI SENIOR HIGH SCHOOL. 2450 SW 1st St. 1927. Spanish Colonial Revival. Kiehnel and Elliott, architects. 4 stories. Rectangular in shape, it encloses 4 interior courtyards. Frontage of over 600 feet along SW 1st. Occupies 19 acres. Entrance is deep set with compound recessed arches of distinct French Romanesque inspiration. First senior high school constructed in Dade County. Public. N.R. 1990.

Miami. MIAMI WOMAN'S CLUB. 1737 N. Bayshore Dr. 1926. Renaissance Revival with Spanish Colonial elements. August Geiger, architect. 4¹/₂ stories, U-shaped, flat tile roof. Built to accommodate the Miami Woman's Club, organized in 1900 and chartered in 1911. Club has been active in numerous civic projects, including the public library. Private. N.R. 1974.

Miami. MOUNT ZION BAPTIST CHURCH. 301 NW 9th St. 1928. Mediterranean Revival. William Arthur Bennett, architect. 2 stories. One of the few examples of Mediterranean Revival style found in the black community of Overtown. The place of worship of one of Miami's oldest black congregations. Private. N.R. 1988.

Miami. OLD U.S. POST OFFICE AND COURTHOUSE (Ameri First Federal). 100–118 NE 1st Ave. 1912–14. Neo-Classical. Oscar Wenderoth, Kiehnel and Elliott, architects. 3 stories. Exterior clad in Bedford limestone from Indiana. The east side parallel to NE 1st Ave. is characterized by a facade 9 bays in length and 3 stories high. Converted to bank in 1937. Private. N.R. 1989.

Miami. OLYMPIA THEATER AND OFFICE BUILDING (Gusman Cultural Center). 174 E. Flagler St. 1925. Mediterranean Revival. John Eberson, architect. 10 stories, faced in brick with terra-cotta and wrought iron detail. The theater is an outstanding example of the "atmospheric" style, with the design suggesting an amphitheater set in a courtyard of a Spanish villa. Public. N.R. 1984.

© 1983, Dan Forer

Olympia Theater and Office Building, south wall of auditorium and proscenium arch

Miami. PALM COTTAGE. 60 SE 4th St. c. 1897. Frame Vernacular. Joseph A. McDonald, architect. 2¹/₂ stories. Moved from its original site in 1980. Believed to be the last known structure in Miami directly associated with Henry Flagler and the early years of the city's development. Oldest known residence in downtown Miami. Presently unoccupied. Public. N.R. 1989.

Miami. PRISCILLA APARTMENTS. 318–320 NE 19th St. store on 1845 Biscayne Blvd. 1925, 1927. Mediterranean Revival. R.A. Preas, architect. 3 stories. A rectangular building with an L-shaped addition (1927). Square 4-story tower on NW corner, smaller tower on SW corner. Part of an effort by an early developer to establish a new shopping area on Biscayne Blvd. Private. N.R. 1989.

Miami. S & S SANDWICH SHOP. 1757 NE 2nd Ave. 1938. Art Deco. 1 story. Sheathed in structural glass in contrasting colors. Its west front is only 12 feet high. Interior retains much of its original elements. Only remaining example of a very popular restaurant style from the early 1930s. Still in use. Private. N.R. 1989.

Miami. ST. JOHN'S BAPTIST CHURCH. 1328 NW 3rd Ave. 1940. Gothic style with Art Deco and Moderne detail. McKissack and McKissack, architects. 2 stories. Masonry, clad in buff brick. A black church designed by a black architectural firm. Church is little altered from when it was built. Private. N.R. 1992.

Miami. SECURITY BUILDING (Capital Building). 117 NE 1st Ave. 1926. Commercial. Robert Greenfield, architect. 16 stories. Its embellishments are in the Second Empire architectural mode. Steel frame, granite facing. Construction began in the last year of Miami's land boom. When finished it was the most imposing building in the city's center. Private. N.R. 1989.

Miami. SHORELAND ARCADE (Dade Federal Savings). 120 NE 1st Ave. 1925. Pfeiffer and O'Reilly, architects. 2 stories. Eight bays, each consisting of a large arched opening flanked by stylized pilasters embellished with masonry medallions sporting symbols of Florida history. The last remaining intact arcade in downtown Miami. Private. N.R. 1989.

Miami. SOUTH RIVER DRIVE HISTORIC DISTRICT. 1908–1914. 6 buildings and 3 outbuildings of historical significance. Predominant architectural style is Frame Vernacular. All buildings of historical importance have projected porches. The buildings within this district are fine representations of early 20th-century Frame Vernacular architecture in Miami. One of the earliest areas of Miami to be settled, it contained a number of boarding houses. Private. N.R. 1987.

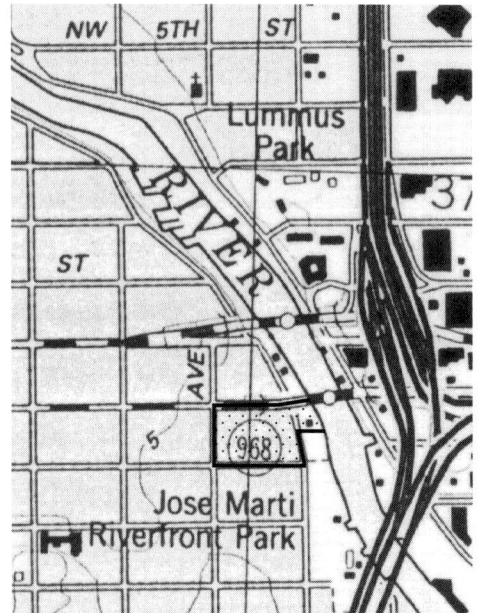

South River Drive Historic District

Miami. SOUTHSIDE SCHOOL. 45 SW 13th St. 1914, additions in 1922, 1925. Mission Revival elements. August Geiger, architect. 2 stories. Sole surviving example of a popular Miami school design. Excellent adaptation of the design to the local climate. One of the oldest public school buildings in Miami. Today serves almost 500 students K-6. Public. N.R. 1989.

Miami. TRINITY EPISCOPAL CATHEDRAL. 464 NE 16th St. 1923. Romanesque Revival. Harold Hasting Mundy, architect. Main facade has a gabled parapet with cross finial. Corners supported by buttresses. Much use of stained glass. Regarded as one of the great monuments of boom architecture. When built, the area was the center of the Episcopal community. Private. N.R. 1980.

Trinity Episcopal Cathedral

Miami. U.S. CAR NO. 1. 12450 SW 152nd St. 1928. Built in 1928 by the Pullman Co., Car No. 1 was rebuilt in 1942 for use by President Franklin D. Roosevelt. The redesign included making the car impenetrable to attack. The interior was redesigned to serve as a mobile presidential suite and includes office, dining room, and sleeping accommodations. Used by President Ronald Reagan to Campaign in Ohio in 1984. Presently in the Gold Coast Railroad Museum. Private. N.R. 1977.

U.S. Car No. 1

Miami. U.S. POST OFFICE AND COURTHOUSE. 300 NE 1st Ave. 1933. Mediterranean Revival. Paist and Steward, architects. 3 stories, East facade has 2-story engaged Corinthian columns. An excellent example of Mediterranean Revival architecture. The largest structure to be built of local limestone in South Florida. N.R. 1983.

Vizcaya

31

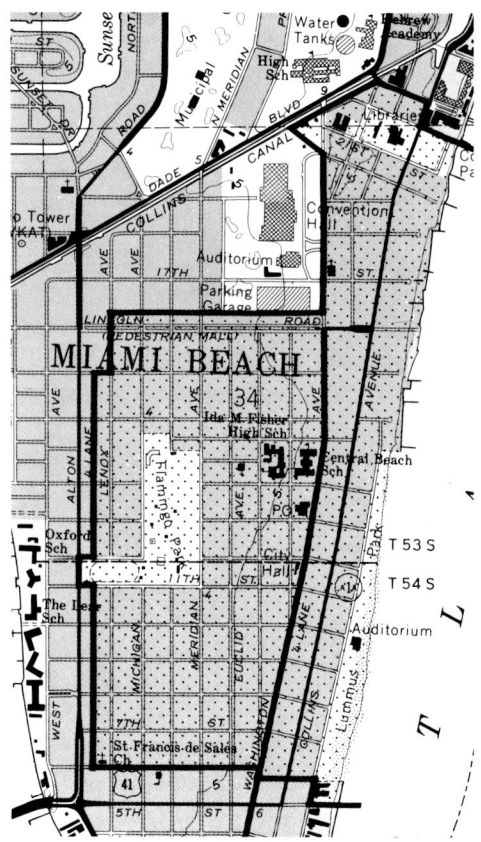

Miami. VIZCAYA (James Deering Estate). 3251 S. Miami Ave. 1914–1916. Italian Renaissance. F. Burral Hoffman and Paul Chalfin, architects. 3 stories, concrete, stuccoed with coral trim; open loggias and arcades with native coral ornamentation. Extensive formal gardens. Many outbuildings. Interior decorated with numerous elements from European palaces. Formerly the 70-room mansion of industrialist James Deering, who employed over 1000 people in its construction. Replica of an Italian Renaissance palace. Museum. Public. N.R. 1970.

Miami. WALGREEN DRUGSTORE. 200 E. Flagler St. 1936. Streamline Moderne style. Zimmerman, Saxe, MacBridge, and Ehmann, architects. 5 stories. One of the most unique commercial buildings in downtown Miami, and one of the best examples of its architectural style in South Florida. Ribbon windows and a curved corner entrance are important identifying features. Private. N.R. 1989.

Miami. J. W. WARNER HOUSE. 111 SW 5th Ave. 1912. Classical Revival. George L. Pfeiffer, architect. $2^{1}/_{2}$ stories, poured concrete, stuccoed, 2-story portico, massive Ionic columns. Interior is distinguished by detailed woodwork and central staircase. Home of the Warner family, which operated a floral business for 66 years. Now private offices. Private. N.R. 1983.

Miami Beach. BETH JACOB SOCIAL HALL AND CONGREGATION. 301 and 311 Washington Ave. 1928, 1936. Classical Revival with Moderne influence. Henry Hohauser, architect. 2 stories, stucco. Large central arched entrance. Social Hall (1928), formerly the synagogue, and the present structure (1936) were the first religious structures of the Orthodox Jewish Congregation of Miami Beach. Private. N.R. 1980.

Miami Beach Architectural District, view northeast from 11th street

Miami Beach. MIAMI BEACH ARCHITECTURAL DISTRICT. 1920–1940. More than 650 architecturally significant buildings in a 125-block area. Predominant styles are Mediterranean Revival and Moderne. Notable buildings are the Cardozo Hotel, Tides Hotel, Victor Hotel, Old City Hall, Bass Museum, Delano Hotel, and Amsterdam Palace. The district contains the largest collection of Art Moderne buildings in the nation. Architectural styles greatly influenced by those of Chicago's Century of Progress (1933) and the New York World's Fair (1939). N.R. 1979.

Miami and Miami Beach. VENETIAN CAUSEWAY. NE 15th St. and Dade Blvd. 1926. Bascule bridge. A series of bridges connecting the Venetian Islands and stretching between Miami and Miami Beach. Total of 12 bridges. Octagonal concrete entrance towers. The oldest causeway in Metropolitan Miami. Public. N.R. 1989.

Miami Shores. GRAND CONCOURSE APARTMENTS. 421 Grand Concourse. 1926. Mediterranean Revival. Robert Law Weed, architect. 4-story central tower, 2-story wings, masonry, stuccoed, 3-bay entrance loggia, 7-bay loggias on wings. The only large, multiunit building constructed from an original plan that would have included a series of grand hotels and apartments. Private. N.R. 1985.

Miami Shores. THEMATIC RESOURCE REGION. NE 91st St. – NE 102nd St. 1926–. Mediterranean Revival. Kiehnel, Elliott and others, architects. 1 and 2 stories. 24 residences, part of a mid 1920s development by the Shoreland Company. Most homes are excellent examples of Mediterranean Revival style. Some were built to suggest a weathered or aged appearance. Private. N.R. 1928.

Miami Springs. COUNTRY CLUB ESTATES THEMATIC RESOURCE AREA. Buildings principally on Deer Run and Hunting Lodge Sts. 1924–1927. 10 buildings, 7 of which are on the National Register of Historic Places. Carl Adams House, 31 Hunting Lodge (1985); Clune Building, 45 Curtiss Pkwy (1985); Lua Curtiss House 1, 85 Deer Run (1985); Lua Curtiss House II, 150 Hunting Lodge (1985); Hequembourg House, 851 Hunting Lodge (1985); Millard-McCarty House, 424 Hunting Lodge (1986); Osceola Apartment Hotel, 200 Azure Way (1985). Pueblo Revival. These structures and several others are the only unaltered of an original 135 which were built in the planned community of Miami Springs. Associated with the development project of Glenn H. Curtiss, internationally recognized aviator and inventor, and James Bright. N.R. 1985 and 1986.

Millard-McCarty House, Country Club Estates Thematic Resource Area

North Miami. ARCH CREEK HISTORIC AND ARCHAEOLOGICAL SITE. 1855 NE 135th St. and Biscayne Blvd. Prehistoric through 19th century. A tropical hardwood hammock near Arch Creek on which there is an Indian midden as well as the sluice of a destroyed 19th-century coontie mill. Coontie is an edible native plant used by Indians and early settlers as a source of starch. Public. N.R. 1986.

North Miami Beach. OLD SPANISH MONASTERY (Monastery of St. Bernard of Clarvaux; Cistercian Monastery of Sacramenia, Segovia, Spain). 16711 W. Dixie Highway. A.D. 1141, reconstructed in Florida 1952–1953. Spanish Romanesque and early Spanish Gothic. The cloister, most notably its chapter house, is a representative example of 12th-century Spanish ecclesiastic architecture. Purchased by William Randolph Hearst in 1925 and reconstructed by Allen Carswell, who built the Cloisters in New York. Presently an Episcopal Church. Private. N.R. 1972.

Old Spanish Monastery

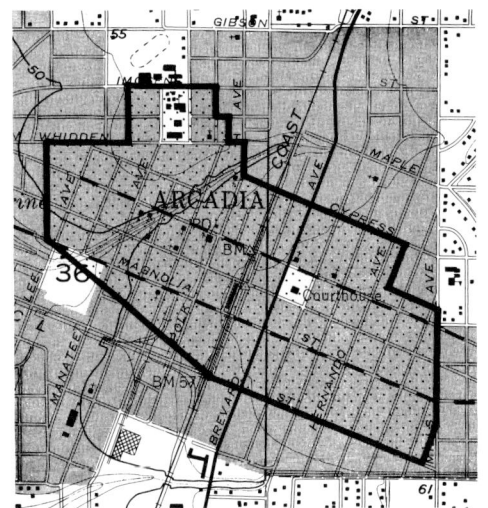

Opa-locka. OPA-LOCKA THEMATIC RESOURCE AREA. 1925–1928. 16 residences and 4 other buildings on the National Register scattered throughout a wide area of the city. Moorish Revival. Bernhardt Emil Muller was commissioned by the developers of the city to design buildings in Moorish Revival style based on visual impressions from stories taken from *1001 Tales from the Arabian Nights*. Outstanding examples of this style are: Opa-locka Company Administration Building, 777 Sharazad Blvd, which got its inspiration from the "Tale of Layn al Asnan," and Opa-locka Railroad Station, 490 Ali Baba Ave., whose design was inspired by the "Tale of Ali Baba and the Forty Thieves." N.R. 1982–1987.

South Miami. HERVEY ALLEN STUDY (The Glades Estate). 8251 52nd Ave. 1934. Masonry Vernacular. 1 story of local limestone. For many years the study of the novelist Hervey Allen, who wrote the novel *Anthony Adverse* and numerous other works of fiction. Most of his later works written here. Private. N.R. 1974.

DE SOTO COUNTY

Arcadia Historic District
Arcadia Business District, c. 1930

Arcadia. ARCADIA HISTORIC DISTRICT. 1886–1930. 374 buildings in 58 blocks. Predominant styles: Masonry and Frame Vernacular. Much use of rusticated concrete block. Several structures show Romanesque and Italianate features. Notable structures: De Soto County Courthouse, Koch Building, and Railroad Station. District contains a concentration of buildings which represent the historic development of the town for almost 50 years. N.R. 1984.

Opa-locka City Hall

DIXIE COUNTY

Horseshoe Beach. GARDEN PATCH ARCHAEOLOGICAL SITE. CR 351 off Old Railroad Grade. 500 B.C.–A.D. 400 Weeden Island period. A site with great potential as a source of information on the Weeden Island culture. Site has 3 sand burial-ceremonial mounds, 2 extensive middens, and 2 other mounds of undetermined function. Public. N.R. 1991.

DUVAL COUNTY

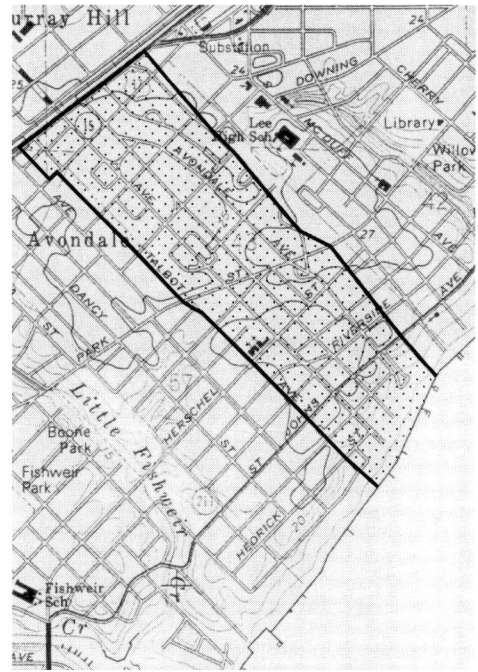
Avondale Historic District

Jacksonville. AVONDALE HISTORIC DISTRICT. 1909–1936. 825 buildings, 729 or historical interest. Colonial and Mediterranean Revival, Bungalow and Craftsman styles common. A residential district of 1- and 2-story single-family residences of many architectural styles. District was laid out for middle-class families, with some custom-made homes for the wealthy. One of the first areas developed in Jacksonville to adapt to widespread use of the automobile. Private. N.R. 1989.

Jacksonville. BETHEL BAPTIST INSTITUTIONAL CHURCH. 1058 Hogan St. 1904. Greek Revival and Romanesque elements. M.H. Hubbard, architect. 1 story, large square bell tower, several different roof types. For years the focal point for the religious and community life of many of Jacksonville's blacks. Present building replaced one that was destroyed in the fire of 1901, which burned much of the city's downtown. Private. N.R. 1978.

Brewster Hospital

Jacksonville. BREWSTER HOSPITAL. 915 W. Monroe St. 1885. Masonry Vernacular. 2 stories, red brick, 2-story, full-width porch. Originally the residence of Hans Christian Peters. House later became the city's first black hospital and nurses' training school. Building became the nucleus of a large complex. Closed in 1966. Private. N.R. 1976.

Jacksonville. NAPOLEON BONAPARTE BROWARD HOUSE. 9953 Heckscher Dr. 1878. Frame Vernacular with Victorian elements. 2 stories, 2-story veranda on front facade, square tower. Napoleon B. Broward was Governor of Florida between 1905 and 1909. Broward, who came from White Springs, owned a steam tugboat, and later became Duval County sheriff, state representative, and finally governor. Private. N.R. 1972.

Jacksonville. BUCKMAN AND ULMER BUILDING. 29–33 W. Monroe St. 1925. Masonry Italian Renaissance. Marsh and Saxelbye, architects. 2 stories. Consists of lower storefront and upstairs office space, cast-stone piers divide the south side into three sections. The piers terminate in a frieze stretching the length of the facade. Private. N.R. 1992.

Church of the Immaculate Conception

Dyal-Upchurch Building, c. 1905

Epping Forest

Jacksonville. CARLING HOTEL (The Roosevelt). 33 W. Adams St. 1926. Italian Renaissance. Thompson, Holmes and Converse, architects. 15 stories. Finished with brick, limestone and terra-cotta. One of Jacksonville's finest hotels. Scene of a fire which killed 22 guests in December 1963. The following year the hotel was closed. Now a retirement facility. Private. N.R. 1991.

Jacksonville. CATHERINE STREET FIRE STATION. 14 Catherine St. 1902. Masonry Vernacular. 2 stories, brick, flat roof. The building accommodated an engine and two horses on 1st floor and men on the 2nd. Closed in 1933. Museum of the city fire of 1901. Public. N.R. 1972.

Jacksonville. CENTENNIAL HALL–EDWARD WATERS COLLEGE. 1658 Kings Rd. 1916. Eclectic. Howell and Stokes, architects. 3 stories, brick, main facade has 2-story pavilion with paired engaged columns. The oldest building on the campus of Edward Waters College, a black Methodist institution founded in 1891. Private. N.R. 1976.

Jacksonville. CHURCH OF THE IMMACULATE CONCEPTION. 121 E. Duval St. 1907. Late Gothic Revival. M.H. Hubbard, architect. 2 stories. One of the finest examples of Late Gothic Revival church architecture in Florida. Rough-faced Kentucky limestone exterior, carved-stone detail, with lancet window and door openings throughout the building. Private. N.R. 1992.

Jacksonville. DYAL–UPCHURCH BUILDING. 4 E. Bay St. 1901–02. Beaux Arts. Henry J. Klutho, architect. 6 stories, brick, external decoration of Bedford limestone. The city's first skyscraper, the first building in the city to be constructed on wood pilings (426), and the first building in Florida designed by Henry J. Klutho, who went on to design many more, including a number in downtown Jacksonville. Private. N.R. 1980.

Jacksonville. EL MODELO BLOCK. 513 W. Bay St. 1886-1889. Eclectic. 3 stories, brick. The largest remaining structure in Jacksonville. Originally it housed El Modelo Cigar Manufacturing Co., one of the largest employers within the city. Functioned as a hotel between 1915 and 1965. Office building. Private. N.R. 1980.

Jacksonville. EPPING FOREST. Christopher Point. 1927. Mediterranean Revival. Marsh and Saxelbye, architects. 2 stories, masonry, stuccoed, front center entrance tower with open belfry. Elaborate interior. Home of Alfred Du Pont, who after improving manufacturing methods in his ancestors' chemical plants, spent much of his later years in Florida promoting the state and his numerous interests within it. Private. N.R. 1973.

Jacksonville. FLORIDA BAPTIST CONVENTION BUILDING (Rogers Building). 218 W. Church St. 1924–1925. Commercial style. H.J. Klutho, architect. 5 stories, brick. One of the last buildings constructed during the city's renaissance, following the great fire of 1901. Housed the Prohibition Bureau and the Intelligence Unit of the U.S. Treasury during the Prohibition Era. Private. N.R. 1984.

Jacksonville. FLORIDA THEATRE. 128–134 E. Forsyth St. 1926–1927. Mediterranean Revival. E. Hall and R. Benjamin, architects. 7 stories. elaborate window surrounds, cartouches, friezes, large marquee. When built it was the finest theater in the city, an excellent example of the "atmospheric" theaters being built during the period. Among others, Eddie Cantor, George Jessel, Sally Rand, Bob Hope, and Elvis Presley have appeared on its stage. Private. N.R. 1982.

Jacksonville. GROOVER-STEWART DRUG COMPANY BUILDING. 25 N. Market St. 1925. Industrial Vernacular. Marsh and Saxelbye, architects. 4 stories. Headquarters of one of the south's leading manufacturers and distributors of pharmaceuticals during the 1920s and 1930s. Now vacant. Private. N.R. 1992.

Jacksonville. JACKSONVILLE TERMINAL COMPLEX. 1000 W. Bay St. 1897, 1919. Union Station (1898). Italianate. W.B.W. Hoe, architect. Terminal (1919). Classical Revival. K.M. Murchison, architect. Terminal: 1 story, reinforced concrete, front has Doric portico with 14 colossal limestone columns. The complex includes the Jacksonville Terminal and a portion of the 1897 Union Terminal, which was gutted by fire in 1979. Presently a convention center. Private. N.R. 1976.

Jacksonville Terminal

Jacksonville. HENRY JOHN KLUTHO HOUSE. 28–30 W. 9th St. 1908 (moved about 1925). Prairie style. Henry John Klutho, architect. 2 stories, masonry and frame, arcaded entrance loggia. Home of Henry J. Klutho, who designed many of the major buildings in downtown Jacksonville. Klutho lived in it, except between 1929 and 1935, until his death in 1964. Private. N.R. 1978.

Jacksonville. LANE-TOWERS HOUSE. 3730 Richmond St. 1927–1928. Tudor Revival. Marsh and Saxelbye, architects. 2^1/$_2$ stories, varicolored red brick, half-timbered and stucco 2nd story. Lavish interior. House is situated on two landscaped acres. Home built for Edward W. Lane, a Georgian who founded the Atlantic National Bank and was a prominent figure in civic and social affairs within the community. Private. N.R. 1982.

Jacksonville. LITTLE THEATRE. 2032 San Marco Blvd. 1938. Art Deco style. Ivan H. Smith, architect. 2 stories. Stucco exterior. Most distinguishing feature is a side facing double entrance stair on the main facade. Long an important element in Jacksonville's amateur little theater movement. Private. N.R. 1991.

Jacksonville. MASONIC TEMPLE. 410 Broad St. 1912–1916. Commercial style. Mark and Sheftall, architects. 5 stories, red brick, ornamentation of the street facades includes use of pressed metal, terra-cotta, and glazed brick. Focal point for the black community's commercial and fraternal activities. Building was designed to hold offices of black businesses as well as the temple. Private. N.R. 1980.

Henry John Klutho House

Jacksonville. MOROCCO TEMPLE. 219 Newnan St. 1910–1911. Prairie style with Egyptian motifs. Henry John Klutho, architect. 3 stories concrete, terra-cotta ornamentation. Main entrance set with a 2-story battered architrave with a massive transom on squat Egyptian-style columns The temple is the oldest Shrine affiliate in Florida. Private. N.R. 1979.

Jacksonville. MOUNT ZION A.M.E. CHURCH. 201 E. Beaver St. 1905. Romanesque Revival. 1905. J.B. Carr, architect. 2 stories. Brick, with arched windows and bell towers. One of 7 churches built in downtown Jacksonville between 1901 and 1910. The church was placed on the Florida Black Heritage Trail in 1992. Private. N.R. 1992.

Jacksonville. OLD JACKSONVILLE FREE PUBLIC LIBRARY (Carnegie Library). 101 E. Adams St. 1903–1905. Classical Revival. Henry J. Klutho, architect. 2 stories, main facade (south) is framed by a 3-bay colossal classical portico with massive stone columns. One of the first public buildings constructed after the disastrous fire of 1901. Private. N.R. 1987.

Mount Zion A. M. E. Church

Jacksonville. OLD ST. LUKE'S HOSPITAL. 314 N. Palmetto St. 1878. Ecletic . George Hoover, architect. 2¹/₂ stories, overhanging hipped roof, small cupola. City's oldest hospital building. Built to provide for penniless or ill travelers at a time when tourism was rapidly growing. Served victims of the 1888 yellow fever epidemic and those of the Great Fire of 1901. Presently used for offices. Private. N.R. 1972.

Jacksonville. PLAZA HOTEL. 353 E. Forsyth St. 1903. Masonry Vernacular. 2 stories. Notable for its circular turret topped by a conical roof. Constructed with rough-faced concrete block. An early hotel, it is one of the few hotel buildings of the early period remaining in the downtown. Private. N.R. 1992.

Jacksonville. THOMAS V. PORTER HOUSE. 510 Julia St. 1902 (moved in 1925). Classical Revival. Henry J. Klutho, architect. 2¹/₂ stories, frame, front portico with 6 fluted Corinthian columns. Home of Texan Thomas V. Porter who came to Jacksonville and established a successful wholesale grocery business. Later he became a developer. Now an architect's office. Private. N.R. 1976.

Jacksonville. RED BANK PLANTATION. 1230 Green Ridge Rd. 1854–1857. Classical Revival elements. 2 stories, brick, painted white, originally the front had a 2-story wood portico, but in 1937 replaced by a Federal-style porch. Main house of what formerly was a 450-acre plantation. The home of several pioneer families of the city. Private. N.R. 1972.

Jacksonville. RIVERSIDE BAPTIST CHURCH. 2650 Park St. 1924–1925. Romanesque, Byzantine, and Spanish elements. Addison Mizner, architect. 1¹/₂ stories, limestone, gabled and hipped tile roof sections, double-door entrance beneath compound round arch, sculptured tympanum. An original design by Mizner and believed to be his only religious structure. The radical nature of the design caused the loss of some of the congregation after its completion. Private. N.R. 1972.

St. Luke's Hospital, 1888

Riverside Baptist Church

Riverside Historic District

Jacksonville. RIVERSIDE HISTORIC DISTRICT. 1871–1935. 2550 buildings, 2120 of historical interest. Styles include Bungalow, Prairie, Queen Anne, Colonial Revival, and Mediterranean Revival. Notable structures include Roberts House (Prairie), 1804 Elizabeth Place; 1116 Acosta St. (Classical Revival); 2063 Oak St. (Mediterranean Revival); Riverside Baptist Church, A. Mizner, architect. Opened up in the late 19th century as a fashionable neighborhood, it expanded steadily into the 1930s. Much of the area has retained its social integrity. Gentrification has begun in some areas that had deteriorated. N.R. 1985.

Jacksonville. ST. ANDREW'S EPISCOPAL CHURCH. 317 Florida Ave. 1887. Gothic Revival. Robert S. Schuyler, architect. 1 story, brick, massive front corner tower with louvered belfry and steep spire roof. The only major church in the city that survived the 1901 fire, and an excellent example of the work of an architect who designed a number of churches in northeast Florida. Private. N.R. 1976.

St. James Building, c. 1920

Jacksonville. ST. JAMES BUILDING (Cohen Bros. Department Store). 117 W. Duval St. 1911–1912. Commercial style. Henry John Klutho, architect. 5 stories, brick, terra-cotta ornamentation, 6-story entrance tower with Sullivanesque cornice ornamentation. At the time of its construction it housed the city's major department store. The name St. James derived from earlier building on site. Used today for offices. Private. N.R. 1976.

Jacksonville. JOHN S. SAMMIS HOUSE. 207 Noble Circle W. c. 1850s. Classical Revival. 2¹/₂ stories, frame, 2-story portico with 4 monumental Ionic columns. Pioneer home of John S. Sammis, an early settler of the county. Born in New York, he came to Florida and eventually became a successful lumberman. He was a Unionist who fled the South during the war. Private. N.R. 1979.

San Jose Estates Gatehouse

Jacksonville. SAN JOSE ESTATES GATEHOUSE. 1873 Christopher Point Rd. N. 1925. Mediterranean Revival. Marsh and Saxelbye, architects. 2 stories. Stucco covered. A cartouche incised with SJE is over the gatehouse keystone. The last of 4 original gatehouses that marked the north and south entrances to San Jose Estates, a late Florida land boom development in Jacksonville. Private. N.R. 1989.

Jacksonville. SAN JOSE ESTATES THEMATIC RESOURCE AREA. 1925–1926. 24 individual structures scattered throughout a wide area of San Jose Estates. Spanish Colonial and Mediterranean Revival. Marsh and Saxelbye were architects of several of the buildings. San Jose neighborhood represents an early Florida example of a planned suburban development with a common architectural theme. N.R. 1985.

Jacksonville. SOUTH ATLANTIC INVESTMENT CORPORATION BUILDING. 35–39 W. Monroe St. 1925. Italian Renaissance. Marsh and Saxelbye, architects. 2 stories, brick. The 2 storefronts are divided by a central bay accentuated with a cast-stone arch. The arch is detailed with stylized dolphin motifs. Private. N.R. 1992.

Jacksonville. SPRINGFIELD HISTORIC DISTRICT. 1882–1930. 119 city blocks with over 1784 buildings over 50 years old. District is mainly composed of frame residential buildings. From the 19th century are examples of Queen Anne, Colonial Revival, and Stick style; from the 20th century are homes in the Prairie, Bungalow, and Mediterranean Revival styles. N.R. 1987.

Jacksonville. SPRINGFIELD MULTIPLE PROPERTY LISTING. 1882–1930. Includes 21 separate properties within the Springfield Historic District, most within Waterworks, Klutho and Confederate parks. Among the properties are 5 footbridges, 3 vehicle bridges, a park comfort station, and a number of monuments. Public. N.R. 1987.

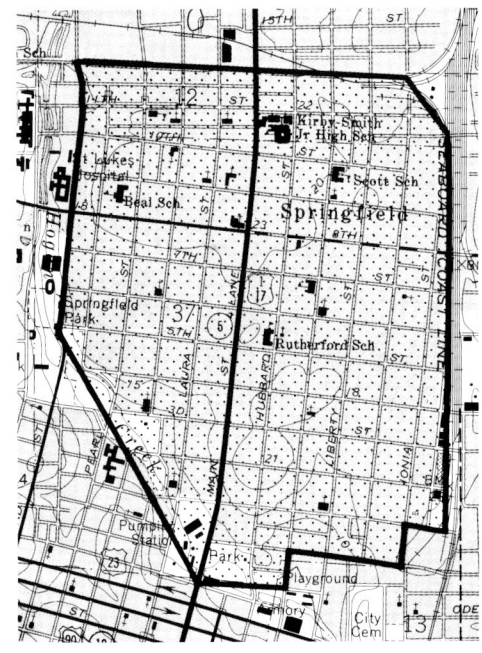

Springfield Historic District

Jacksonville. EDWIN M. STANTON SCHOOL. 521 W. Ashley St. 1917. Masonry Vernacular. Mellen C. Greeley, architect. 3 stories, brick, T-shaped with central block and 3 wings. At the time of its completion it was the only high school for blacks in the county. Closed in 1971. Its construction was the result of a legal suit against the Duval County Board of Public Instruction. The suit was the earliest documented example of Jacksonville's blacks pressing for equal educational opportunity. Undergoing restoration for community center. Private. N.R. 1983.

Jacksonville. 310 W. CHURCH STREET APARTMENTS (Ambassador Hotel). 420 N. Julia St. 1923. Georgian Revival, with Beaux-Arts elements. Hentz, Reid and Adler, architects. 6 stories, brick, main entrance has massive rusticated ashlar stonework, set with a scroll keystone. Built in the midst of the Florida boom, the building first served for apartments, then was converted to a hotel. Private. N.R. 1983.

Klutho Studios, Springfield Historic District

Jacksonville. TITLE AND TRUST COMPANY (Florida Building). 200 E. Forsyth St. 1929. Classical Revival. Marsh and Saxelbye, architects. 2 stories. Steel frame encased in concrete. Brick and limestone detail on outside. Main facade has entrance with engaged columns and Doric pilasters. Building played a critical role in the development of Jacksonville following the Great Fire of 1901. Private. N.R. 1990.

Jacksonville. THE VILLAGE STORE. 4216 Oxford Ave. 1923–1938. Masonry Vernacular with Classical Revival elements. Marsh and Saxelbye, architects. 1 story. Gabled wall dormers irregularly placed around the building. One of 3 buildings in the center of the village of Ortega, now absorbed by Jacksonville. Building housed 6 stores. Private. N.R. 1988.

Young Men's Hebrew Association

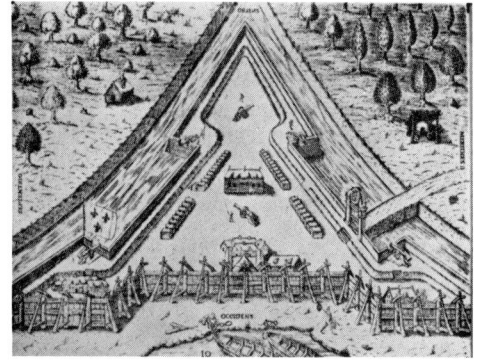

Ft. Caroline, Theodore de Bry's engraving made after painting by Jacques Le Moyne de Morgues, 1562-1565.

Outbuilding, Kingsley Plantation, thought to be slave quarters.

Jacksonville. WOMAN'S CLUB OF JACKSONVILLE. 861 Riverside Ave. 1927. Tudor Revival. Mellen C. Greeley, architect. 2 stories. Exterior covered with brick, stucco with half timbering, and rustic wood siding. Complex gabled roof. Club was an early leader in addressing a multitude of social, health, educational, and environmental issues, and provided numerous cultural opportunities for the community. Private. N.R. 1992.

Jacksonville. YOUNG MEN'S HEBREW ASSOCIATION (Maceo Elk Lodge #8). 712 W. Duval St. 1914. Masonry Vernacular. J.W.H. Hawkins, architect. 1 story. One of the 2 remaining buildings in downtown Jacksonville constructed during the city's historic period. Later the building housed a Black Elk's Lodge. Private. N.R. 1992.

Vicinity of Jacksonville. FORT CAROLINE NATIONAL MEMORIAL. 12713 Fort Caroline Rd. 1564. Reconstruction (1964) of old fort. Here the struggle between France and Spain for supremacy in Florida began and for the French virtually ended. The fort, built by the French, was the first in what is today the U.S. Overrun in 1565 by Spanish forces under Pedro Menéndez de Avilés, founder of St. Augustine, and renamed Fort San Mateo. In 1568 burned by the French. Museum. Public. N.R. 1966.

Vicinity of Jacksonville. GRAND SITE. N of Jacksonville. A.D. 500– A.D. 1600. St. Johns IIA through St. Johns IIB periods. Shell ring midden 30 feet wide and 175 feet in diameter. Sand mound on west edge of ring. Private. N.R. 1975.

Vicinity of Jacksonville. KINGSLEY PLANTATION. North tip of Fort George Island. Early 19th century. Plantation house is 2 stories, tabby foundation, remainder frame. Adjoining is the 1791 Don Juan McQueen house built of tabby on 1st floor and frame on 2nd. Also a large brick and tabby barn, a tabby and brick house, and the remains of 24 slave cabins. Originally received from the Spanish Crown by John McQueen in 1791. By 1817 it had been purchased by Zephaniah Kingsley who raised cotton, sugarcane, and other cash crops which were shipped to Charleston. The main plantation house may be the oldest in Florida. Museum. Public. N.R. 1970.

Vicinity of Jacksonville. MISSION OF SAN JUAN DEL PUERTO ARCHAEOLOGICAL SITE. Fort St. George Island. c. 1578–1763. One of the oldest and most long-standing Spanish missions in Florida. Established by Franciscans to missionize the Timucuan and Guale Indians who lived along the coast. Site also was involved in the struggles of Britain and Spain over control of Georgia and Florida in 1702. Private. N.R. 1986.

Vicinity of Jacksonville. YELLOW BLUFF FORT. New Berlin Rd. 1 mi. S of Fl. 105. 1862. Trenches and earthworks built by Confederates on the St. Johns River in the summer of 1862. Housed cannon to prevent the Union forces from reaching Jacksonville. Changed hands 4 times during the Civil War. Public. N.R. 1970.

Jacksonville Beach. CASA MARINA HOTEL. 12 6th Ave. N at First St. 1925. Mission style. Marsh and Saxelbye, architects. 2 stories. Features arched windows, a loggia, wrought iron work, vigas, niches, and other decorative detail. A major hotel during the 1920s, when Jacksonville's beaches were being developed. Private. N.R. 1993.

Mayport. OLD ST. JOHNS LIGHTHOUSE. U.S. Naval Station. 1858. Conical. Brick, 85 feet high. The third lighthouse built in Mayport. Shifting sands caused the first two to be abandoned. Present light ceased functioning in 1929 and was replaced by a light ship. Public. N.R. 1976.

Old St. Johns Lighthouse, c. 1900

ESCAMBIA COUNTY

Century. THE ALGER-SULLIVAN LUMBER COMPANY RESIDENTIAL HISTORIC DISTRICT. 1900–1934. 51 buildings, 46 of historical interest. Frame Vernacular predominates. One of the few remaining examples of a mill town in Florida. A little village named Teaspoon existed on the site before the lumber company developed it. Churches and community buildings as well as residences in the district. Private. N.R. 1989.

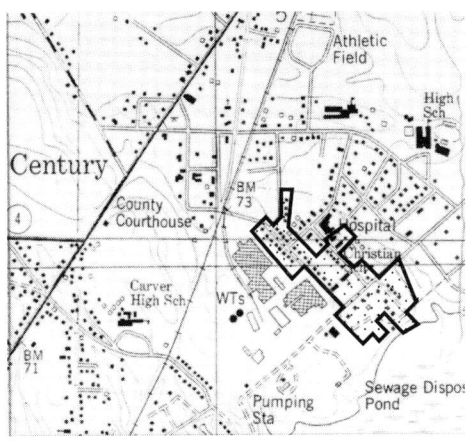

The Alger-Sullivan Lumber Company Residential Historic District

Pensacola. AMERICAN NATIONAL BANK BUILDING. 226 S. Palafox St. 1908+. Commercial style with Sullivanesque elements. J.E.R. Carpenter, architect. 11 stories, masonry, heavily ornamented on main facade. A product of a boom period in the city's history. Believed to have been the tallest building in Florida when completed. Tallest in Pensacola until 1974. Private. N.R. 1978.

Pensacola. CRYSTAL ICE COMPANY BUILDING. 2024 N. Davis St. c. 1932. Masonry Vernacular. Steve Fulghum, architect. 1 story, stucco ornamentation to convey the impression of a block of ice. One of the few remaining examples of vernacular roadside commercial architecture in Pensacola. Building used to sell ice to motorists. Private. N.R. 1983.

Pensacola. CLARA BARKLEY DORR HOUSE. 311 S. Adams St. 1871. Greek Revival. 2 stories, frame, 2-story full-width front porch. One of Pensacola's best-preserved examples of post-Civil War Classical Revival architecture. House Museum. Public. N.R. 1974.

Crystal Ice Company Building

First Christian Church

Pensacola. JOHN EDMUNDS APARTMENT HOUSE (Mirador). 2007 E. Gadsden St. 1927+ . Mediterranean Revival. Walker Dorr Willis, architect. 3 stories, masonry, stuccoed, 5 cast-iron balconies on 3rd floor. One of the most fashionable apartments in Pensacola for 30 years. Until 1956 it was the only major apartment complex in the city. Private. N.R. 1983.

Pensacola. FIRST CHRISTIAN CHURCH (Greater Mount Lily Baptist Church). 619 E. Gadsden St. 1913. Medieval Eclectic. Front-facing parapetted gables, 18 colorful, well-executed art-glass windows. Private. N.R. 1994.

Fort San Carlos and Fort Barrancas

Pensacola. FORT BARRANCAS HISTORIC DISTRICT. Pensacola Naval Air Station. 17th to 19th century. 3 structures: Fort Barrancas, Battery San Antonio, and the Advanced Redoubt. The most notable structure is Fort Barrancas, a semicircular brick fortification surrounded by a moat, which replaced a fort built in 1698, and destroyed by French in 1719. Present fort was captured from the Spanish in 1814 by forces commanded by Andrew Jackson. Public. N.R. 1982.

Pensacola. FORT GEORGE SITE. La Rua at Palafox St. 1778. Site of a log fort built by the British to protect Pensacola. Captured by Spanish in 1781 following the Spanish alliance with the American colonies during the Revolution. Renamed Fort San Miguel, but allowed to deteriorate by the Spanish. Public. N.R. 1974.

Pensacola. CHARLES WILLIAM JONES HOUSE. 302 N. Barcelona St. 1869+ . Frame Vernacular. 2 stories, frame wraparound porch. Jones was a leader in the Democrat Party after the Civil War. Born in Ireland, he settled in Florida where he first became a carpenter, but then studied law. He served in the U.S. Senate from Florida. Private. N.R. 1977.

Pensacola. KING-HOOTON HOUSE. 512–514 N. 7th Ave. 1871. Frame Vernacular. 1$^1/_2$ stories. Built as a single dwelling, it was converted into a duplex in mid-1950s. Built for Margaret E. King, one of Pensacola's most prominent real estate holders in the late 19th century. Detached kitchen wing. Private. N.R. 1991.

Pensacola. L AND N MARINE TERMINAL BUILDING. Bayfront Parkway. 1902+ (moved in 1972) . Eclectic. 2$^1/_2$ stories, frame, wraparound porch on 2nd floor. Served as the focal point for the Louisville and Nashville Railroad's export trade prior to World War II. This trade was considerable and included local lumber as well as coal from northern Alabama. Public. N.R. 1972.

Pensacola. L AND N PASSENGER STATION AND EXPRESS OFFICE. 239 N. Alcaniz St. 1912–1913. Spanish Mission and Italianate elements. 2-story, masonry passenger terminal, 1-story masonry express wing. Raised limestone and terra-cotta ornamentation on facades. Built to serve the city's most important land transportation artery, its railway. Incorporated into a new hotel in 1984. Private. N.R. 1979.

Pensacola. LAVALLE HOUSE. 203 E. Church St. c. 1803–1815 (moved in 1969). Frame Vernacular raised Creole cottage. 1 story, gallery porch. One of the few remaining early 19th-century frame houses in the city. An excellent example of early Gulf Coast Vernacular style. House Museum. Public. N.R. 1971.

Pensacola. NORTH HILL PRESERVATION DISTRICT. 1870–1930s. 542 structures, of which 404 are considered of historical interest, within 65 blocks. Queen Anne, Frame Vernacular, Tudor Revival, and Mediterranean Revival are the predominant styles. An early upper-middle-class suburb of the city. Included within it are the remains of the British fortifications of Fort George used in the 1781 Battle of Pensacola. One of the finest collections of Victorian and early 20th-century houses in northwest Florida. N .R. 1983.

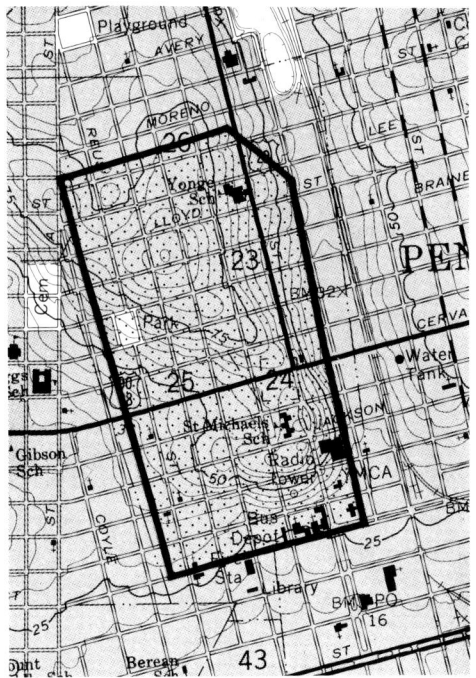

North Hill Preservation District

Pensacola. OLD CHRIST CHURCH. 405 S. Adams St. 1830–1832. Gothic Revival. 1 story, brick, square bell tower. The oldest building used for religious purposes in northwest Florida. Built as an Episcopal Church, but used by several other denominations. From 1937 to 1957, it served as the Pensacola Public Library. Public. N.R. 1974.

Pensacola. PENSACOLA ATHLETIC CLUB (Rafford Hall). SW corner of Baylen and Belmont Sts. 1889–1890. Frame Vernacular. 2¹/₂ stories, 2nd-story balcony. One of the oldest gymnasiums and private athletic clubs in the state. An important reflection of American social history in the Victorian era. Sold to Odd Fellows in 1906. Presently returned to use as athletic club. Private. N.R. 1975.

Pensacola. PENSACOLA HISTORIC DISTRICT (Seville Historic District). 18th century to 19th century. Approximately 20 blocks. A significant concentration of French influenced Gulf Coast Vernacular cottages with some excellent examples of Greek Revival and Victorian-era houses. The typical Gulf Coast cottage is a distinctive 1¹/₂-story house on piers with a steep pitched gable roof and a gallery porch on the main facade. Design is from the Caribbean by way of New Orleans. District contains historic Seville Square and Pensacola Village, a state-owned museum complex. N.R. 1970.

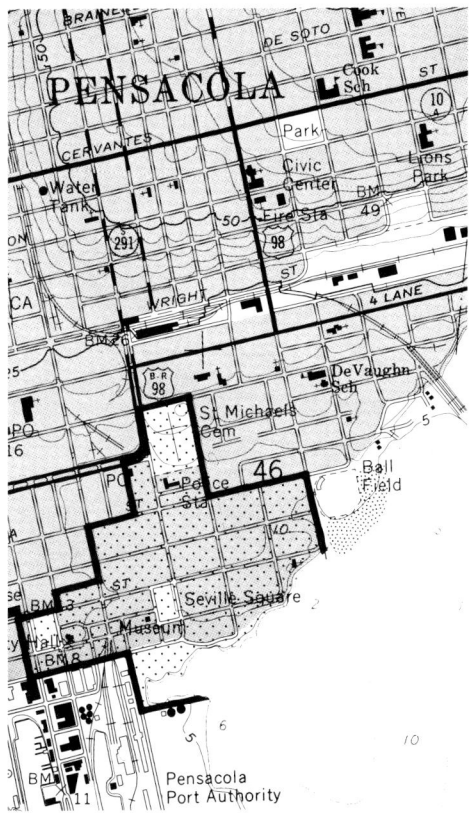

Pensacola Historic District

Pensacola Hospital

Pensacola. **PENSACOLA HOSPITAL.** N. 12th Ave. 1915+. Late Gothic Revival. A.O. Von Herbulis, architect. 4 stories, sandstone veneer, main block flanked by 2 3-story wings, raised basement. Quoins, lintels and belt courses of Indiana limestone. The first major hospital in Pensacola and for its time a major undertaking. Building ceased being used as hospital in 1965. Private. N.R. 1982.

Pensacola. **PENSACOLA LIGHTHOUSE AND KEEPER'S QUARTERS.** Pensacola Naval Air Station. 1859. Conical. Brick. 160 feet high. Keeper's quarters (1869): 2 stories with a 2-story gallery. Present lighthouse built to replace an earlier one (1824). Damaged during the Civil War. Public. N.R. 1974.

Pensacola. **PENSACOLA NAVAL AIR STATION HISTORIC DISTRICT.** 1824–1899, 1914. 55 structures of historical interest within 82 acres. Notable are the octagonal armory and chapel (1854), and 6 metal seaplane hangars (1916-1918). First permanent U.S. Naval Air Station and first Navy pilot training center in the nation. Public. N.R. 1976.

St. Michael's Creole Benevolent Association Hall

Pensacola. **PLAZA FERDINAND II.** Palafox and Government Sts. 1821. Site of the formal transfer of Florida from Spain to U.S. in 1821. Present square is remnant of original city square laid out by the British in 1765, a large part of which was subdivided and sold in 1802. Public. N.R. 1966.

Pensacola. **SAENGER THEATER.** 118 S. Palafox St. 1924–1925. Spanish Baroque. Emile Weil, architect. 2 stories, masonry, terra-cotta ornamentation on front facade as well as grille-work. Auditorium has elaborate columns and is notable for outstanding use of color in decoration. The theater itself, one of the "atmospheric" variety built throughout the nation in the period , served for live theater as well as movies. Public. N.R. 1976.

Pensacola. **ST. JOSEPH'S CHURCH BUILDINGS.** 140 W. Government St. Church, 1892; Convent, 1857 +; School-orphanage, 1920–1928. Church: 1 story, brick, asymmetrical towers on main facade; convent: 1$^1/_2$ stories, frame, incised veranda; school-orphanage: 2$^1/_2$ stories, frame. A religious center for Pensacola's black community since mid-19th century. Also served the city's large Creole community. Private. N.R. 1979.

Pensacola. **ST. MICHAEL'S CREOLE BENEVOLENT ASSOCIATION HALL.** 416 E. Government St. 1895–1896. Frame Vernacular with Queen Anne elements. 1$^1/_2$ stories, frame, front and side porches. Built to accommodate the social and cultural activities of the city's Creoles, a racially mixed group which remained socially isolated from the white and black communities. Private. N.R. 1974.

Pensacola. SAN CARLOS HOTEL. 1 N. Palafox St. 1909+ . Mediterranean Revival. W.L. Stoddart, architect. 8 stories, concrete and masonry, 2 central blocks and 2 wings (added between 1922 and 1927). 2-story interior lobby with an art glass dome. The hotel has played a major role in the city's cultural and social life throughout its history. Early example of Mediterranean Revival architecture in Pensacola. Hotel closed in 1984. Private. N.R. 1982.

San Carlos Hotel

Pensacola. THIESEN BUILDING . 40 S. Palafox St. 1901+ . Commercial style. Morgan and Dillon, architects. 5 stories, brick, terra-cotta ornamentation on west and south facades. Built by Christian Thiesen, a Danish immigrant who settled in the city in 1882 and became a developer. The building was one of the first modern office blocks in the city and represents the early 20th-century optimism of the city business leaders. Private. N.R. 1979.

Vicinity of Pensacola Beach. FORT PICKENS. U.S. 98 W of Pensacola Beach. 1834. Pentagonal brick fort with bastions at each corner, partial moat, 40-foot-high walls, 12 feet thick. Built to defend Pensacola's deep water harbor. Never captured by Confederates despite several attempts. Public. N.R. 1972.

Vicinity of Warrington. PERDIDO KEY HISTORIC DISTRICT. Small island south of Pensacola in Pensacola Bay. 1828, 1862, 1898, 1905, 1940. On the eastern end of the key a series of artillery batteries was built to defend Pensacola. Fort McRee built by U.S. in 1828. In 1861 fort fell to Union forces. Fort McRee eroded by sea currents and finally abandoned. In 1898 another battery built, followed by another in 1905 and another in 1940. The newer batteries also have been undermined by sea erosion. Public. N.R. 1980.

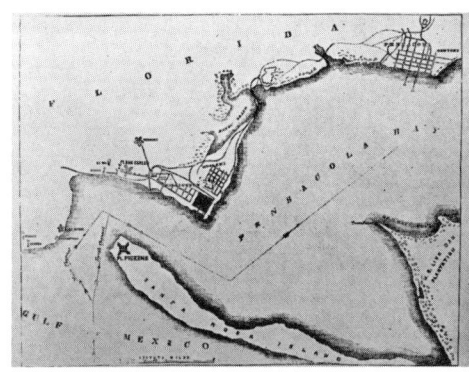

Strategic location of Ft. Pickens, c. 1860

FLAGLER COUNTY

Bunnell. OLD BUNNELL STATE BANK (Citizens Bank of Bunnell). 101–107 N. Bay St. 1917. Masonry Vernacular. 2 stories. Decorative brickwork on north side. Some wood paneling in interior. The only bank in Flagler County from 1917 until 1932, and again from 1938 to 1942. Private. N.R. 1992.

Bulow Plantation Ruins

Vicinity of Bunnell. BULOW PLANTATION RUINS. Fl. S-5, 9 mi. SE of Bunnell. 1826. Bulow Plantation, founded in 1821, employed approximately 300 slaves growing sugarcane and cotton. Evacuated in 1835 during the Second Seminole War. Indians plundered it in that year, destroying all buildings. Museum. Public. N.R. 1970.

Marine Studios (Marineland)

Vicinity of St. Augustine. **MARINE STUDIOS** (Marineland). Fl. A1A, 18 mi. S of St. Augustine. 1937. Moderne style. John Walter Wood and M.F. Hasbrouch, architects. A complex of buildings and tanks, stuccoed, open grandstand. The world's first oceanarium and underwater motion picture studio. Leading Florida tourist attraction. Private. N.R. 1986.

FRANKLIN COUNTY

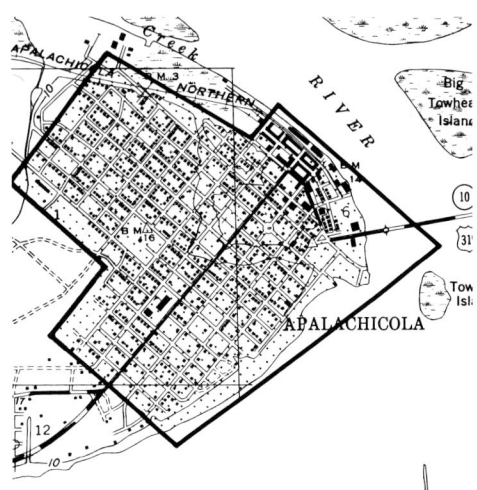

Apalachicola Historic District

Apalachicola. **APALACHICOLA HISTORIC DISTRICT.** 1835–c. 1900. 146 city blocks. Predominantly Frame Vernacular and Classical Revival buildings. Notable structures include David G. Raney House and Trinity Episcopal Church. A high concentration of Vernacular buildings are found within the district which is a well-preserved 19th-century setting. Within district is the John Gorrie State Museum. N.R. 1980.

Apalachicola. **DAVID G. RANEY HOUSE.** SW corner of Market St. and Ave. F. c. 1840. Greek Revival. 2 stories, frame, classical front portico with 4 fluted Doric columns. According to tradition, the house was built in Port St. Joseph in 1838 and moved to its present site. Mr. Raney was a prosperous merchant and owner of the Apalachicola Race Track. Private. N.R. 1972.

Apalachicola. **TRINITY EPISCOPAL CHURCH.** Ave. D and 6th St. 1839. Greek Revival. 1$^{1}/_{2}$ stories, clapboarding, full-height fluted Ionic columns on front facade. The building was prefabricated in New York from white pine and shipped by sea to Apalachicola. Peg fasteners used instead of nails. Private. N.R. 1972.

Vicinity of Apalachicola. **PIERCE SITE.** Approximately 1 mi. NW of Apalachicola on 12th St. 500 B.C.–A.D. 1400 Late Deptford to Fort Walton period. 5 shell middens and 2 mounds. Private. N.R. 1974.

Vicinity of Carrabelle. **CROOKED RIVER LIGHTHOUSE.** City Park on U.S. 98. 1895. Wrought-iron skeleton. 115 feet high. Replaced an older lighthouse on Dog Island, which had been destroyed in 1873. Public. N.R. 1978.

Vicinity of Eastport. **PORTER'S BAR SITE.** 2 mi. NE of Eastport off U.S. 319. c. A.D. 500 Swift Creek and Weeden Island periods. Site of village and burial mound complex which exhibits Hopewellian and Kolomoki cultural influences. Private. N.R. 1975.

Little St. George Island. CAPE ST. GEORGE LIGHTHOUSE. Southernmost point on Little St. George Island. 1852. Conical. Brick, 70 feet high. This is the third lighthouse built on the site, the first having been built in 1833, destroyed by hurricane. The second built in 1847 was also damaged by wind. Public. N.R. 1974.

Vicinity of St. Teresa. YENT MOUND. On E side of Fl. 370, approximately 2.5 mi. from jct. of U.S. 98. c. 500 B.C.–A.D. 500. Between Deptford and early Swift Creek periods. Platform mound originally 7^1/$_2$ feet high, 106 feet long, and a maximum of 74 feet wide. Greatly altered through uncontrolled digging. One of the best-known examples of a Hopewellian ceremonial complex found in North Florida. Private. N.R. 1973.

Vicinity of Sumatra. FORT GADSDEN HISTORIC MEMORIAL (Negro Fort). 6 mi. SW of Sumatra off Fl. 65. 1814–1818. Fort turned over to Indian and black allies of British traders during Second Spanish Period. After an attack by the U.S. in 1815, in which 270 black defenders were killed when a powder magazine exploded, the U.S. garrisoned it until 1821. Museum. Public. N.R. 1972.

Replica of Fort Gadsden

GADSDEN COUNTY

Chattahoochee. U.S. ARSENAL–OFFICERS' QUARTERS. Florida State Hospital. 1839. Masonry Vernacular. 2-story, brick main building, 1^1/$_2$-story wings, carved bracketing and framing of front and rear porches. Originally officers' quarters of Chattahoochee arsenal. Used to muster Confederate troops in Civil War, later a penitentiary and now part of Florida State Hospital. Public. N.R. 1973.

Vicinity of Mt. Pleasant. JOSHUA DAVIS HOUSE. 2.5 mi. NW of Mt. Pleasant. 1827. Frame Vernacular. 1^1/$_2$ stories, log construction, clapboarding, full-width front porch. The oldest documented building in Gadsden County, it is a good example of a pioneer homestead. Private. N.R. 1975.

Joshua Davis House, Esther Elizabeth Davis Bates in yard

Quincy. WILLOUGHBY GREGORY HOUSE (Krausland). Fl. 274 and Krausland Rd. c. 1843. Masonry Vernacular. 2 stories, brick, 2-story entrance facade porch. Built by Gregory, an immigrant from North Carolina, who acquired 700 acres and 30 slaves and raised cotton and tobacco. Private. N.R. 1983.

Quincy. E.C. LOVE HOUSE. 219 N. Jackson St. c. 1850. Greek Revival elements. 2 stories, frame, clapboarding, 1-story entrance veranda. Edward C. Love practiced law, served as judge and mayor of Quincy, and also was a planter. Private. N.R. 1974.

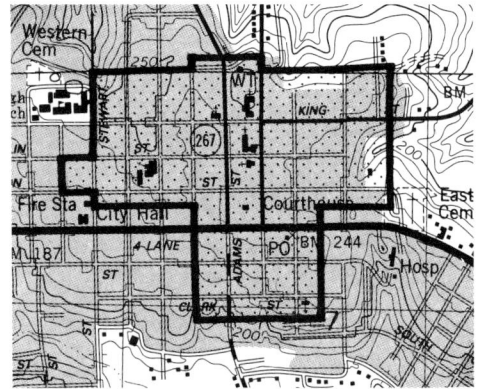
Quincy Historic District

Judge P.W. White House

Old Philadelphia Presbyterian Church

Quincy. JOHN LEE McFARLIN HOUSE. 305 E. King St. c. 1895. Queen Anne. 2¹/₂ stories, frame, gabled roof sections, full-width front porch, front polygonal turret. Home of John Lee McFarlin, second largest independent shade tobacco producer in the county and a pioneer in shade-grown tobacco cultivation. Private. N.R. 1974.

Quincy. QUINCY HISTORIC DISTRICT. 1840s–1910. 28 structures of historical significance within a 16-block area. Predominant styles are Classical Revival and Queen Anne. Notable structures are the County Courthouse, Quincy Library, Stockton-Curry House. The architectural styles reflect the growth and decline of the tobacco boom periods (1840-1860 and 1890-1920). N.R. 1978.

Quincy. QUINCY LIBRARY (Quincy Academy). 303 N. Adams St. 1850–1851. Federal elements. 2 stories, brick, center entrance porch. Housed the Quincy Academy until 1912, later served as temporary courthouse, meeting house, library, and public school. Private. N.R. 1974.

Quincy. QUINCY WOMAN'S CLUB. 300 N. Calhoun St. 1852–1853. Italian Villa and Greek Revival elements. 1 to 2 stories, southwest corner has Doric entrance portico. Originally built as a Masonic lodge. In 1922 taken over by the Woman's Club. Private. N.R. 1975.

Quincy. E.B. SHELFER HOUSE. 205 N. Madison St. 1903. Frame Vernacular with Queen Anne elements. 2¹/₂ stories, gabled roof sections, front and side wraparound porch. Built during the second tobacco boom of Quincy by E.B. Shelfer, a pioneer shade tobacco grower. Private. N.R. 1975.

Quincy. STOCKTON-CURRY HOUSE. 121 N. Duval St. c. 1845. Classical Revival. 2¹/₂ stories, frame, pedimented portico with 2-story fluted Doric columns. Philip A. Stockton, who came to Quincy from Pennsylvania to operate a mail coach line, but later practiced law, lived here until his death in 1879. Later sold to C.H. Curry, pioneer in the shade-grown tobacco industry. Private. N.R. 1974.

Quincy. JUDGE P.W. WHITE HOUSE. 212 N. Madison St. c. 1843. Greek Revival. 2 stories, frame, 2-story front and rear pedimented Doric porticos with fluted columns. The home of Judge P.W. White, important local civic leader who served in the Civil War as Chief Confederate Commissary Officer for Florida. Private. N.R. 1972.

Vicinity of Quincy. OLD PHILADELPHIA PRESBYTERIAN CHURCH. Off Fl. 65, 5 mi. N of Quincy. 1859. Classical Revival elements. 1¹/₂ stories, frame, clapboarding, interior slave gallery. Built for one of the earliest Presbyterian congregations in the state. County's oldest surviving church. Private. N.R. 1975.

HAMILTON COUNTY

Jasper. OLD HAMILTON COUNTY JAIL. 501 NE 1st Ave. 1893. Romanesque Revival. 2 stories, brick, 3-story tower with a pyramidal roof. Oldest functioning jail building in Florida and oldest public building in the county. Public. N.R. 1983.

Jasper. UNITED METHODIST CHURCH. Central Ave. and 5th St. 1878. Gothic Revival elements. 1 story, frame, bell tower with 2 setbacks and a steeple. One of the oldest surviving structures in the county. Private. N.R. 1978.

HARDEE COUNTY

Vicinity of Bowling Green. PAYNE'S CREEK MASSACRE–FORT CHOKONIKLA SITE. ³/₄ mi. SE of Bowling Green on Fl. 664A. 1849–1859. On July 17, 1849, Seminole Indians attacked a store on this site, killing the manager and his assistant. News of the incident precipitated massive retaliation. A string of forts built in the area, including one on the store site. Public. N.R. 1978.

Wauchula. CARLTON ALBERT ESTATE. 302 E. Bay St. 1903. Colonial Revival and Queen Anne elements. 2¹/₂ stories. 4 buildings within a 26-acre orange grove. An excellent example of an early 20th-century orange grove and residence. In 1903 the first seedless orange discovered in the grove. Private. N.R. 1991.

Hamilton County Jail, c. 1893

Carlton Albert Estate

Clewiston Inn

Avon Park Historic District

Central Station

HENDRY COUNTY

Clewiston. CLEWISTON INN. U.S. 27. 1926. Classical Revival. L. Phillips Clarke and Edgar S. Wortman, architects. 2 stories. Built in 1926 by the Southern Sugar Company, rebuilt in 1938 following a fire. Oldest hotel in the Lake Okeechobee area. Still owned and operated by the U.S. Sugar Corporation. Private. N.R. 1991.

La Belle. OLD HENDRY COUNTY COURTHOUSE. Corner of Bridge St. and Hickpochee Ave. 1927. Mediterranean Revival. E.C. Hosford, architect. 3 stories. A large Italian Renaissance clock tower and 3 subsidiary towers with pyramidal roofs at the corners of the building. Center of the county's civic and political gatherings. Weather and market reports vital to the agricultural economy are still placed on a blackboard on the front veranda. Public. N.R. 1990.

HIGHLANDS COUNTY

Avon Park. AVON PARK HISTORIC DISTRICT. 1912–1935. 20 buildings, 16 of historical interest. Masonry Vernacular, Neo-Classical and Art Deco styles. Main Street Mall is the most significant feature of the district. The mall was laid out between 1920 and 1927. Numerous trees and monuments dot this mall. Public and Private. N.R. 1990.

Lake Placid. OLD LAKE PLACID A.C.L. RAILROAD DEPOT. 19 Park, W. 1926. Masonry Vernacular. 1 story. The building is covered by a gable roof and is distinguished by a loggia on 3 elevations. The station now functions as a museum of railroading and local history. Public. N.R. 1993.

Sebring. CENTRAL STATION (Sebring Fire Station). 1927. Art Deco. William J. Heim, architect. 2 stories. Flat roof with steeped parapet and a prominent 4-story domed hose drying tower. First fire station in Florida of this style and served as model for several others. Private. N.R. 1989.

Sebring. ELIZABETH HAINES HOUSE. 605 Summit Drive. 1928. 2 stories. Stucco, with barrel-tile roof. Among the last of the "grand" residences of Sebring to be built. Elizabeth Haines, a wealthy Massachusetts widow, built the first house as a winter home. Private. N.R. 1993.

Sebring. EDWARD HAINZ HOUSE. 155 W. Center Ave. 1919. Bungalow and Craftsman styles. 2 stories. Japanese influence in design, including peaked truss work and in roof lines. House became an important model for Sebring residential architecture during the 1930s. Design was derived from the "bengali bangla," a house style used as a wayside shelter for British travelers in India during the 18th and 19th centuries. Private. N.R. 1989.

Edward Hainz House

Sebring. HARDER HALL. 3300 Golfview Dr. 1927. Spanish Colonial Revival. William Manley King, architect. 7 stories. Rough stucco finished facade, arcaded loggias at various elevations, barrel-tile roof. A popular resort hotel of the 1920s. Private. N.R. 1990.

Sebring. HIGHLANDS COUNTY COURTHOUSE. 430 S. Commerce Ave. 1926. Classical Revival. Fred Bishop, architect. 3 stories. Colossal portico in the Ionic order. Built as an expression of confidence in the economic future of the county. Public. N.R. 1989.

Sebring. OLD SEABOARD AIR LINE DEPOT. E. Center Ave. 1924. Masonry Vernacular. 1 story. A common design for a railroad station of that period. The railroad provided Sebring with a far higher degree of access to northern visitors than previously. Private. N.R. 1990.

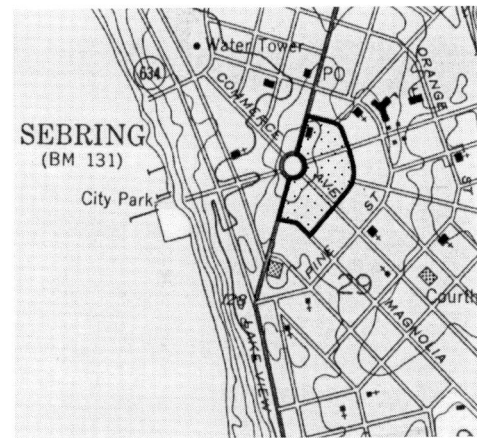

Sebring Downtown Historic District

Sebring. SEBRING DOWNTOWN HISTORIC DISTRICT. 1916–1927. 27 buildings, 22 of historical interest. Masonry Vernacular, Classical Revival. One of the distinguishing features of the district is the curvilinear facades of the main buildings that surround the central circular park. Private. N.R. 1990.

Sebring. H. ORVEL SEBRING HOUSE. 483 S. Lake View Dr. 1919. Spanish Colonial Revival. M. Leo Elliot, architect. 2 stories. Smooth stucco finishing, red-clay barrel-tile roof, numerous archways. The owner, Sebring, aided in attracting settlers to the community. He was the son of the city's founder. Private. N.R. 1989.

Sebring. PAUL L. VINSON HOUSE. 309 N. Lake View Dr. 1920. Mission and Spanish Colonial Revival. 2 stories. Primarily Mission style with Spanish Colonial and Art Deco elements in the design. Private. N.R. 1989.

Paul L. Vinson House

53

① North Plant City Residential District
② Downtown Plant City Commercial District

HILLSBOROUGH COUNTY

Brandon. MOSELEY HOMESTEAD. 1820 W. Brandon Blvd. 1886. Frame Vernacular. 1 story, rambling modified dogtrot, exterior sided with wood shingles, metal roof. The Moseley Homestead occupies 15 acres and consists of a house and four outbuildings. Charles Scott Moseley and his wife were pioneers of Brandon. One of the oldest surviving rural residences in the county. Private. N.R. 1985.

Plant City. DOWNTOWN PLANT CITY COMMERCIAL DISTRICT. 1901–1925. 56 buildings, 38 of historical interest. Masonry Vernacular, Beaux-Arts and Mediterranean Revival styles. City's early commercial district. Although the commercial life of the city has moved elsewhere, the district retains some of the character it had when it was the focus of the town's business activities. Public and Private. N.R. 1993.

Plant City. HILLSBORO STATE BANK BUILDING. 121 N. Collins St. 1914. Classical Revival and Beaux-Arts Classical elements. Francis Kennard, architect. 3 stories, brick, 2-story front portico with twin concrete columns with ornate capitals. Plant City's first and oldest successful bank. Organized in 1902. The architect, Francis Kennard, from England, designed several notable buildings in the Tampa Bay area. Private. N.R. 1984.

"The Palm," largest room in the Moseley House, 1984

Plant City. NORTH PLANT CITY RESIDENTIAL DISTRICT. 1898–1942. 90 buildings, 74 or historical interest. Masonry and Frame Vernacular and several examples of Revival style. The neighborhood contains the largest concentration of residential structures in the city dating from before World War II. Contains a church and former schoolhouse. Public and Private. N.R. 1993.

Plant City. PLANT CITY HIGH SCHOOL. N. Collins St. 1914+. Modified Georgian Revival. Willis R. Biggers, architect. 3 stories, red brick, east and west facades feature central, 4-bay, pedimented portico with fluted Doric columns. Public. N.R. 1981.

Plant City. PLANT CITY UNION DEPOT. East N. Drane St. 1908–1909. Eclectic. J.F. Leitner, architect. 1-story, brick passenger depot, separate 2-story brick freight terminal. Important element in the early development of the city, since it depended so heavily on railroad transportation. Private. N.R. 1974.

George Miller House

Ruskin. GEORGE MILLER HOUSE. 508 Tamiami Trail. 1914. Swiss Chalet influence with elements of Stick and Prairie styles. 2 stories, frame with stucco, large eave braces. Only remaining structure of Ruskin College, founded by George McA. Miller, who was influenced by the theories of John Ruskin, 19th-century British social thinker. Private. N.R. 1974.

Vicinity of Ruskin. COCKROACH KEY. 3 mi. S of Little Manatee River. A.D. 700–A.D. 1500. Glades period. Two large shell heaps, long shell ridge at center of key, shell burial mound, small shell hummocks situated on the key. Private. N.R. 1973.

Anderson-Frank House

Tampa. ANDERSON-FRANK HOUSE. 341 Plant Ave. 1898+. Colonial Revival. Miller and Kennard, architects. 2½ stories, brick and granite, veranda with Ionic columns and a turned balustrade wrap the main and side facades. James B. Anderson was an important member of the city's banking community. Private. N.R. 1982.

Tampa. CENTRO ASTURIANO. 1913 Nebraska Ave. 1914. Beaux-Arts Classicism, Mannerist elements. Bonfoey and Elliott, architects. 2 stories, yellow brick, balustraded parapet, window bays articulated by engaged columns. Club formed in 1902 when the more radical Asturian Spaniards withdrew from the Centro Español. Best preserved of the city's clubs, it includes a 1200-seat theater, ballroom, and cantina. Private. N.R. 1974.

Centro Asturiano

Tampa. CIRCULO CUBANO DE TAMPA (Cuban Club). 10th Ave. and 14th St. 1918. Beaux-Arts Classicism. M. Leo Elliott, architect. 4 stories, yellow brick with stone trim, balustrade. Main entrance has double glass doors with transom, stained-glass Diocletian window above. The second structure of this ethnic men's club and mutual aid society organized in 1902. Facilities include a theater, cantina, and 4th-floor ballroom with lavishly decorated ceiling. Private. N.R. 1972.

Tampa. WILLIAM E. CURTIS HOUSE. 808 E. Curtis St. c. 1905–1906. Dutch Colonial Revival. 2 stories, frame, gambrel roof. One of the first residential structures erected in what is now Seminole Heights. Curtis was a nurseryman who developed the area. Private. N.R. 1987.

Tampa. DAVIS ISLAND MULTIPLE PROPERTY LISTING. 1925–1932. 22 buildings of historical interest. Mediterranean Revival and Mission styles. The Davis Island section of Hyde Park was developed as a fashionable residential area in the late 1920s and early 1930s. Most residences were large and of Mediterranean style. Area remains well cared for. Many homes retain their original integrity. Private. N.R. 1989.

Tampa. EL CENTRO ESPAÑOL OF WEST TAMPA. 2306 N. Howard Ave. 1912. Mediterranean Revival with Moorish details. Fred J. James, architect. 2 stories, red and yellow brick, decorative corbeling on cornice and in frontispiece around Howard Ave. entrance. Built after the growth of the cigar industry in West Tampa brought thousands of new members to Ybor City's Centro Español. Large ballroom has Moorish influence. Private. N.R. 1974.

Tampa. EL PASAJE (Cherokee Club). 1318 9th St. 1886. Eclectic with Italian Renaissance elements. 2 stories, brick, 1st-floor open arcade on the north and east sides, general style is modeled after Italian Renaissance villa. The Cherokee Club, as it was originally known, was established in 1895 for the promotion of "social intercourse among its members," which at the time included many of Tampa's most prominent businessmen and cigar manufacturers. Private. N.R. 1972.

Tampa. EPISCOPAL HOUSE OF PRAYER. 2708 Central Ave. 1923. Gothic Revival. 1 story. Rubble stone exterior. Church has all the features associated with the Gothic Revival, including steeply pitched roof, a tower and crenelation and stained glass windows. When built the church was situated in a fashionable neighborhood. Private. N.R. 1991.

Tampa. FEDERAL BUILDING, U.S. COURTHOUSE, POSTAL STATION. 601 Florida Ave. 1902–1905. Second Renaissance and Classical Revival elements. James Knox Taylor, architect. 4 stories, granite faced with marble at 2nd floor, central entrance section with full height Corinthian portico. The oldest significant building in Tampa originally designed for government use. Public. N.R. 1974.

Episcopal House of Prayer

Tampa. HUTCHINSON HOUSE. 304 Plant Ave. 1908+. Second Empire style. 3 stories, brick, high mansard roof, large porch with tall Corinthian columns. One of the few structures of this style erected in Florida. The builder, Currie J. Hutchinson, was a local merchant. Private. N.R. 1977.

Tampa. HYDE PARK HISTORIC DISTRICT. 1886–1933. 1695 structures within 860 acres. Predominant styles are Frame and Masonry Vernacular, Bungalow, Queen Anne, English Romantic Revival, Classical Revival. The oldest and best preserved of Tampa's early residential neighborhoods. Includes the Bayshore Blvd. Esplanade. N.R. 1985.

Tampa. JOHNSON-WOLFF HOUSE. 6823 S. De Soto St. 1885. Masonry Vernacular. 2¹/₂ stories, hipped roof, front and side balustraded porch. Major alterations in 1893. Home of Capt. Henry L. Johnson, Norwegian immigrant who was a pilot on Tampa Bay. Private. N.R. 1974.

Tampa. S.H. KRESS AND COMPANY BUILDING. 811 N. Franklin St. 1929. Renaissance Revival. G.E. McKay, architect. 4 stories, masonry, suspended bronze marquee, extensive use of terra-cotta ornamentation on 2 facades. One of the last major commercial structures built in Tampa before the Great Depression. Private. N.R. 1983.

Tampa. LE CLAIRE APARTMENTS. 3013–3015 San Carlos. 1926. Masonry Vernacular. Fred J. James, architect. 2 stories. 2 "mirror-image" structures linked by a passage on the second floor. Stucco-covered arcade. Each second floor has a full-width porch. An early fashionable apartment complex. Private. N.R. 1988.

Hyde Park Historic District

Hutchinson House

57

Leiman House

Tampa. LEIMAN HOUSE. 716 S. Newport St. 1916. Prairie style. M. Leo Elliott, architect. 2 stories, frame, stuccoed, hipped roof with eaves, front walls enclose raised patio. Good example of fully developed Prairie style house. Home of Henry Leiman (1857–1931), manufacturer of cigar boxes. Private. N.R. 1974.

Tampa. MASONIC TEMPLE OF TAMPA, NUMBER 25. 508 E. Kennedy Blvd. 1928. Mediterranean Revival with Beaux-Arts detail. M. Leo Elliott, architect. 2 stories, brick, ornamental glazed terra-cotta detailing and elaborate brick work. Considerable interior wall and ceiling ornamentation. Private. N.R. 1986.

Tampa. OLD SCHOOL HOUSE. University of Tampa Campus. 1858 (moved twice). Greek Revival. 1 story, frame, clapboarding, pedimented tetrastyle portico. One of area's oldest buildings, typical of small private schools which dominated the state's early educational system. Private. N.R. 1974.

S.H. Kress and Company Building

Tampa. OLD TAMPA FREE PUBLIC LIBRARY. 102 E. 7th Ave. 1915. Classical Revival. 1 story. T-plan, masonry building faced with yellow and brown brick resting upon a rusticated granite basement. Barrel-tile roof. Constructed with funds provided by the Carnegie Foundation. Presently vacant. Public. N.R. 1991.

Tampa. STOVALL HOUSE. 4621 Bayshore Blvd. 1909. Classical Revival. 2 stories, brick, central entrance has 2-story center Ionic entrance portico and a 1-story Ionic balustraded veranda. In 1915 became the home of Col. Wallace Stovall, founder of the Tampa Tribune. House has recently undergone radical alterations. Private. N.R. 1974.

Tampa. T.C. TALIAFERRO HOUSE. 305 S. Hyde Park. 1893. Classical Revival. Grable, Weber and Groves, architects. 2 stories, frame, 2-story pedimented portico with coupled Ionic columns, balustraded balconies. Home of prominent member of the Tampa banking community. Private. N.R. 1974.

Taliaferro House

Tampa. TAMPA BAY HOTEL. 401 W. Kennedy Blvd. 1888–1891. Moorish Revival. J.A. Wood, architect. 4 stories, brick, 12 towers with bulbous domes and cupolas, covered cornices, ornate porches, elegant interior once included rotunda lobby. Built by railroad magnate Henry Bradley Plant. An excellent example of an early luxury hotel. Used as headquarters for the U.S. Army in the Spanish-American War. Now the home of the University of Tampa and Henry B. Plant Museum. Public. N.R. 1972.

Tampa. TAMPA CITY HALL. 315 John F. Kennedy Blvd. E. 1915. Eclectic. Bonfoey and Elliott, architects. 3-story main block with 8-story central office tower. 2nd and 3rd floors have Doric columns, balustrade around main block, terra-cotta detail and clock tower. Recognized as the finest of the architect M. Leo Elliott's commercial-municipal structures. Public. N.R. 1974.

Tampa Bay Hotel

Tampa. TAMPA THEATER AND OFFICE BUILDING. 709–711 Franklin St. 1925. Mediterranean Revival. John Eberson, architect. 9 stories, brick, highly ornate facade, 2 tower-like extensions on south wall, auditorium extremely ornate. Typical of the "atmospheric" theaters of the 1920s. Public. N.R. 1978.

Tampa. TAMPANIA HOUSE. 4611 N. A St. 1927. Prairie style. 1 story, masonry, stuccoed, tiled roof, raised patio at main entrance. 1 of 5 Prairie-style structures in the Tampa Bay area. House displays an unusual and distinctive use of stained glass. Private. N R. 1985.

Tampa Theater

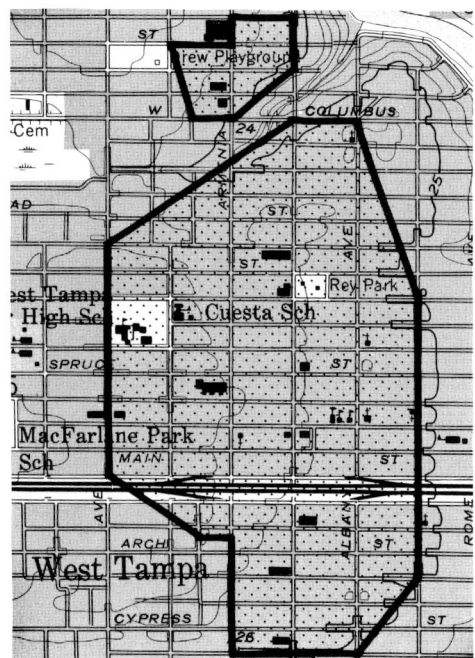

West Tampa Historic District

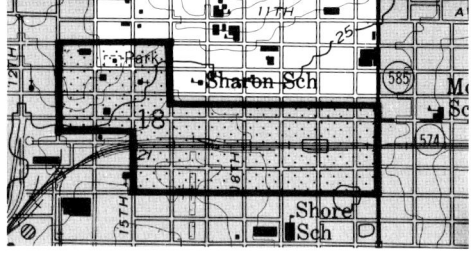

Ybor City Historic District

Ybor Factory Building

Tampa. UNION RAILROAD STATION. 601 N. Nebraska St. 1912. Italian Renaissance Revival. J.F. Leitner, architect. 1 story, brick, terracotta and stone trimming. Built to combine the passenger operations of the Atlantic Coast Line and the Seaboard Air Line. Private. N.R. 1974.

Tampa. WEST TAMPA HISTORIC DISTRICT. 1895–1925. 1287 structures within 77 blocks. Frame Vernacular row houses (many shotgun style) and bungalows are predominant styles. Notable buildings include 11 brick cigar factories and the Centro Español. Established as a working-class town. Many of the employees who worked in the numerous cigar factories lived there. Today it architecturally appears much as it did in 1925. Many of the original brick streets and granite curbs survive. N.R. 1983.

Tampa. YBOR CITY HISTORIC DISTRICT. 1886–early 20th century. 26 blocks. Brick and Frame Vernacular residential and commercial buildings predominate, with some Victorian and Mediterranean Revival. Wrought-iron balconies survive on 7 commercial buildings. Notable structures are Ybor Factory, El Pasaje, and 3 mutual aid society clubhouses. Remains of once thriving city within a city developed by Cuban cigar manufacturer Vincent Martinez Ybor, who relocated his Key West factory there and provided housing for immigrant workers. Now primarily a commercial area. N.R. 1974.

Tampa. YBOR FACTORY BUILDING. 7th Ave. between 13th and 14th Sts. 1886. Eclectic. C.E. Parcell, architect. 3 stories, brick, flat roof, central cupola, gabled portico replaces original. Cigar factory built by Vincent Martinez Ybor. Served as meeting place for Cuban patriots during 1890s. Portico was where José Martí, leader of Cuban Revolution, gave famous speech. Original portico removed to Havana. Private. N.R. 1972.

Vicinity of Tampa. EGMONT KEY. At entrance to Tampa Bay. 1840–1945. The site of a variety of military activities throughout the 19th and 20th centuries. Lighthouse established in 1848 and served the Union during Civil War. In the Spanish-American War a coastal artillery battery was installed (Fort Dade). Patrol station in World War II. Public. N.R. 1978.

Vicinity of Tampa. UPPER TAMPA ARCHAEOLOGICAL DISTRICT. 8001 Double Branch Rd. 1000 B.C.–A.D. 1400. Linear shell middens along the shoreline of Tampa Bay. Public. N.R. 1985.

Vicinity of Zephyrhills. FORT FOSTER (Camp Foster, Fort Alabama). 9 mi. S of Zephyrhills on U.S. 301. 1836. Site of military post built during the Second Seminole War to replace Fort Alabama as a supply depot. The fort was occupied and maintained as a depot until August 1837. In November 1837 again garrisoned and finally abandoned in 1849. Private. N.R. 1972.

INDIAN RIVER COUNTY

Sebastion. BAMMA VICKERS LAWSON HOUSE. 1133 U.S. 1. c. 1911. Frame Vernacular. 2 stories. Well-preserved example of local vernacular architecture. The most intact building remaining from Sebastion's days of first settlement. Its first occupants were pioneer families. Presently a doctor's office. Private. N.R. 1990.

Vicinity of Sebastion. PELICAN ISLAND NATIONAL WILDLIFE REFUGE. E of Sebastion on the Indian River. 1903. Pelican Island, largest of several mangrove islands, and surrounding waters were declared the first National Wildlife Refuge in 1903 by Theodore Roosevelt. These islands form a large rookery for brown pelicans, cormorants, egrets, herons, ibis, and other water birds. Public. N.R. 1966.

Vicinity of Sebastion. SPANISH FLEET SURVIVORS AND SALVORS CAMP SITE. Fl. A1A in Sebastion Inlet State Park. 1715. When 12 Spanish merchant ships sank in area, about 1500 survivors gathered on this site. Later Spanish built a temporary settlement here while salvage operations were underway to regain the lost gold and silver aboard the sunken vessels. Public. N.R. 1970.

Driftwood Inn and Restaurant

Vero Beach. DRIFTWOOD INN AND RESTAURANT (The Breezeway). 3150 Ocean Dr. 1937. Frame Vernacular. Waldo E. Sexton, architect. 2 stories. 2 Frame Vernacular buildings, 1 a restaurant, the other an inn. Began as a summer retreat for the Sexton family. Later converted to an inn. Presently an inn and restaurant associated with a time-share community. Private. N.R. 1994.

Vero Beach. FLORIDA THEATER. 2036 14th Ave. 1924. Mediterranean Revival. F.H. Trimble, architect. 2 stories. Flat roof, with parapets, walls finished in stucco. One of the few remaining structures of the original downtown. First motion picture theater in town. Presently vacant. Private. N.R. 1992.

Judge Henry F. Gregory House

Vero Beach. JUDGE HENRY F. GREGORY HOUSE. 2179 10th Ave. 1937. Monterey style. Bruce Kitchell, architect. 2 stories. Unusual style for area, most interesting feature is two-story porch. The Monterey style is Californian in origin. Built as winter residence for a Cook County, Illinois, circuit court judge and Florida land investor. Private. N.R. 1994.

Vero Beach. OLD PALMETTO HOTEL. 1889 Old Dixie Hwy. 1921, 1926. Frame Vernacular, with Mediterranean Revival elements. 2 stories. Originally a hotel, it was converted to apartments in the 1930s. Enlarged in 1926 and rehabilitated in 1990. Presently an apartment complex. Private. N.R. 1991.

Florida Theater

Vero Beach. **OLD VERO BEACH COMMUNITY CENTER**. 2146 14th Ave. 1935, 1943. Frame Vernacular. 1 story. The original U-shaped building altered by an addition in 1943. Throughout its history the building has served as a social gathering place, playhouse, and meeting hall. Built as a federal project during the Depression. Public. N.R. 1993.

Vero Beach. **VERO BEACH (FEC) RAILROAD STATION**. 2336 14th Ave. 1903, enlarged and remodeled 1916 and 1936, relocated in 1984. Frame Vernacular. 1 story, shingle-sided. The building served the transportation needs of the community and its surrounding agricultural area for over 70 years. Now a county historical exhibit center. Private. N.R. 1987.

Vero Beach Railroad Station, 1917

JACKSON COUNTY

Greenwood. **ERWIN HOUSE** Fort Rd. E of Fl. 71. c. 1840. Frame Vernacular. 2 stories, clapboarding, front veranda. Built by John A. Syfrett with lumber shipped from Apalachicola. Antebellum stage stop. Private. N.R. 1974.

Greenwood. **GREAT OAKS** (Bryan Mansion). S of Jct. of Fl. 69 and Fl. 71. 1857–1861. Greek Revival. 2 stories, 2-story, full-width portico with fluted Doric columns. Main house of Great Oaks, an antebellum plantation which acquired its name from a row of live oaks lining the road in front of it. Restored in 1961. Private. N.R. 1972.

L.S. Pender General Store

Greenwood. **L.S. PENDER GENERAL STORE.** Near Jct. of Fl. 77 and Fl. 71. c. 1869. Frame Vernacular. 1^1/$_2$ stories. Typical rural commercial structure. It has been in continuous use as a store since construction. Private. N.R. 1974.

Marianna. **ELY-CRIGLAR HOUSE**. 242 W. Lafayette St. c. 1840. Greek Revival. 2 stories, brick, 2-story portico with Doric columns. Francis R. Ely, for whom the house was built, came from North Carolina in 1839 and became owner of a plantation of 1629 acres and 63 slaves. Private. N.R. 1972.

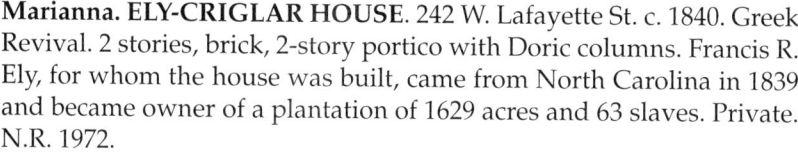

Marianna. **JOSEPH W. RUSS, JR., HOUSE**. 310 W. Lafayette St. 1892–1896, 1910. Classical Revival with Queen Anne elements. 2^1/$_2$ stories, frame, conical turret, monumental, semicircular, 2-story porch supported by Corinthian columns. Built by Joseph W. Russ, member of an old Marianna family, in the Queen Anne style. Later (1910) altered to conform to the Classical Revival style. Private. N.R. 1983.

Joseph W. Russ, Jr., House, 1983

Marianna. THEOPHILUS WEST HOUSE. 403 Putnam St. c. 1840. Greek Revival elements. 1$\frac{1}{2}$ stories, frame, full-width veranda. Home of Dr. Theophilus West, prominent local physician and druggist. He also was the county's first superintendent of schools. Private. N.R. 1972.

Vicinity of Marianna. WADDELLS MILL POND SITE. 7 mi. NW of Marianna. A.D. 1200–A.D. 1500 Fort Walton period. Cave sites and rock shelters which yielded aboriginal ceramics, projectile points, scrapers, and shell ear plugs. Private. N.R. 1972.

JEFFERSON COUNTY

Capps. ASA MAY HOUSE. N of Jct. of U.S. 19 and U.S. 27. c. 1840. Greek Revival. 1$\frac{1}{2}$ stories, frame, gabled roof, full-width porch. Home of Asa May, owner of Rosewood Plantation. May, a cotton planter, owned 3500 acres within the county. Private. N.R. 1972.

Vicinity of Lamont. SAN MIGUÉL DE ASILE MISSION SITE. 30 mi. SE of Tallahassee. 1607–1704. Site of a mission with a 39-foot-by-64 foot mission structure. The mission was the most westward of 4 set among the Yustaga (Timucua) Indians. Believed to have been burned by English and Creek Indians in 1704. Private. N.R. 1974.

Theophilus West House

Vicinity of Lamont. TURNBULL-RITTER HOUSE. NW of Lamont off U.S. 19. 1856. Classical Revival. 2$\frac{1}{2}$ stories, frame, facades have full length porches. Private. N.R. 1979.

Lloyd. DENNIS-COXETTER HOUSE. Fl. 59 and Fl. 158 (Bond St.). c. 1859. Frame Vernacular. 1 story. Side gables, crimped seam metal roof, two interior red brick chimneys. George Elliott Dennis was a prominent Jefferson County cotton planter. Purchased in 1908 by Winifred and Sydney Coxetter. Winifred was granddaughter of Dennis. Private. N.R. 1988.

Lloyd. LAFITTE LOG HOUSE. Fl. 59. c. 1844. Log Vernacular. 1 story. If construction data are correct (oral tradition), it is the oldest of two antebellum hewn log houses in the county. In poor condition. Private. N.R. 1991.

Dennis-Coxetter House

Lloyd. LLOYD-BOND HOUSE. Bond St. c. 1864. Frame Vernacular with Classical Revival elements. 1 story, portico and full-width porch at entrance. House the result of joining of 2 double-pen cabins. Home of Walter Lloyd, who enticed the railroad to lay its tracks through Lloyd. During the Civil War it served as a hospital for Confederate soldiers wounded at the Battle of Olustee in Baker County. Private. N.R. 1984.

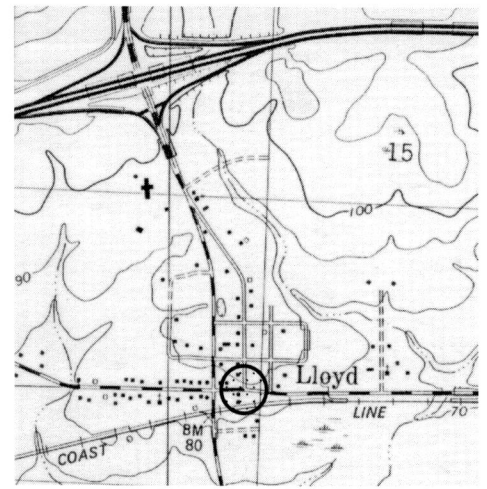

Lloyd Historic District

Lloyd. LLOYD HISTORIC DISTRICT. c. 1840–1920. 24 buildings, 20 of historical interest. Frame Vernacular, some with Classical elements. Buildings in Lloyd were built in 2 and possibly 3 periods. c. 1855–1859 and 1870–1890. Some evidence suggests buildings were on the site as early as 1840. Public and Private. N.R. 1991.

Lloyd. LLOYD RAILROAD DEPOT. Jct. of Fl. 59 and Lester Lawrence Rd. c. 1858. Masonry Vernacular. 1 story, brick. Built by Pensacola and Georgia Railroad to provide cotton producing county access to Atlantic and Gulf coast seaports. Decline of use began with the boll weevil infestation and the growth of highway transportation. Private. N.R. 1973.

Vicinity of Lloyd. SAN JOSÉ DE OCUYA SITE. 17 mi. E of Tallahassee. 1600–1703. 1 of 18 Franciscan missions established by the Spanish among the Apalachee Indians between 1633 and 1683. Believed to be the first mission destroyed in one of the English-led raids of Creek Indians, which began in 1703 and continued until 1707. Raids destroyed 32 Spanish settlements in North Florida. Private. N.R. 1973.

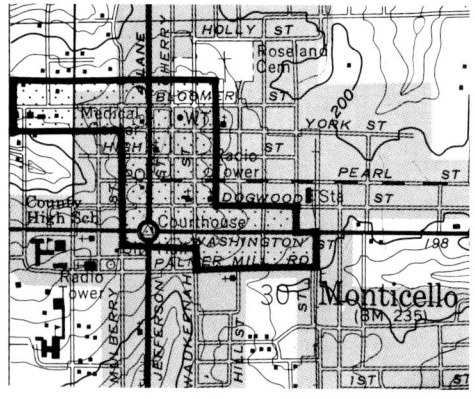

Monticello Historic District

Monticello. DENHAM-LACY HOUSE. 555 Palmer Mill Rd. 1874+. Italianate. 2 stories, frame, octagonal cupola, monumental portico added to west side. One of a few Italianate structures in North Florida. Built for John Denham, Scottish immigrant and cotton merchant. Private. N.R. 1982.

Monticello. MONTICELLO HISTORIC DISTRICT. 1828-c. 1900. 42 19th-century buildings within 27 blocks. Predominant styles are Frame Vernacular, Victorian, and Classical Revival. Notable structures: Perkins Opera House (Romanesque) and Mays House (Greek Revival). With rare exception, the buildings within the district are 19th century and reflect the typical architectural development of a North Florida town of the period. N.R. 1977.

Monticello. PALMER HOUSE. Palmer Mill Rd. and S. Jefferson. c. 1867. Classical Revival. 1¹/₂ stories, frame. Home of Dr. J. Dabney Palmer until his death in 1909. Private. N.R. 1978.

Monticello. PALMER-PERKINS HOUSE. 625 W. Palmer Mill Rd. c. 1836. Classical Revival. 2¹/₂ stories, brick 1st floor. 2nd floor is frame, 2-story pedimented portico with 2nd-story porch. Built for Martin Palmer who came to county in 1820s and established himself as a planter. Private. N.R. 1979.

Denham-Lacy House

Monticello. PERKINS OPERA HOUSE. Washington St. and Courthouse Sq. 1890. Masonry Vernacular with Romanesque Revival elements. 2 stories, red brick, round, arched 2nd-floor windows. Center of social activities for the county with traveling opera companies, vaudeville shows, and local talent performing there from the turn of the century through the late 1920s. Private. N.R. 1972.

Monticello. WIRICK-SIMMONS HOUSE. Jefferson and Pearl Sts. 1830s. Greek Revival. 2 stories, frame Doric porticos on end and side with 2nd-story balcony. Believed to be the oldest building in Monticello. Built for Methodist circuit rider Adam Wirick. Private. N.R. 1972.

Vicinity of Monticello. LYNDHURST PLANTATION. Off Ashville Rd. 1850–1855. Greek Revival. 2½ stories, brick 1st floor, frame upper floor, with pedimented 2-story portico. Main house of a typical 19th century Middle Florida plantation. Private. N.R. 1973.

Vicinity of Tallahassee. SAN JUAN DE ASPALAGA SITE. 16 mi. E of Tallahassee. 1640–1704. Site of one of the oldest Spanish Franciscan missions established in the Province of Apalachee. Indian village to the south of the mission. Destroyed by English and Creek Indian raiding party in 1704. Private. N.R. 1973.

LAKE COUNTY

Vicinity of Astor. BOWERS BLUFF MIDDENS ARCHAEOLOGICAL DISTRICT. In the Ocala National Forest, 5 mi. SE of Astor. 2000 B.C.–300 B.C. Archaic period. 3 snail-shell middens, the largest being 380 feet long, 100 feet wide, and 15 feet high. Public. N.R. 1980.

Vicinity of Astor. KIMBALL ISLAND MIDDEN ARCHAELOGICAL SITE. Ocala National Forest. 3000 B.C.–2000 B.C. Archaic period. Giant preceramic snail-shell midden 700 feet by 390 feet and 17 feet high. Public. N.R. 1979.

Clermont. CLERMONT WOMAN'S CLUB. 655 Broome St. 1923, 1927. Frame Vernacular. George Hartford, architect. 1 story. T-shaped building with aluminum siding. Built as a community project. Served as the central meeting place for the community until 1940. During World War II used for several defense-related projects. Public. N.R. 1993.

Eustis. CLIFFORD HOUSE. 536 N. Bay St. 1910. Classical Revival. 2½ stories, frame, clapboarding, full-height entrance portico with paired Doric columns. Built by Guilford David Clifford, Lake County pioneer merchant and a founder of Eustis. Private. N.R. 1975.

Eustis. FERRAN PARK AND THE ALICE McCLELLAND MEMORIAL BANDSHELL. Ferran Park Rd. 1918. Mission/Spanish Colonial Revival. Alan J. MacDonough, architect. Ferran Park is a 4.5-acre public recreational area developed between 1918 and 1921. The bandshell is a 2-story stucco building erected in 1926. In 1992 bandshell was restored by a state preservation grant. Public. N.R. 1994.

San Juan de Aspalaga Church Structure
(Conjectural reconstruction)

Clermont Woman's Club

Alice McClelland Memorial Bandshell

Eustis. WILLIAM KIMBROUGH PENDLETON HOUSE. (The Palms). 1208 Chesterfield Rd. c. 1876, c. 1886. Queen Anne. William Kimbrough Pendleton, architect. 2¹/₂ stories, frame, originally 2-story Frame Vernacular, hexagonal observatory tower and other features added (1886). Owner was a pioneer citrus grower from West Virginia. His home became a showplace of Central Florida. Private. N.R. 1983.

Eustis. WOMAN'S CLUB OF EUSTIS. 227 N. Center St. 1931. Classical Revival. 1 story. Concrete block with stucco walls. Main entrance pavilion. Continues to serve as a social and cultural center. Private. N.R. 1991.

Fruitland Park. HOLY TRINITY EPISCOPAL CHURCH. Spring Lake Rd. 1888. Gothic Revival. J.J. Nevitt, architect. 1 story, frame, fishscale shingles in the gable. First church in Fruitland Park, a community of English settlers founded in 1879. Private. N.R. 1974.

Howey-in-the-Hills. HOWEY HOUSE. Citrus St. 1926. Mediterranean Revival. Katherine Cotheal Budd, architect. 2 stories, masonry, stuccoed, tile roof, front entrance has spiralled engaged columns, bas-relief panels. Home of the founder of the town, a Northerner who established citrus groves in the area and urged his friends from the North to settle there. Private. N.R. 1983.

Donnelly House

Leesburg. MOTE-MORRIS HOUSE. 1021 N. Main St. 1892. Frame Vernacular. 2 stories, clapboarding and shingle siding, full-width 1-story entrance porch, slender turret. E.H. Mote, from Washington, D.C., was an early developer and hotel owner in the city. Private. N.R. 1974.

Mount Dora. DONNELLY HOUSE. Donnelly Ave. 1893. Queen Anne. 2¹/₂ stories, frame, clapboarding, carpenter decorations, octagonal turret, wraparound porch. John Phillip Donnelly, from Pittsburgh, was one of the founders of Mount Dora. Private. N.R. 1975.

Mount Dora. LAKESIDE INN. 100 N. Alexander St. 1883+ . Frame Vernacular. Complex of 5 buildings, 2 to 3 stories, the first having been built in 1883. 2 built in 1926 and 1929 are stuccoed and have Jacobethan-style elements. The main building, 2 stuccoed buildings, and an Olympic-size pool (1929) define a quadrangle. A highly successful tourist facility of the late 19th century and early 20th century. Recently restored to its 1920s appearance. Private. N.R. 1987.

Lakeside Inn

Mount Dora. OLD MOUNT DORA A.C.L. RAILROAD STATION. 341 Alexander St. 1915. Frame Vernacular. 1 story. The first railroad to reach Mount Dora was in 1886, when a line connected it to Jacksonville and Tampa. The Mount Dora depot cost $8,223 to build. The last passenger train left Mount Dora in 1950 and freight was discontinued in 1973. Private. N.R. 1992.

LEE COUNTY

Boca Grande. CHARLOTTE HARBOR AND NORTHERN RAILWAY DEPOT. Park and 4th Sts. 1909–1910, 1912–1913. Mediterranean Revival elements. 2 stories, beige brick, arcaded loggia, tile roof. A symbol of the importance of railroads in the opening of the area for phosphate exports as well as tourism. Private. N.R. 1979.

Boca Grande. JOURNEY'S END. Beachfront at 18th St. 1914 (moved). Frame Vernacular. 2 stories, porch on 3 sides, 4 cottages and a garage added later. Main house built of virgin heart-of-pine timber grown and milled near Arcadia, Florida. One of town's earlier buildings. Private. N.R. 1985.

Boca Grande Lighthouse, Assistant Keeper's quarters, and U.S. Coast Guard Beacon, 1978

Vicinity of Boca Grande. BOCA GRANDE LIGHTHOUSE. S tip of Gasparilla Island. 1890. Frame. 44 feet tall, assistant keeper's quarters nearby also frame. The light opened up shipping into Boca Grande Harbor, permitting the export of large quantities of phosphate. Public. N.R. 1980.

Buckingham. BUCKINGHAM SCHOOL. Intersection of Buckingham Rd. and Cemetery Rd. 1895. Frame Vernacular. T.M. Parks and M.S. Gonzalez, architects. 1 story. Metal hipped roof. Area settled by homesteaders who practiced truck farming, citrus cultivation and cattle ranching. Classes were held from 1–8th grade. Oldest known schoolhouse in Lee County. Now used for social functions. Public. N.R. 1989.

Estero. KORESHAN UNITY SETTLEMENT HISTORIC DISTRICT. U.S. 41 at Estero River. 1894. Community complex of 20 buildings from the original 30; includes auditorium, residences, dormitories, post office, bakery, store, and machine shop. Frame Vernacular is predominant style. Settled by Koreshan Unity, a communal sect based on scientific and economic theories emphasizing education, culture, and landscaping. Declined after death of Cyrus Teed (1908), its founder. State Park. N.R. 1976.

Buckingham School

Vicinity of Estero. MOUND KEY. In Koreshan State Park. Prehistoric, 15th–16th centuries. Glades period. 2 large oval, earth-and-shell mounds, a large truncated temple mound, a low burial mound, several smaller mounds, and a man-made canal. A large village center believed to have been visited by Pedro Menéndez de Avilés in 1565. Site of Jesuit mission. Public. N.R. 1970.

Fort Myers. ALDERMAN HOUSE. 2572 1st St. 1925. Spanish Colonial Revival. 2 stories. Patio in front with Italian blue and white tile. Arcaded loggia with twisted columns. Residence of a local banker. Presently used as store. Private. N.R. 1988.

Koreshan Unity Store, c. 1890s

Thomas Edison Winter Estate

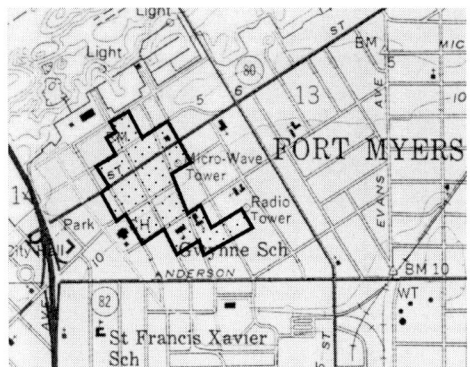

Fort Myers Downtown Commercial District

Lee County Courthouse

Fort Myers. PAUL LAWRENCE DUNBAR SCHOOL. 1857 High St. 1927. Mission Revival. L.N. Iredell, architect. 2 stories. T-shaped cement block building with stuccoed exterior walls. From 1927 to 1962 it was the only secondary school facility for black children in Lee County. Prior to its construction county only provided black children instruction through the 10th grade. Public. N.R. 1992.

Fort Myers. THOMAS EDISON WINTER ESTATE. 2350 McGregor Blvd. 1886+. The winter estate is a 14-acre property with 8 buildings of historical interest. Seminole Lodge, the main residence, is 2 connecting buildings. Purchased in 1885 by Edison at a time when Fort Myers was still a little cattle town, Edison developed the property into a winter home and secondary research facility. Now a museum. Public. N.R. 1991.

Fort Myers. HENRY FORD ESTATE. 2400 McGregor Blvd. c. 1895. Frame Vernacular with Craftsman elements. 1$^{1}/_{2}$ stories. Located next to the Edison home, it remains in virtually the same condition as when the automobile maker lived there. Was his winter home from 1916 to 1931. Curiously, Ford never built a garage or driveway. Public. N.R. 1988.

Fort Myers. FORT MYERS DOWNTOWN COMMERCIAL DISTRICT. 1888–1939. 76 buildings, 70 of historical interest. Commercial, Classical Revival, Moderne, Mediterranean Revival styles predominate. Commercial district evolved from Fort Harvie, a Seminole Indian War army post. Settlers took apart the fort to build Fort Myers' first buildings. Perhaps the best example of early 20th century commercial styles in SW Florida. Public and Private. N.R. 1990.

Fort Myers. JEWETT-THOMPSON HOUSE. 1141 Wales Dr. 1926. Spanish Colonial Revival. Nat Walker, architect. 2 stories. U-shaped with a 2-story center block. One of the most elaborate Spanish Colonial structures built in Fort Myers. Jewett was an actor from Australia who married into a wealthy New York banking family. Private. N.R. 1988.

Fort Myers. LEE COUNTY COURTHOUSE. 2120 Main St. 1915. Classical Revival. Francis J. Kennard, architect. 2 stories. Buff-colored brick Classical Doric columns at main entrance. Second courthouse of Lee County. Built with considerable objection from those who did not want to replace the old frame courthouse with a $85,000 new one. Public. N.R. 1989.

Fort Myers. MURPHY-BURROUGHS HOUSE. 2505 1st St. 1901. Georgian Revival. C.S. Caldwell and G.T. Barker, architects. 2$^{1}/_{2}$ stories, frame, balustraded widow's walk, wide lst-floor porch. One of the first and one of the few remaining residences of its style and quality built in Fort Myers. House Museum. Public. N.R. 1984.

Vicinity of Pine Island. DEMERE KEY. In Pine Island Sound. A.D. 800–A.D. 1700. Glades and Historic periods. Several mounds, canals, 12-foot conch-shell seawall, and flat truncated conch-shell pyramid presumed to have been a temple foundation. One of the finest examples of late prehistoric through early historic Calusa settlements in southwest Florida. Private. N.R. 1972.

Pine Island Sound. DORMITORIES AND ICE HOUSES ASSOCIATED WITH FISHING INDUSTRY. 1920–1945. 9 Frame Vernacular buildings set on pilings in Pine Island Sound. 8 were used as dormitories for commercial fisherman and 2 as ice houses to preserve fish until they could be brought to Fort Myers for sale. Most used today as fish camps for sports fishermen. Private. N.R. 1989,1991.

Pineland. JOSSLYN ISLAND SITE. Between Pine Island and Cayo Costa. A.D. 1300–A.D. 1600. Glades and Historic periods. Island on which are found mounds divided by deep channels, platforms, and a central plaza. Site of historic Calusa Indian settlement and of prehistoric habitation. Private. N.R. 1978.

Pineland. PINELAND SITE. Pine Island. A.D. 1300–A.D. 1600 Glades and Historic periods. Pyramidal and truncated mounds, section of ceremonial canal, and a burial mound. One of the largest extant Calusa sites in area, though smaller than that of Mound Key. Private. N.R. 1973.

Sanibel Island. SANIBEL LIGHTHOUSE AND KEEPER'S QUARTERS. Eastern Tip of Sanibel Island. 1884. Screw pile. Iron, 98 feet high. Two adjacent Frame Vernacular keeper's houses supported on iron piers. Verandas surround both. Public. N.R. 1974.

Sanibel Lighthouse and Keeper's Quarters

LEON COUNTY

Vicinity of Iamonia. TALL TIMBERS PLANTATION DISTRICT. 2 mi. E of intersection of CR 155 and CR 12. c. 1895. 13 buildings, 11 of historical interest. Frame Vernacular. The oldest is the Beadel House (1895). Antebellum cotton plantation converted to a quail hunting plantation in 1895. Site of extensive experimentation in woodland and game management. Private. N.R. 1989.

Tallahassee. BROKAW-McDOUGALL HOUSE (Peres-Brokaw House). 329 N. Meridian Rd. c. 1850. Classical Revival. 2 stories, frame, full-width veranda with Corinthian columns, balustraded balcony, square cupola. The house at one time was situated on an estate of several hundred acres, part of the Lafayette Grant. The former farmland is now part of Tallahassee's downtown. Public. N.R. 1972.

Brokaw-McDougall House

Carnegie Library

Coles-Buzzett Farm House

Tallahassee. CALHOUN STREET HISTORIC DISTRICT. 19th century to early 20th century. The district, an old residential neighborhood, is now mainly offices. Contains approximately 39 buildings of historical interest, ranging from Frame Vernacular to Classical Revival. In the 19th century Calhoun Street was known as "Gold Dust Street." N.R. 1979.

Tallahassee. CARNEGIE LIBRARY. Florida Agricultural and Mechanical University. 1908. Classical Revival. 2 stories, brick, front portico with 4 Ionic columns. One of the oldest buildings of what formerly was Florida's black university. Money for construction donated by the Carnegie Foundation. Public. N.R. 1978

Tallahassee. CASCADES PARK. Bounded by Apalachee Pkwy, Bloxham, Suwannee, Monroe and Meridian Sts. 1820–1840. 35 acres which formed the nucleus of the area selected for the capital. Included within it is the Prime Meridian marker, which determines the starting point of all state land surveys. Public. N.R. 1971.

Tallahassee. COLES-BUZZETT FARM HOUSE. 411 E. Oakland Ave. 1885. Frame Vernacular. 1 story. Side gables, rear hipped-roof porch. Originally built in a rural area, the house is now located in an urban residential neighborhood within sight of the state capitol. Private. N.R. 1992.

Tallahassee. THE COLUMNS. 100 N. Duval St. c. 1830 (moved in 1971). Greek Revival. 2½ stories, brick, 2-story pedimented entrance portico. Built for William W. Williams, first president of the Bank of Florida. Originally the house served as residence and bank. One of the oldest houses in Tallahassee. Houses the Tallahassee Chamber of Commerce. Private. N.R. 1975.

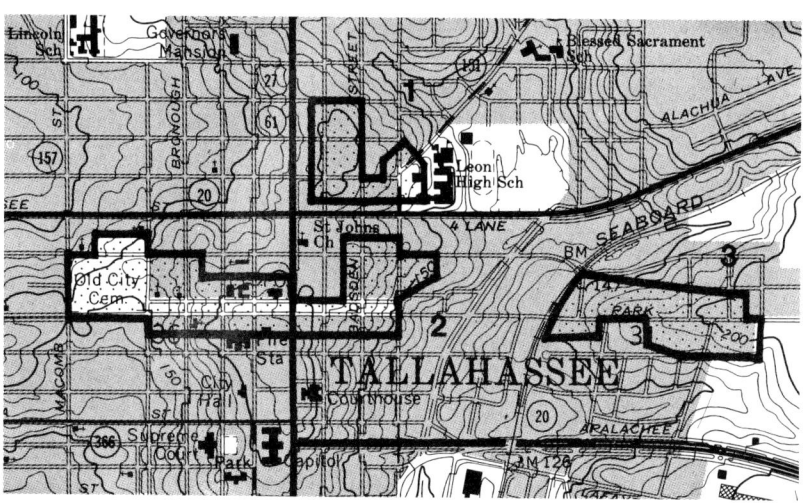

Calhoun Street Historic District (1), Park Avenue Historic District (2), and Magnolia Heights Historic District (3)

Tallahassee. COVINGTON HOUSE. 328 Cortez St. 1927. French Renaissance. William A. Edwards, architect. 1¹/₂ stories. Stuccoed, hollow-clay tile roof. Includes garage and servants' quarters and stable. Built in Los Robles subdivision. Blanche Covington was one of Florida's best known horticulturalists. Private. N.R. 1989.

Tallahassee. EXCHANGE BANK BUILDING. 201 S. Monroe St. 1927. Eclectic. Edwards and Sayward, architects. 6 stories, buff brick, limestone trim, terra-cotta wall ornamentation in a Neo-Egyptian and Greek design. The first modern private office building in Tallahassee. One of the few downtown buildings to have maintained its architectural integrity. Private. N.R. 1984.

Tallahassee. FIRST PRESBYTERIAN CHURCH. 102 N. Adams St. 1835–1838. Greek Revival with Gothic Revival elements. 2 stories, brick, front pedimented Doric portico, rectangular tower. One of the oldest buildings in the city and the only church still standing which dates from the territorial period. Private. N.R. 1974.

First Presbyterian Church

Tallahassee. FLORIDA STATE CAPITOL (The Old Capitol). S. Monroe St. 1839+. Classical Revival. 3 stories, brick, stuccoed, east and west facade have Doric porticos, central dome with cupola. This structure, the third state capitol, housed the first session of the state legislature when Florida received statehood. Original building expanded in 1902, 1923, 1936 and 1947. Building restored to 1902 appearance and contains a museum and offices. Public. N.R. 1973.

Tallahassee. GALLIE'S HALL AND BUILDINGS. Jefferson and Adams Sts. 1873–1874. 2¹/₂ stories, brick. Contained the first theater and only public hall in the city from the late 1800s into the 1900s. Because of completion of a new theater and the construction of school auditoriums, it closed in 1910. Recently restored to its 1890s appearance. Private. N.R. 1980.

Florida State Capitol (The Old Capitol), c. 1977

Tallahassee. GOODWOOD (Old Croom Mansion). 1500 Miccosukee Rd. 1844. Greek Revival. George Anderson, architect. 2 stories, brick, large octagonal cupola, 1-story veranda, numerous outbuildings. Located on a tract of land originally part of the Lafayette Land Grant. On the grounds were once a private race track, formal English gardens and bridle paths. Private. N.R. 1972.

Tallahassee. THE GROVE. Adams St. and 1st Ave. c. 1825. Greek Revival. 2 stories, brick, 2-story, 4-column pedimented portico. Built by Richard Call, territorial governor from 1836 to 1839, and again from 1841 to 1844. Also the home of LeRoy Collins, governor from 1955 to 1961. Public. N.R. 1972.

Gallie's Hall and Buildings

Photo and Drawing of Falcon Dancer from reverse view of large repousse copper breastplate from Burial 7 (female), Lake Jackson Mound 3.

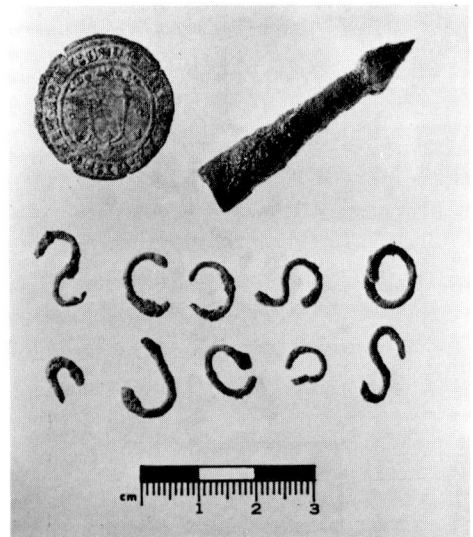

Spanish copper 4 maravedis coin (c. 16th century), **cross bow quarrel, chain mail links,** de Soto winter encampment, John W. Martin House.

Tallahassee. JOHNSON-CALDWELL HOUSE. Village Green (moved 1987). c. 1852. Greek Revival. 2¹/₂ stories, frame, 2-story front portico. Originally sat within a 320-acre plantation. First identified with Robert Butler, friend of Andrew Jackson. Purchased in 1941 by Millard F. Caldwell, governor from 1945 to 1949. Public. N.R. 1979.

Tallahassee. LAKE JACKSON MOUNDS . Off U.S. 27, N of Tallahassee. A.D. 1300–A.D. 1600. Fort Walton period. The largest known Fort Walton ceremonial center in North Florida. Included on the site are truncated temple mounds, a plaza, and village area. Largest mound has an estimated height of 25 feet and a base of approximately 200 feet by 150 feet. Public. N.R. 1971.

Tallahassee. LEWIS HOUSE. 3117 Okeeheepkee Rd. 1954. Hemicycle style. Frank Lloyd Wright, architect. 2 stories, masonry and frame, plan of the house is characterized by both concentric and intersecting circles. The only home designed by Wright within Florida, it is associated with the architect's last and shortest stylistic phase, called *Hemicycle*. Private. N.R. 1979.

Tallahassee. LEON COUNTY HIGH SCHOOL. 550 E. Tennessee St. 1936. Italian Renaissance. M. Leo Elliott, architect. E-shaped building. Masonry accented by terra-cotta friezes. Additions are music and science building (1965), gymnasium (1965), and graphic arts building (1983). The school has played a major role in the education of a number of the state's political leaders. Public. N.R. 1993.

Tallahassee. LOS ROBLES GATE. Intersection of Thomasville Rd. and Meridian Rd. 1926. Spanish Colonial Revival. George Kerr Armes, architect. A 104-foot wide gate with a 33-foot elliptical arch. Includes barrel-tile roof. When constructed the subdivision was outside the city's northern limits. Area was mainly farm and pasture land. Public. N.R. 1989.

Tallahassee. MAGNOLIA HEIGHTS HISTORIC DISTRICT. 701 to 1005 E. Park Ave. and Cadiz St. 1899–1934. Approximately 45 buildings, 30 of which were built between 1899 and 1934, in a 5-block area. Predominant styles are Frame Vernacular and Queen Anne. Locally significant because it illustrates the early stages of suburban development in the city. Settled mainly by newcomers, many of whom came to work for the state. Governor LeRoy Collins grew up here. N.R. 1984.

Tallahassee. GOVERNOR JOHN W. MARTIN HOUSE (Apalachee). 1001 Governor's Drive. 1933–1934. Georgian Revival. 1 story, red brick, small pedimented portico with paired Tuscan columns. Home of Governor Martin, who held office from 1925 to 1929. When constructed, it was regarded as a country estate, although today it is well within the city. Believed to be the site of the 1539–40 winter encampment of the Hernando de Soto expedition. Private. N.R. 1986.

Tallahassee. OLD CITY WATERWORKS. E. Gaines St. and S. Gadsden St. 1923. Masonry Vernacular. 1 story, brick, stuccoed, 2 steeply pitched truncated pyramids accent the roof. The last of several waterworks built on the site. Significant as the remnant of a "modern" civil engineering improvement implemented in the city. Public. N.R. 1979.

Tallahassee. OLD FORT BRADEN SCHOOL. Jackson Bluff Rd. 1926. Frame Vernacular. E.D. Fitchner, architect. 1 story. Gable on hipped roof, 6 chimneys. Was the most important educational facility in western Leon County for many years. Built to consolidate the area's many one-room school houses. Presently not in use. Public. N.R. 1994.

Old Fort Braden School

Tallahassee. PARK AVENUE HISTORIC DISTRICT. 19th century to early 20th century. Includes both residential and commercial buildings located along Park Ave. from Macomb St. to Gadsden St. Frame Vernacular is the most common style, but a number of homes are Classical Revival. A chain of public parks links this district. N.R. 1979.

Tallahassee. JOHN GILMORE RILEY HOUSE. 419 E. Jefferson St. 1892. Frame Vernacular. 2 stories. Owner was an early black educator who worked for the Tallahassee School Board from 1880s until 1926 and was a leader in the black community. Private. N.R. 1978.

Tallahassee. ST. JOHN'S EPISCOPAL CHURCH. 211 N. Monroe St. 1881+ . Gothic Revival. 1 story, red brick, south facade has a tower. Excellent example of Gothic Revival within the city. Congregation formed in 1827, the 3rd oldest Episcopal congregation in the state. Within its congregation have been several governors and other high-ranking state political figures. Private. N.R. 1978.

St. John's Episcopal Church

Tallahassee. SAN LUIS DE APALACHE. Tennessee St. and Ocala Rd. 1633, 1663. Site of mission and fort complex, typical of Spanish mission system in Florida. Administrative center for Apalachee missions of the Franciscan religious order. Burned by British and Creek Indians in 1704. Museum. Public. N.R. 1966.

Tallahassee. UNION BANK. Apalachee Pkwy. and Calhoun Sts. 1841 (moved in 1971). Federal and Greek Revival elements. 1 story, brick, stuccoed. The Union Bank, established in 1830, was an early major financial institution in the state. Restored and presently a museum. Public. N.R. 1971.

Tallahassee. DAVID S. WALKER LIBRARY. 209 E. Park Ave. 1903. Eclectic. 2 stories, brick, 2-story columns at entrance. Named after an early supporter of a library in Tallahassee on land donated by his widow. The library contributed greatly to the educational and cultural life of early 20th century Tallahassee. Private. N.R. 1976.

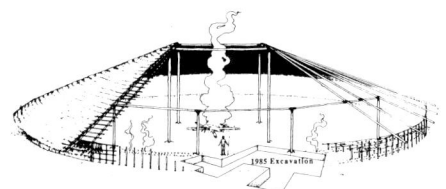
San Luis Council House, artist's rendition based on 1985 test excavation

Bellevue

Vicinity of Tallahassee. BELLEVUE (Murat House). Tallahassee Museum of History and Natural Science. Early 19th century (moved in 1967). Colonial Revival elements. 1^1/$_2$ stories, frame, recessed full-width front and rear porches. Once the main residence of a 500-acre plantation. Home of Catherine Murat, widow of Napoleon's nephew Prince Achille Murat, following his death. House museum. Public. N.R. 1971.

Vicinity of Tallahassee. BRADLEY'S COUNTRY STORE COMPLEX. Fl. 151, 15 mi. NE of Tallahassee. 1893–1970. 17 buildings on 31 acres, mainly Frame Vernacular. Homestead built between 1893 and 1903, other structures newer. For 3 generations the Bradleys have maintained a store on the premises. The related homestead and farm buildings with the store make-up a complex which could be described as a living museum. Private. N.R. 1984.

Bradley's Country Store, 1987

Vicinity of Tallahassee. ESCAMBE (San Cosmo y San Damias de Escambe). 3 mi. NW of Tallahassee. mid-17th century. Site of Spanish Franciscan mission burned by the British in 1704. Contains the church complex, cemetery, Indian village. There is evidence of an earlier, pre-historic village. Private-Public. N.R. 1971.

Vicinity of Tallahassee. PISGAH UNITED METHODIST CHURCH. Off Fl. 151, N of Tallahassee. 1858–1859. Greek Revival elements. 1^1/$_2$ stories, frame. The third structure built to accommodate the area's Methodists. Following the Civil War the congregation dwindled, but today it has regained its former vitality. Private. N.R. 1974.

Vicinity of Tallahassee. SAN PEDRO Y SAN PABLO DE PATALE. 6 mi. E of Tallahassee on Buck Lake Rd. mid-17th century. Site of one of the first of 9 missions established in the Apalachee Province by Franciscans during the westward expansion of the Spanish from St. Augustine. Attacked and burned by British and Creek Indian forces in 1704. Private. N.R. 1972.

Vicinity of Woodville. NATURAL BRIDGE BATTLEFIELD. Natural Bridge Rd. In March 1865 site of a battle between a Federal force of approximately 650 men and a Confederate force of roughly the same number. Confederates occupied defensive positions beside a narrow stretch of firm land which the Union forces endeavored to cross. Union forces routed with heavy casualties. Public. N.R. 1970.

LEVY COUNTY

Cedar Key. CEDAR KEY HISTORIC AND ARCHAEOLOGICAL DISTRICT. c. 1839–1920. 311 buildings, 155 of historical interest. Frame Vernacular. An early Florida community that first gained importance when it became the terminus of an antebellum railroad that ran to Fernandina on the east coast. Later the center of cedar cutting for the nation's pencil industry. Presently a fishing port and tourist center. Archaeological sites from Deptford and Weeden Island periods nearby. Also wildlife sanctuary. Public and Private. N.R. 1989.

Cedar Key. ISLAND HOTEL. 224 2nd St. 1861. Masonry Vernacular. 2 stories, tabby walls, stuccoed, 2-story porch. Built as a general store when railroad reached the town. Following the decline of the cedar industry, local economy languished and store closed (1910). Operated as a hotel since 1946. Private. N.R. 1984.

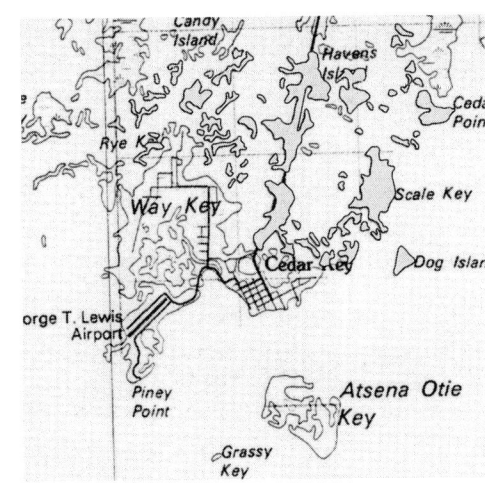

Cedar Key Historic and Archaeological District

LIBERTY COUNTY

Blountstown. OTIS HARE ARCHAEOLOGICAL SITE. at mile 73 on E bank of the Apalachicola River. c. A.D. 100–A.D. 700. Swift Creek and Weeden Island periods. Midden contains numerous lithic and ceramic artifacts as well as shell, faunal, and other food remains. Private. N.R. 1989.

Island Hotel, 1984

Vicinity of Bristol. TORREYA STATE PARK (Gregory House). 13 mi. NE of Bristol on Fl. 12. Pre-Columbian period to 19th century. Focal point of park is Gregory House (c. 1830), 2-story, frame, Greek Revival home. Within park are 6 gun pits dug by Confederates on the bank of the Apalachicola River for cannon to prevent Union Army use of the river. Archaeological sites from Weeden Island period within park. Public. N.R. 1972.

Vicinity of Bristol. YON MOUND AND VILLAGE SITE. 2 mi. W of Bristol. 0–A.D. 350 and A.D. 800–A.D. 1500. Swift Creek and Fort Walton periods. Well-preserved, 29-foot-high temple mound and village complex on a natural levee of the east bank of the Apalachicola River. Private. N.R. 1978.

Gregory House (Torreya State Park)

MADISON COUNTY

Greenville. BISHOP ANDREWS HOTEL. 1902. 109 Redding St. Queen Anne. 3 stories. Most notable feature is a wraparound porch. The only remaining historic hotel in Greenville. It served this function until c. 1954. Presently vacant. Private. N.R. 1990.

Madison. DIAL-GOZA HOUSE. 105 NE Marion St. c. 1880. High Victorian Italianate. 2 stories, square cupola, front and side entrance portico. Built for William M. Dial, local planter, as his town residence. Private. N.R. 1973.

Madison. FIRST BAPTIST CHURCH. Pickney and Orange Sts. 1898+. Queen Anne. Stephen Crockett, architect. 1 story, frame, 2½-story tower, semioctagonal wing, large semicircular bay. Rare example of Queen Anne style in church architecture. Designed by the Reverend Stephen Crockett, English immigrant, who was pastor of the church for a time. Private. N.R. 1978.

Madison. WARDLAW-SMITH HOUSE. 103 N. Washington St. c. 1860. Greek Revival. William A. Hammerly, architect. 2-story colonnade on all 4 sides. Built for Benjamin F. Wardlaw, prominent local civic leader. Served as a hospital following the Civil War Battle of Olustee in Baker County. Private. N.R. 1972.

First Baptist Church, 1977

MANATEE COUNTY

Bradenton. BRADEN CASTLE PARK HISTORIC DISTRICT. 1850, 1924–1929. 206 structures on 34 acres. Predominant style: Frame Vernacular bungalows, many reflecting Craftsman style in design. Notable structures: H.E. Robbins home, Community Hall, and ruins of Braden House (1850). A remarkably complete assemblage of small frame cottages, trailer sites, and large communal buildings designed to serve as seasonal campground for the Camping Tourist of America. Laid out in 1924. N.R. 1986.

Bradenton. BRADENTON CARNEGIE LIBRARY. 1405 4th Ave. W. 1918. Masonry Vernacular with Classical Revival elements. 2 stories, brick, tile roof, classically derived porch at front entrance with 2 Tuscan columns. Built with one of the Carnegie Corporation's last grants for library construction. In 1978 the facility became the Historic Records Library of the county. Public. N.R. 1987.

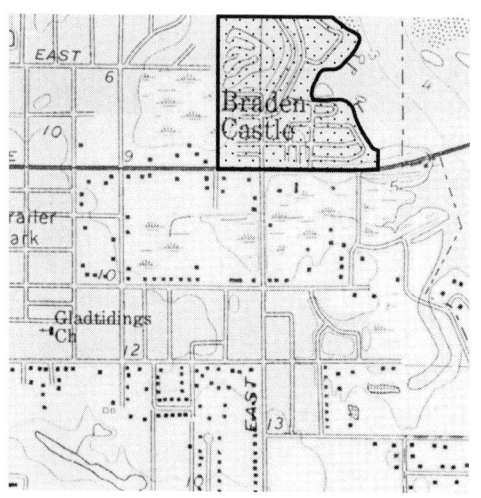

Braden Castle Park Historic District

Bradenton. MANATEE COUNTY COURTHOUSE (Original). Manatee Ave. and 15th St. 1859–1860 (moved 4 times). Oldest remaining county courthouse in Florida built explicitly for that purpose. Later served as church, parsonage, and private residence. Public. N.R. 1976.

Bradenton. WHITFIELD ESTATES BROUGHTON STREET HISTORIC DISTRICT. 1925–1943. 9 buildings, 8 of historical interest. Classical and Mediterranean Revival. The only concentration of buildings from the formative years of the Whitfield Estates Subdivision. Private. N.R. 1993.

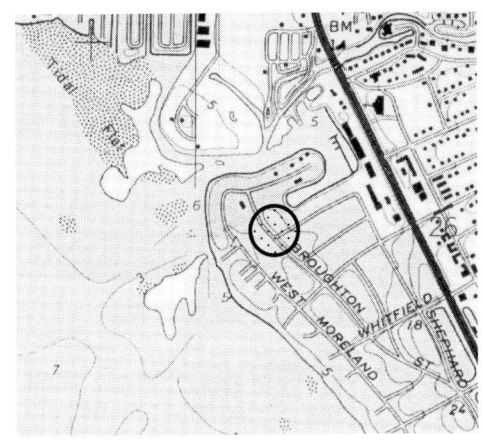

Whitfield Estates Broughton Street
Historic District

Vicinity of Bradenton. DE SOTO NATIONAL MEMORIAL. 5 mi. W of Bradenton. 1539–1543. Site commemorates landing of Hernando de Soto in Florida and the initiation of the first extensive organized exploration of the interior of the U.S. Museum. Public. N.R. 1966.

Ellenton. ROBERT GAMBLE HOUSE. U.S. 301. 1845–1850. Greek Revival influence. 2 stories, brick, 18 25-foot-high pillars support the roof and form upper and lower verandas. Plantation home of Major Gamble. At the close of the Civil War, Confederate Secretary of State Judah P. Benjamin hid there until he could flee to England. Museum. Public. N.R. 1970.

Robert Gamble House

Palmetto. PALMETTO HISTORIC DISTRICT. 1890–1930. 292 buildings, 208 of which are of historical significance. Predominant styles are Frame and Masonry Vernacular, Queen Anne, Bungalow, and Colonial Revival. Notable structures are Parrish House, Lamb House, and Carnegie Library. Includes a major portion of the historic residential, commercial, and industrial sections of the town of Palmetto. Reflects the development of the town, which was a service center for the surrounding agricultural community. N.R. 1986.

Palmetto. WOMAN'S CLUB OF PALMETTO. 910 6th St. W. 1930. Mediterranean Revival. 1¹⁄₂ stories, masonry, stuccoed, 4-bay porte cochere. The Woman's Club of Palmetto played a major role in cultural, social, and civic life of the town for many years. For years the only public facility in the county north of the Manatee River large enough to hold various meetings. Private. N.R. 1986.

Vicinity of Sarasota. SEAGATE (Powel Crosley, Jr., House). 6565 N. Tamiami Trail. 1929. Mediterranean Revival. Paul W. Bergman and George Albee Freeman, architects. 2 to 2¹⁄₂ stories, cast stone, stuccoed, cast-stone quoins, decorative cast-stone wall ornamentation, wrought-iron balcony rails. Seasonal estate built by Crosley, owner of WLW radio station in Cincinnati. Private. N.R. 1983.

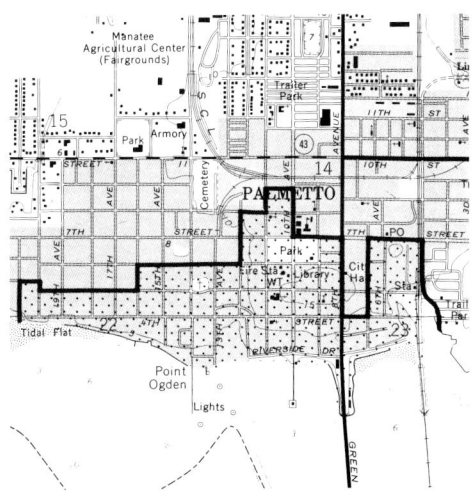

Palmetto Historic District

Terra Ceia Island. **MADIRA BICKEL MOUND**. On U.S. 19. 1000 B.C.–A.D. 1600. Archaic period to Safety Harbor period. Large oblong ceremonial mound and a smaller sand mound begun in middle Weeden Island period and used through the Safety Harbor period. Public. N.R. 1970.

MARION COUNTY

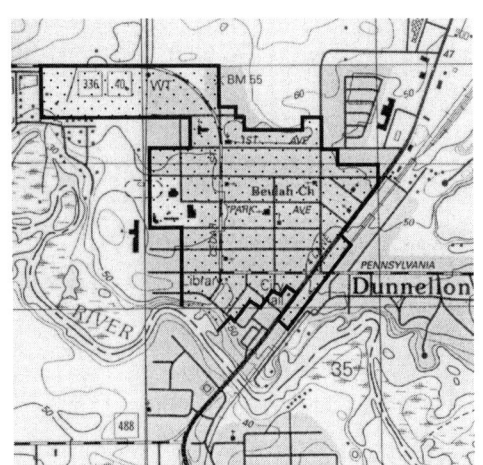

"Boomtown" Historic District

Dunnellon. "BOOMTOWN" HISTORIC DISTRICT. 1887–1920. 105 buildings, 70 of historical interest. Frame Vernacular and Bungalow predominate. A small, mainly residential district whose period of significance was when the town was the center of hard-rock phosphate mining. Public and Private. N.R. 1988.

East Lake Weir. JAMES RILEY JOSSELYN HOUSE. 13845 Alt. U.S. 27. c. 1895. Frame Vernacular, Colonial Revival elements. $2^1/_2$ stories. Original owner was one of Marion County's most successful citrus growers. Josselyn came from Massachusetts. Most citrus growers of the area came from the North. Private. N.R. 1993.

East Lake Weir. LAKE WEIR YACHT CLUB. New York Ave. 1913. Frame Vernacular. 1 story. Center of recreation for early settlers in the area, many of whom were citrus grove owners. Area also attracted many visitors from the North in the winter. Club still operates. Private. N.R. 1993.

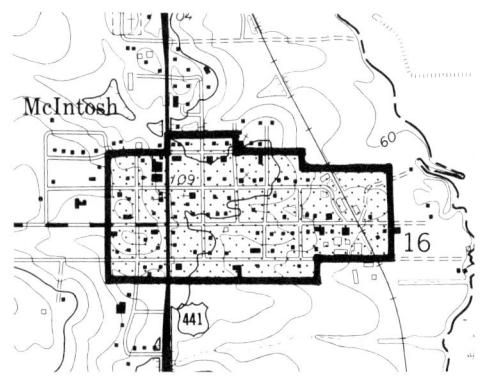

McIntosh Historic District

McIntosh. McINTOSH HISTORIC DISTRICT. 1885–1930. 38 blocks in area. Predominant structures are 2-story Frame and Masonry Vernacular buildings, many with Victorian, Gothic, and Queen Anne stylistic influences. A number of bungalows built in early 20th century. Town developed as a citrus and vegetable center following the completion of the Florida Southern Railroad to it. N.R. 1983.

Ocala. COCA-COLA BOTTLING PLANT. 939 N. Magnolia Ave. 1939. Mediterranean Revival. Courtney Stewart, architect. 2 stories, masonry, stuccoed, corner 3-story entrance tower, tile roof. Private. N.R. 1979.

Ocala. MARION HOTEL. 108 N. Magnolia Ave. 1927. Mediterranean Revival. Peebles and Ferguson, architects. 7 stories, with flanking 2-story wings, masonry, stuccoed, red tile roof. One of the last remaining Mediterranean Revival buildings of the 1920s within the county. Private. N.R. 1980.

Coca-Cola Bottling Plant, 1978

Ocala. MOUNT ZION A.M.E. CHURCH. 623 S. Magnolia Ave. 1891. Masonry Vernacular. Levi Alexander, Sr., architect. 1 story, brick, with a 2-story pyramidal roofed tower. Important center for social and civic functions of the black community. The only surviving brick 19th-century religious structure in Ocala. Private. N.R. 1979.

Ocala. OCALA HISTORIC DISTRICT. 1880-1930. Total area of 173 acres. Various Revival styles, Frame Vernacular, and bungalows. Notable structure is the Dunn Residence, 416 SE Fort King Ave., ornate Queen Anne. The district was associated with many of the most prominent residents of Ocala during its formative period. N.R. 1984.

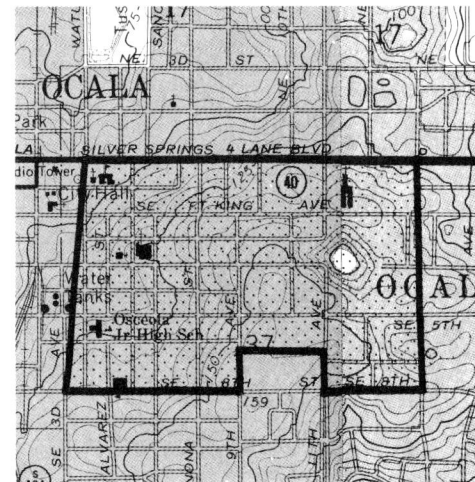
Ocala Historic District

Ocala. RITZ APARTMENTS. 1205 E. Silver Springs Blvd. 1925. Mediterranean Revival. Frederick T. Uezzell, architect. 4 2^1/$_2$ story buildings connected by a 1-story wing. Masonry, stuccoed, balconies with wrought-iron rails. The apartments introduced a new architectural style to Ocala during the Florida land boom; one of the first apartment complexes in the city. Private. N.R. 1986.

Ocala. E.C. SMITH HOUSE. 507 NE 8th Ave. 1894. Queen Anne Revival. 2 stories. Excellent example of this architectural style. House has been owned by only 2 families since constructed. Private. N.R. 1990.

Ocala. TUSCAWILLA PARK HISTORIC DISTRICT. 1877–1930. 46 buildings, 36 of historical interest. Frame Vernacular with a few Revival structures. One of the oldest sections of Ocala. The district comprises mainly wood frame residences and included a former synagogue, a former woman's club and a park. Public and Private. N.R. 1988.

E. C. Smith House

Oklawaha. T.R. AYER HOUSE. 11885 SE 128th Place. c. 1885. Queen Anne Revival. 2^1/$_2$ stories. Best example of Queen Anne Revival in rural Marion County. Located along the north side of Lake Weir, it is one of a number of surviving homes of early citrus grove owners. Private. N.R. 1993.

Oklawaha. GENERAL ROBERT BULLOCK HOUSE. SE 119th Ct. 1885. Vernacular with Classical elements. 2 stories. An excellent example of a Vernacular building with many Classical elements. Located on Lake Weir, a site for many fine homes of early citrus growers in the county. Private. N.R. 1993.

Vicinity of Oklawaha. ALFRED AYER HOUSE. on U.S. 441A. c. 1885. Frame Vernacular with Classical Revival elements. 2 stories. Excellent example of Classical Revival style as applied to a simple vernacular form. Original owner was one of the pioneer citrus growers in the county. Private. N.R. 1993.

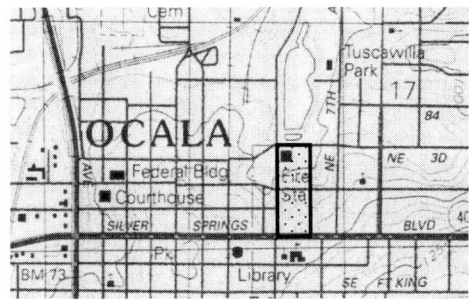
Tuscawilla Park Historic District

Orange Springs Methodist Episcopal Church

Orange Springs. ORANGE SPRINGS METHODIST EPISCOPAL CHURCH AND CEMETERY. S.R. 315 and Church St. c. 1852, 1867. Frame Vernacular. Only structure remaining from town's earliest period. Oldest extant church in Marion County. Local materials used. Private. N.R. 1988.

Orange Springs. JAMES W. TOWNSEND HOUSE. NW corner of Main and Spring Sts. 1912. Frame Vernacular. Owner was instrumental in developing the turpentine industry in central Florida during the latter part of the last century. Owner was also a banker, rancher, and grove owner. Private. N.R. 1988.

MARTIN COUNTY

Lyric Theatre

Stuart. LYRIC THEATRE. 59 SW Flagler Ave. 1926. Mediterranean Revival, Beaux-Arts elements. John N. Sherwood, architect. 2 stories. Played a very important social and recreational function in Stuart before World War II. Presently a performing arts theater. Private. N.R. 1993.

Vicinity of Stuart. HOUSE OF REFUGE AT GILBERT'S BAR. Hutchinson Island. 1876. Frame Vernacular. 2 stories, erected on pilings, clapboarding, covered by shingles. Following a hurricane in 1873 in which a crew from a wrecked vessel came ashore on Hutchinson Island and found no shelter, the U.S. Government ordered a refuge to be built. Eventually 10 were constructed on Florida's east coast. Deactivated in 1940. Museum. Public. N.R. 1974.

MONROE COUNTY

Dry Tortuga Islands. FORT JEFFERSON NATIONAL MONUMENT. 68 mi. W of Key West. 1846+ . Massive ruins of the largest of a chain of 19th-century American coastal forts. Hexagonal structure encompasses 16 acres. Walls 8 feet thick, 50 feet high, brick. Used in the Civil, Spanish-American and both World Wars to control the entrance to the Gulf of Mexico. Used as a military prison following the Civil War. Abandoned after World War II. Museum. Public. N.R. 1970.

Florida Keys. OVERSEAS HIGHWAY AND RAILWAY BRIDGES. Connects Florida Keys. 1912+. The 3 railroad bridges, now used as a highway, which span the major channels along U.S. 1 connecting Key West to the mainland, are among the few extant elements of the Key West Extension of the Florida East Coast Railway. These bridges were converted to vehicular use and incorporated into the federal highway program. Public. N.R. 1979.

Bahia Honda Bridge, Overseas Highway and Railway Bridges

Islamorada. SAN FELIPE SHIPWRECK. 1526–1769, San Felipe was one of a fleet of merchant ships that sailed from Havana in 1733 bound for Spain. The fleet encountered a hurricane and was wrecked on the keys. Cargo was mainly organic, such as food, dyes, snuff. No evidence of bullion. Public. N.R. 1994.

Key Largo. AFRICAN QUEEN. 99701 Overseas Highway. c. 1912. 30-foot open-hulled steam launch built in England. The hull is galvanized steel. Used on the rivers of Central Africa during its work life. Was used in the filming of the African Queen starring Humphrey Bogart and Katharine Hepburn. Private. N.R. 1992.

African Queen

Vicinity of Key Largo. CARYSFORT LIGHTHOUSE. 12 mi. NE of Key Largo on Fl. 905. 1852. Screw pile. Howard Stanbury and Thomas E. Lannard, architects. Iron, 106 feet tall. 2-story keeper's quarters of iron and wood. Oldest of 6 screw-pile lighthouses on the Florida east coast. In continuous operation since built, it is now automated. Public. N.R. 1984.

Vicinity of Key Largo. JOHN PENNEKAMP CORAL REEF STATE PARK AND RESERVE. Offshore of Key Largo. A.D. 1700–A.D. 1900. First underseas park designed to protect an area of seabed containing an unknown number of shipwrecks. There are also believed to be early aboriginal sites, now under water. N.R. 1972.

Vicinity of Key Largo. ROCK MOUND ARCHAEOLOGICAL SITE. $^1/_2$ mi. W of U.S. 1. A.D. 100–A.D. 1300. Glades period. Large limestone mound, village and limestone ridges. Mound 1000 feet long, 55 feet wide. Possible ceremonial center. The only surviving rock mound in southeast Florida. Private. N.R. 1975.

Key West. THE ARMORY. 600 White St. c. 1900. Frame Vernacular with Italianate details. T.F. Russell, architect. 2$^1/_2$ stories, frame, 2 turrets. Built to house men and arms of the Island City National Guard. Public. N.R. 1971.

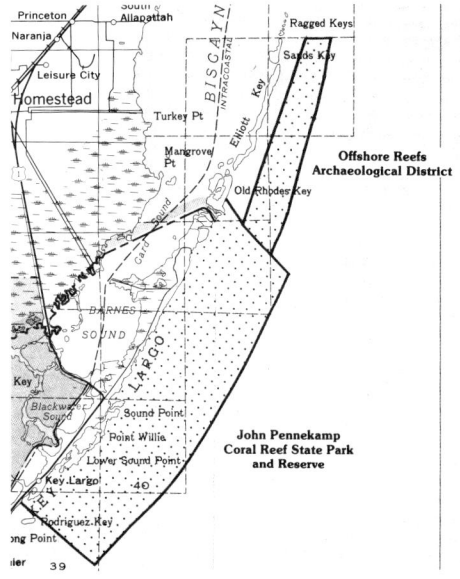

John Pennekamp Coral Reef State Park and Reserve

Ernest Hemingway House

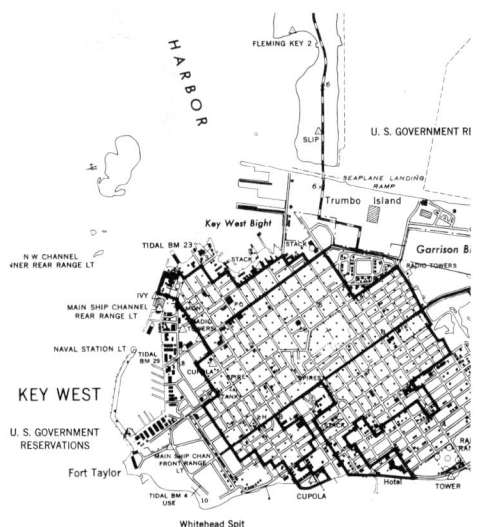

Key West Historic District

Old Post Office and Customhouse

Key West. FORT ZACHARY TAYLOR. U.S. Naval Station. 1845–1866. 3 stories, trapezoid-shaped, 3 seaward walls of 225 feet and a barracks area measuring 495 feet, walls 5 to 8 feet thick, reduced in height following Spanish-American War. Built at the time of the Mexican War to defend Key West, then Florida's largest city. Designed to withstand a long siege. Controlled by Federal forces in Civil War. Public. N.R. 1971.

Key West. EDUARDO H. GATO HOUSE. 1209 Virginia St. c. 1890. Classical Revival with Italianate influence. 2 stories, frame, 2-tier porch. Built by Cuban immigrant Eduardo Gato, who founded the city's largest cigar factory (1876). Only briefly occupied by Gato. Later a school and then a hospital. Private. N.R. 1973.

Key West. ERNEST HEMINGWAY HOUSE. 907 Whitehead St. Late 19th century. Masonry Vernacular with classical elements. 2 stories, coquina limestone, stuccoed, 2-story veranda. French doors at main entrance. Built after the Civil War by Asa Tift, a prominent merchant. Made famous by Ernest Hemingway, the novelist, who purchased it in 1931 and resided in it for long periods throughout the rest of his life. Museum. Private. N.R. 1968.

Key West. KEY WEST HISTORIC DISTRICT. 1822–1920. Approximately 3100 buildings within 190 blocks. The district contains the greatest and most important concentration of wooden buildings in Florida. Buildings are of architectural, commercial, industrial, and military significance. Notable structures are Hemingway House, Audubon House, Porter House, Gato House. Key West throughout much of the 19th century was Florida's largest city. It maintained close relations with Cuba and had a cosmopolitan population. N.R. 1971, extended 1983.

Key West. LITTLE WHITE HOUSE (Quarters A). U.S. Naval Station. 1890. Frame Vernacular. 2^1/$_2$ stories, clapboard, porches enclosed by wooden jalousies. Originally the commandant's quarters but often used during the administration of President Harry S. Truman as his fall and winter vacation home. He continued to use it after his term in office until 1969. N.R. 1974.

Key West. MARTELLO GALLERY–KEY WEST ART AND HISTORY MUSEUM. S. Roosevelt Blvd. 1862. Fortified martello towers. Masonry Vernacular. Tower commissioned in 1862 and incorporated with Fort Zachary Taylor into the defense of the city. Unlike true martello towers, which were circular, the central tower of East Martello is square. Public. N.R. 1972

Key West. OLD POST OFFICE AND CUSTOMHOUSE. Front St. 1889–1891. Richardsonian Romanesque. William Kerr, architect. 3^1/$_2$ stories, central block with 2 wings, decorative terra-cotta and brickwork. Regarded as the finest example of Richardsonian Romanesque in the state. Functioned as post office and customhouse until 1932. Private. N.R 1973.

Key West. DR. JOSEPH Y. PORTER HOUSE. 429 Caroline St. 1838 (later additions). Eclectic. 2¹/₂ stories, frame, clapboard siding, mansard roof, 2-tier veranda. Birthplace of Dr. Joseph Yates Porter, III, Key West's first native-born physician. House combines Bahamian, New England, and French architectural elements. Private. N.R. 1973.

Key West. THOMPSON FISH HOUSE, TURTLE CANNERY AND KRAALS. 200 Margaret St. 1918–1944. Masonry Vernacular. The fish house is a 1¹/₂-story concrete building with a gable roof. Long associated with the maritime industry in Key West, Thompson was mayor of the city and played a big role in Key West's political as well as economic life. Kraals were used to confine turtles. Private. N.R. 1994.

Key West. U.S. COAST GUARD HEADQUARTERS, KEY WEST STATION. NW corner of Front St. and Whitehead St. 1856–1861. Masonry Vernacular. J.M. Scarpitt, architect. 1 story, brick and limestone. Established as Naval Supply Depot (1856), served as Naval Administration Building until 1923. Absorbed by U.S. Coast Guard (1939). Private. N.R. 1973

Thompson Fish House

Key West. U.S. NAVAL STATION. W side of Key West. 1845–1942. 23 structures built between 1845 and 1923, 1 erected in 1942, 4 freshwater cisterns and 4 elevated storage tanks. Masonry Vernacular is dominant style. The Post Office–Customhouse (1891) is a notable structure, as is the Little White House. Known as "the Gibraltar of the Gulf," the station commanded the entrance of the Gulf of Mexico from the Atlantic. N.R. 1984.

Key West. WEST MARTELLO TOWER. Between Reynolds and White Sts. 1861–1866. Fortified martello tower. Masonry Vernacular. Remnants of a Civil War fortification designed to support Fort Zachary Taylor's defense of the city. Ruins presently occupied by the Key West Garden Club. Private. N.R. 1976.

Vicinity of Key West. SAND KEY LIGHTHOUSE. 7 mi. SW of Key West. 1853. Screw pile. W.P. Lewis, architect. Iron, 132 feet high. Second oldest of 6 screw-pile lighthouses on Florida's east coast. Illustrates early application of metal in construction. Public. N.R. 1973.

Vicinity of Lower Matecumbe Key. INDIAN KEY. 1 mi. SE of Lower Matecumbe Key. 1825–1849. A low-lying island covered with tropical vegetation where Jacob Housman, in 1825, began a ship salvage empire. Later Henry Perrine, a physician and botanist, moved to the key to pursue botanical research. Indians attacked the island in 1840, killing 7 of its residents. Public. N.R. 1972.

Sand Key Lighthouse

Marathon. GEORGE ADDERLEY HOUSE. 5550 Overseas Highway. c. 1906. Masonry Vernacular. Bahamian style. Owner was a black Bahamian. Crane Hammock, on which the house is situated, had a black Bahamian settlement in the early 20th century. Private. N.R. 1992.

Pigeon Key. PIGEON KEY HISTORIC DISTRICT. 1912. 17 buildings, 15 of historical interest. Frame and Masonry Vernacular. A base camp in the construction of the Florida East Coast Railroad's Florida Keys extension and later in the construction of the Overseas Highway. Includes workers quarters and other buildings. Hugh concrete trestles on the key are reminders of the difficulty of construction. Public and Private. N.R. 1990.

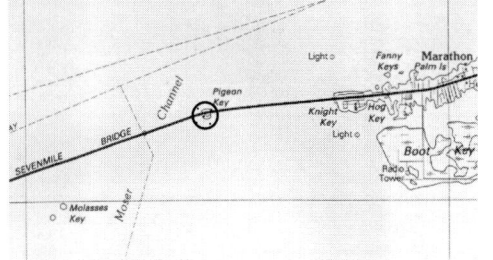

Pigeon Key Historic District

Vicinity of Plantation Key. SAN JOSÉ SHIPWRECK SITE. 4.06 mi. SE of Plantation Key. 1733. Site of buried shipwreck. Most of the wooden keel and lower portion of the ship's ribs remain. Cannon still on site. On July 13, 1733, a fleet of 22 ships set sail for Havana. All but one were lost or crashed on the reefs of the keys, including the 326.5-ton San José y Las Animas, carrying silver coin and bullion. Public. N.R. 1975.

Sugarloaf Key. BAT TOWER. Sugarloaf Key. 1929. Frame Vernacular. A tower to shelter bats. The tower was an early effort at mosquito control undertaken by Richter Clyde Perky, a fish lodge owner on the keys in the 1920s. The effort proved ineffective. Private. N.R. 1982.

NASSAU COUNTY

Fernandina Beach. BAILEY HOUSE. 7th St. and Ash St. 1895. Queen Anne. George Barber, architect. 2¹/₂ stories, frame, clapboarding, shingle gables, polygonal corner towers, wraparound porch. One of finest Victorian homes in the city. Presently used as a bed-and-breakfast. Private. N.R. 1973.

Fernandina Beach. FAIRBANKS HOUSE. 227 S. 7th St. 1885. Italianate elements. R.V. Schuyler, architect. 2¹/₂ stories, frame, arcaded front and side porches, 3-story central tower. Home of George Rainsford Fairbanks, state senator, newspaper editor, and author of three popular books of Florida history. Present use is for apartments. Private. N.R. 1973.

Bat Tower

Fernandina Beach. FERNANDINA BEACH HISTORIC DISTRICT. 19th century–20th century. 347 buildings, of which 296 are of historical significance, within a 50-block area. Predominant styles: Victorian and Frame Vernacular. Notable are the elaborate High-Victorian, Italianate Fairbanks House, Queen Anne-style Humphrey House and Bailey House, and the Nassau County Courthouse. Although the city lost much importance after dredging permitted Jacksonville better access to the sea, Fernandina Beach had a brief period of prosperity in the late 19th century, when many of its finer homes were built. Area extended in 1987. N.R. 1973, 1987.

Fernandina Beach. MERRICK-SIMMONS HOUSE. 102 S. 10th St. 1861+. Greek Revival. 2^1/$_2$ stories, frame, front portico has 2-story porch. One of the few remaining buildings constructed in the city before the Civil War. Early owner was Miss Chloe Merrick, a school teacher from the North who ran an orphanage after the Civil War. Presently used for apartments. Private. N.R. 1983.

Fernandina Beach. OLD TOWN FERNANDINA HISTORIC SITE. 1811–1821. 40 buildings, 1 of historical interest. Also contains the Plaza Lot, site of Fort San Carlos, constructed in 1816. Old Town reflects the original plot of the town of 1811. By the end of the Spanish period the town had about 40 houses, all built of wood. Public and Private. N.R. 1990.

Fernandina Beach. JOHN DENHAM PALMER HOUSE. 1305 Atlantic Ave. c. 1891. Frame Vernacular with Colonial Revival elements. 2^1/$_2$ stories, frame, hipped roof, 2-story wraparound porch. Home is associated with an important period in the architectural history of the city. John Denham Palmer was an early physician within the community. Presently a funeral home. Private. N.R. 1986.

Fernandina Beach. TABBY HOUSE (C.W. Lewis House). 7th and Ash Sts. 1885. Eclectic. R.S. Schuyler, architect. 2^1/$_2$ stories, 2-story veranda with carved posts and brackets. Although called the "Tabby House," the walls are of concrete with aggregate being local shell, and not tabby. Private. N.R. 1973.

Vicinity of Fernandina Beach. FORT CLINCH. Fl. A1A, at N end of Amelia Island. 1847+. Pentagonal brick fort with corner bastions and loopholes in outer walls. Several structures in interior courtyards, including a 2-story barracks. Occupied by Confederates in 1861, recaptured by Federal troops in March 1862, giving the Union control of the Georgia coast. Museum. Public. N.R. 1972.

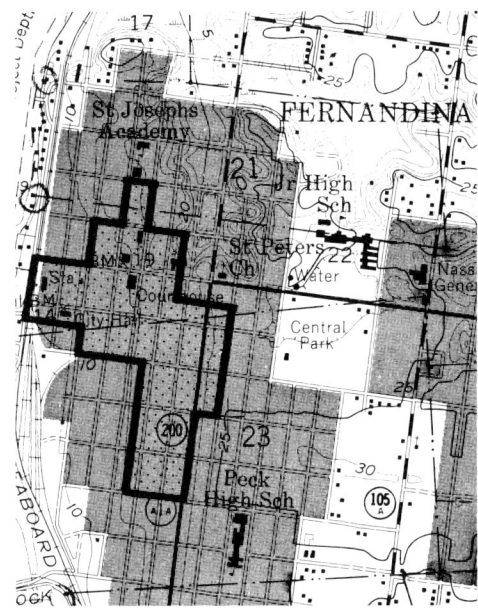

Fernandina Beach Historic District

Tabby House

Fort Clinch

85

Thought to be **Burial Urn,** found in Buck Burial Mound, just south of Fort Walton Mound, located at Fort Walton Museum.

Carroll Building

OKALOOSA COUNTY

Fort Walton Beach. FORT WALTON MOUND. N shore of Santa Rosa Sound. A.D. 0–A.D. 50. Deptford to Fort Walton period. 12-foot-high temple mound from which many artifacts have been excavated. Type site of the Fort Walton culture. Museum. Public. N.R. 1966.

Fort Walton Beach. GULFVIEW HOTEL. 12 Miracle Strip Pkwy SE. 1906. Frame Vernacular. 2 stories. A hotel that operated continuously until 1986. Now vacant. 9 cottages surround the hotel. Private. N.R. 1992.

OKEECHOBEE COUNTY

Okeechobee. FREEDMAN-RAULERSON HOUSE. 600 S. Parrott Ave. 1923, 1925 (moved in 1983). Masonry Vernacular with Mediterranean Revival addition. 2 stories, concrete block, stuccoed. House built by Abraham Freedman, an early merchant. Later owned by Hiram H. Raulerson, civic figure. Early use of cement block in the city. Now private office. Private. N.R. 1985.

Vicinity of Okeechobee. OKEECHOBEE BATTLEFIELD. 4 mi. SW on Fl. 78. 1837. Site of a Second Seminole War battle between U.S. troops led by Zachary Taylor and the Seminole and Miccosukee warriors. The U.S. Army won a decisive victory, which proved the turning point in the war. Private. N.R. 1966.

ORANGE COUNTY

Apopka. APOPKA SEABOARD AIR LINE RAILWAY DEPOT. 36 E. Station St. 1918. Frame Vernacular. 1 story. The only remaining transportation element of Apopka's early period. Presently in use as a warehouse. Private. N.R. 1993.

Apopka. CARROLL BUILDING. 407–409 S. Park Ave. 1932. Masonry Vernacular. 2 stories. First used as a medical office. Now a local history museum. Public. N.R. 1993.

Apopka. MITCHELL-TIBBETTS HOUSE. 21 E. Orange St. 1887. Frame Vernacular. 2 stories. The home of several of Apopka's early developers. Private. N.R. 1991.

Apopka. RYAN AND COMPANY LUMBERYARD. 215 E. 5th St. 1924. Industrial Vernacular. 2 1-story buildings and 2 1-story structures. Associated with one of Apopka's oldest businesses and with the local lumber industry. Private. N.R. 1993.

Waite-Davis House

Apopka. WAITE-DAVIS HOUSE. 5 S. Central Ave. 1886. Frame Vernacular. 1¹/₂ stories. 1-story veranda, with a gazebo at the SW corner. Original owner came from New Hampshire in 1876 to start an orange grove. Later entered real estate. The community around the house had many New Englanders and was called Yankee Town. Private. N.R. 1990.

Maitland. MAITLAND ART CENTER. 231 W. Packwood Ave. 1937. Aztec-Mayan motifs. Andres Smith, architect. 6 principal buildings and several utility buildings, courtyard, and ornamental pool. Buildings and walls are ornamented with bas reliefs cast in concrete. Richly decorated garden. Winter home of Andres Smith, architect, etcher, painter, author, and outspoken advocate of modern art. Formerly an artists' village. Public. N.R. 1982.

Maitland Art Center

Maitland. WILLIAM H. WATERHOUSE HOUSE. 820 S. Lake Lily Dr. 1884. Frame Vernacular. William H. Waterhouse, architect. 2¹/₂ stories. Built by William H. Waterhouse, a pioneer developer in Maitland. Waterhouse, a New Yorker, took a traditional Northeast architectural style and adapted it for the Florida environment. Private. N.R. 1983.

Ocoee. WITHERS-MAGUIRE HOUSE. 16 E. Oakland Ave. c. 1884. Frame Vernacular with Stick-style elements. 2 stories, gabled roof, 1st-story veranda on west, south, and east facades. 2nd-story veranda on south facade. Original owner, William T. Withers (1825–1889), a Kentuckian, who wintered in the city. Later sold to David O. Maguire, a Georgian, who came to the town to grow citrus and vegetables. Public. N.R. 1987.

Withers-Maguire House

Orlando. J.J. BRIDGES HOUSE. 704 S. Kuhl Ave. 1916. Colonial Revival. Wilson C. Ely, architect. 2 stories, frame, gabled roof, main entrance has portico, on west facade is portico with balcony. The first of the highly academic, Colonial-Revival-style homes built in the area. Built for the Rev. J.J. Bridges, a retired New York clergyman. Private. N.R. 1984.

Orlando. FIRST CHURCH OF CHRIST SCIENTIST (St. George Orthodox Church). 24 N. Rosalind Ave. 1926–1927. Classical Revival. George Foote Durham, architect. 2¹/₂ stories, masonry, the main facade has a Doric portico, copper dome. The Christian Scientist congregation abandoned the church in 1975 and it was acquired by the Greek Orthodox congregation. Private. N.R. 1980.

Orlando. JOHN N. HUTTIG ESTATE. 435 Peachtree Rd. 1934. Tudor Revival. James Gamble Rogers, architect. 1½ stories. Large house on 2-acre lot. Formal entrance gate. The architect had a national reputation. Private. N.R. 1993.

Orlando. LAKE EOLA HEIGHTS HISTORIC DISTRICT. 1890–1940. 662 buildings, 487 of historical interest. The buildings in the district provide an important link with Orlando's history. Excellent selection of popular architectural styles. Public and Private. N.R. 1992.

Orlando. OLD ORLANDO RAILROAD DEPOT. Depot Pl. and W. Church St. 1889. Eclectic Victorian. 2½ stories, brick, hipped roof section, 3-story corner tower with 3-story open porch. Built for Henry B. Plant, 19th-century railroad and hotel magnate, during the large-scale development of the area. Private. N.R. 1976.

Orlando. DR. P. PHILLIPS HOUSE. 135 Lucerne Circle, NE. 1893. Shingle style. L.M. Boykin, architect. 2½ stories, frame, 3-story tower and monumental Ionic portico. Owned by Dr. P. Phillips, one of Florida's most successful early citrus growers. It is the only Shingle-style residence in the city. Phillips added the Ionic portico. Public. N.R. 1979.

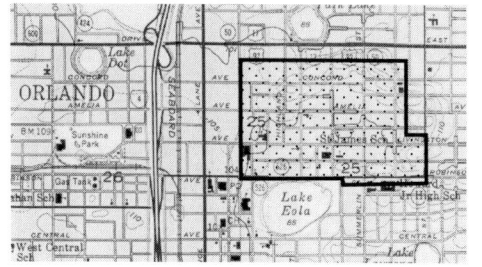

Lake Eola Heights Historic District

Rogers Building

88

Orlando. ROGERS BUILDING (English Club). 37–39 S. Magnolia Ave. 1886+. Eclectic. 2 stories, exterior fabric is pressed zinc cladding, main facade has heavily embossed friezes. One of the most distinctive late 19th-century buildings in Central Florida and one of the best-preserved examples of sheet-metal construction in the state. Second floor served for a time as a club for English immigrants. Private. N.R. 1985.

Orlando. TINKER BUILDING. 16–18 W. Pine St. 1925+. Masonry Vernacular. 2 stories, brick, detail on front facade of brick, terra-cotta, and tile. Associated with Joe (Joseph B.) Tinker, one of baseball's legendary personalities, member of the Baseball Hall of Fame and a major Orlando developer. Private. N.R. 1980.

Vicinity of Sorrento. TWIN MOUNDS ARCHAEOLOGICAL DISTRICT. W bank of the Wekiva River, 7 miles S of its confluence with the St. Johns River. 2000 B.C.–A.D. 1565. Orange, Transitional, St. Johns I and II. 2 snail and mussel shell middens. The dense deposit of shell and aboriginal food remains in the midden is a record of 3000 years of cultural adaptation to the central Florida wetlands. Public. N.R. 1992.

Windermere. WINDERMERE TOWN HALL. 520 Main St. 1922. Colonial Revival. 1½ stories. First used as a woman's club. Moved to its present site in 1938 for use as a community center. Public. N.R. 1994.

Winter Park. EDWARD HILL BREWER HOUSE (The Palms). 240 Trismen Tr. 1899+. Colonial Revival. 2½ stories, enlarged in 1923 to include porticos with fluted Ionic columns, an altered veranda, balustraded 2nd-story decks. Edward Hill Brewer was a prominent Cortland, New York, manufacturer who used the house as a winter residence. Private. N.R. 1982.

Winter Park. COMSTOCK-HARRIS HOUSE (East Bank) . 724 Bonita Dr. 1878–1883. Queen Anne. 2½ stories, frame, cypress-shingle siding, porte cochere. All principal interior spaces have panelled wainscoting. Excellent example of Queen Anne style. Built for William C. Comstock, prominent Chicago businessman and Florida realtor. At one time was a showplace of Winter Park. Private. N.R. 1983.

Comstock-Harris House

OSCEOLA COUNTY

Kissimmee. COLONIAL ESTATE. 2450 Old Dixie Hwy. 1916. Frame Classical Revival. 2½ stories. Portico has colossal Ionic columns that support a full entablature. Constructed for J. Wade Tucker, a leading businessman. Private. N.R. 1994.

Colonial Estate

Osceola County Courthouse, dedication, July 4, 1890

Kissimmee. OLD HOLY REDEEMER CATHOLIC CHURCH. 120 N. Sproule Ave. 1912. Gothic Revival. George A. Ledvina, architect. 1 story. Battlemented entrance porch, wall buttresses, stained-glass windows. Originally a Catholic Church. In 1978 sold to First United Methodist Church. Used today by an Hispanic congregation. Private. N.R. 1994.

Kissimmee. OSCEOLA COUNTY COURTHOUSE. Emmett, Bryan, Rose, and Vernon Sts. 1886–1890. Romanesque Revival. F.C. Johnson, architect. 3 stories, brick, main facade has central portico, building surmounted by tower. The oldest courthouse in Florida retaining its architectural integrity and continuing to house county government functions. Public. N.R. 1977.

PALM BEACH COUNTY

Boca Raton. ADMINISTRATION BUILDINGS. 2 Camino Real. 1925. Mediterranean Revival. Addison Mizner, architect. 2 2-story buildings arranged around a large open courtyard. L-shaped porches, ceilings supported by unique cast-stone Moorish columns. Excellent example of the mature style of Mizner. They housed the offices of his development corporation, but shortly after their completion the Florida land boom ended and the corporation failed. Private. N.R. 1985.

Old Holy Redeemer Catholic Church

Boca Raton. FRED C. AIKEN HOUSE. 801 Hibiscus St. 1926. Mediterranean Revival. Addison Mizner, architect. 2 stories. The house is located in one of the most modest neighborhoods of early Boca Raton. Aiken, a film executive, helped develop the area. He lived in the house until his death in 1959. Private. N.R. 1992.

Boca Raton . BOCA RATON OLD CITY HALL . 71 N. Federal Highway. 1926. Mediterranean Revival. William E. Alsmeyer, architect. 1 to 2 stories, tile roof, entrance section has a curvilinear gabled roof surmounted by a domed bell tower. One of the important elements in Addison Mizner's dream city of Boca Raton. Restored in 1984 by Boca Raton Historical Society. Public. N.R. 1980.

Administration Buildings, Boca Raton

Boca Raton. FLORIDA EAST COAST RAILWAY PASSENGER STATION. 741 S. Dixie Hwy. 1930. Mediterranean Revival. Chester G. Henninger, architect. 1 story, with 2-story tower, 5-bay arcaded loggia on east side; addition added in 1957 on north side. Built for Clarence Geist, who purchased the Boca Raton holdings of the Mizner Development Corporation after the collapse of the Florida land boom. Private. N.R. 1980.

Boynton Beach. BOYNTON SCHOOL. 141 E. Ocean Ave. 1913. Masonry Vernacular. William W. Maughlin, architect. 2 stories. The site has been associated with community affairs since 1900. There is a 1927 high school building to the west of it. Site originally had one-room school house. School still in use. Public. N.R. 1994.

Boynton School

Boynton Beach. BOYNTON WOMAN'S CLUB. 1010 S. Federal Highway. 1925. Mediterranean Revival. Addison Mizner, architect. 2 stories, masonry with painted stucco, tile roof. Loggia on 3 sides. The social hub of Boynton Beach in the 1930s. Until 1961 it housed the local library, founded by the Woman's Club. Private. N.R. 1979.

Vicinity of Canal Point. BIG MOUND CITY. 10 mi. E of Canal Point off U.S. 98. 300 B.C.–A.D. 1600. Glades period. Mound and earthwork complex situated between the Everglades and the Piney Flatwoods. One of the finest examples of Calusa ceremonial complexes in South Florida. Private. N.R. 1973.

Delray Beach. DELRAY BEACH SCHOOLS. N Swinton Ave. 1913–1926. Mediterranean Revival. 3 detached buildings. The oldest was built in 1913. The high school, built in 1926, is 2 stories and of Mediterranean Revival style. The gymnasium, also built in 1926, is 2-story Mediterranean. Schools are still in use. Public. N.R. 1988.

Delray Beach. SEABOARD AIR LINE RAILWAY STATION. 1525 W. Atlantic Ave. 1927. Mediterranean Revival. Harvey and Clarke, architects. 1 story, masonry, stuccoed, barrel-tile roof, 2-story tower. Served the commercial and transportation needs of the community during the period when highway transportation was just beginning. Private. N.R. 1986.

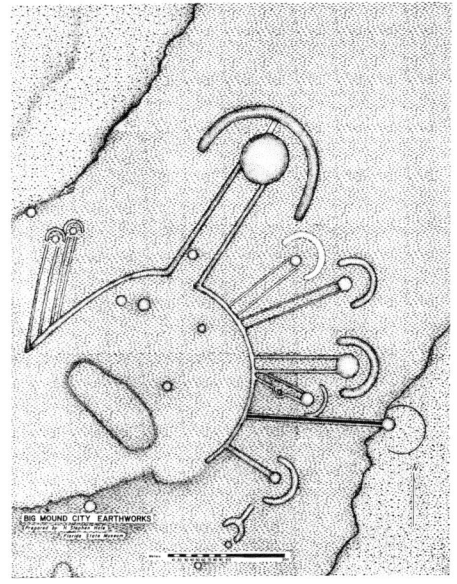

Big Mound City Earthworks, based on aerial photo.

Delray Beach. JOHN AND ELIZABETH SHAW SUNDY HOUSE. 106 S. Swinton Ave. 1902. Frame Vernacular with Queen Anne elements. 2 stories. Home of first mayor of town. Sundy also was a truck farmer and citrus grower. Presently a restaurant. Private. N.R. 1992.

Vicinity of Jupiter. JUPITER INLET HISTORIC AND ARCHAEO- LOGICAL SITE. Off Fl. A1A. 500 B.C.–19th century. Glades period and Historic period. Irregular mound of shell approximately 80 yards by 25 to 50 yards. Varies in height from 3 to 15 feet. Site of long human occupation. There is evidence that Indians at this site had contact with early Spanish. 19th-century structure on site. Public. N.R. 1985.

Vicinity of Jupiter. JUPITER INLET LIGHTHOUSE. Jct. of Loxahatchee River and Jupiter Sound. 1854–1859. Conical tower. George G. Meade and John W. Nystrem, architects. Brick, 105 feet high. Built to improve navigation along the Florida east coast. Confederates put light out during Civil War. Public. N.R. 1973.

John and Elizabeth Shaw Sundy House

Lake Park. KELSEY CITY CITY HALL. 535 Park Ave. 1927. Mediterranean Revival. Bruce Kitchell, architect. 2 stories, masonry, stuccoed, decorative detail on main entrance. Town hall of Kelsey City (Lake Park), a 1920s land boom town, which was one of the area's first luxury winter resorts. Public. N.R. 1981.

Gulf Stream Hotel

Lake Worth. GULF STREAM HOTEL (El Nuevo Hotel). 1 Lake Ave. 1923. Masonry Vernacular with Mediterranean Revival elements. G. Lloyd Preacher, architect. 6 stories, masonry, stuccoed, arcade on its 2 street sides. Stucco shields and other decorations. 135-room luxury hotel built during a time when Lake Worth was among the most important tourist centers of South Florida. Private. N.R. 1983.

Lake Worth. OLD LAKE WORTH CITY HALL. 414 Lake Worth Ave. 1929. Mediterranean Revival. Floyd King, architect. 2 stories. Barrel-tile roof. Today it is used as the city museum. Public. N.R. 1989.

Palm Beach. BREAKERS HOTEL COMPLEX. S. County Rd. 1925. Classical Revival. Schultze and Weaver, architects. 6 to 8 stories, concrete, clay tile, cast-stone trim, enclosed east loggia, decorative engaged and freestanding columns and pilasters, twin towers, central courtyard. One of the few remaining grand hotels in the nation with its original public rooms. Hotel retains the elegance of a past era, when it played a major role in the tourist industry of South Florida. Private. N.R. 1973.

The Breakers

Palm Beach. HENRY MORRISON FLAGLER HOUSE (Whitehall). Whitehall Way. 1901. Classical Revival. Carrere and Hastings, architects. 2 stories (3 stories in front). Brick, stuccoed, tile roof, 2-story Doric portico. Henry M. Flagler (1830–1913), founding partner of Standard Oil Co., began a hotel and railroad empire in the 1880s along Florida's east coast. Key figure in the development of Palm Beach. House museum. Private. N.R. 1972.

Palm Beach. MAR-A-LAGO NATIONAL HISTORIC LANDMARK. 1100 S. Ocean Blvd. 1923–1927. Mediterranean Revival. Marion Sims Wyeth, architect; Joseph Urban, interior designer. 2-story main block, 1-story wings, masonry, stuccoed, crescent-shaped facade, tile roof, 75-foot tower. Built for Mrs. Marjorie Meriweather Post of Post Cereals. Outstanding example of a lavish mansion built in one of the nation's most fashionable winter resorts. Each interior room a different style. Private N.R. 1980.

Henry Morrison Flagler House

Palm Beach. PALM BEACH DAILY NEWS BUILDING. 204 Brazilian Ave. 1925. Mediterranean Revival. 2 stories, masonry, stuccoed, entry tower, barrel-tile roof. The building reflects the influence of architect Addison Mizner. Ceased serving as newspaper office in 1974. Private. N.R. 1985.

Palm Beach. PARAMOUNT THEATRE BUILDING. 145 N. County Rd. 1926. Mediterranean Revival. Joseph Urban, architect. 2½ stories, masonry, stuccoed, 2½-story entrance, breezeway terrace. Designed as a complete cultural center that included theater, residences, restaurant, shops, and offices. In 1930s and 1940s center of live entertainment as well as films. Now offices. Private. N.R. 1973.

Palm Beach. U.S. POST OFFICE. 95 N. County Rd. 1937. Mediterranean Revival. Louis A. Simon, architect. 2 stories, masonry, stuccoed, barrel-tile roof, decorative exposed cypress beams on lobby ceiling. Murals in postbox lobby are by Charles Rosen and depict Seminole Indian scenes. Public. N.R. 1983.

Palm Beach. VIA MIZNER. 337–339 Worth Ave. 1923,1925. Mediterranean Revival. Addison Mizner, architect. A complex of 1 -, 2 -, 3 - and 5-story buildings used for commerce and as residences. Addison Mizner lived in an apartment within the complex from 1925 to 1933. Area recently restored. Private. N.R. 1993.

Via Mizner

Palm Beach. VINETA HOTEL. 363 Cocoanut Row. 1926. Mediterranean Revival. 3 stories, masonry, stuccoed, walled interior courtyard, arched tower. Hotel closely associated with Atwater Kent, famous inventor. Representative of the type of resort hotel designed during the Florida land boom of the 1920s. Private. N.R. 1986.

Palm Beach. WILLIAM GRAY WARDEN RESIDENCE (Warden House). 112 Seminole Ave. 1922. Mediterranean Revival. Addison Mizner, architect. 2 stories, masonry with stone balusters and stairs, stained pecky-cypress ceilings, barrel-tile roof. Open cloister connects north and south wing. Outstanding example of Mediterranean Revival. Notable adaptive re-use as condominiums. Private. N.R. 1984.

Vineta Hotel

West Palm Beach. DIXIE COURT HOTEL. 301 N. Dixie Hwy. 1926. Mediterranean Revival. Harvey and Clarke, architects. 7 stories, 2 elaborate classically derived entrances and large window openings with elaborate cast-stone surrounds. Architecturally as well as commercially significant because of its close association with the Florida land boom of the 1920s. Private. N.R. 1986.

West Palm Beach. HATCH'S DEPARTMENT STORE. 301–307 Clematis St. 1903, 1915. Masonry Vernacular with Moderne elements. John L. Volk, architect. 3 stories. 2 buildings, 1 built in 1903, the other in 1915. Remodeled in 1936 into present structure. Was a department store. Private. N.R. 1994.

Hatch's Department Store

Mickens House

West Palm Beach. HIBISCUS APARTMENTS. 619 Hibiscus St. 1926. Mediterranean Revival. Chalker, Lund and Crittenden, architects. 3 stories, masonry, stuccoed, classical entrance, wrought-iron window grilles on front. An early Mediterranean Revival apartment building in West Palm Beach. Private. N.R. 1984.

West Palm Beach. MICKENS HOUSE. 801 4th St. 1917. Frame Vernacular. 2 stories, front porch spans the first floor, weatherboard siding. Home of Dr. Alice F. Mickens, black educator who was a driving force in the cause of black education in the state. Private. N.R. 1985.

West Palm Beach. NORTHWEST HISTORIC DISTRICT. 1915–1941. 469 buildings, 316 of historical interest. Frame Vernacular, Craftsman and Bungalow styles predominate. Area was an integral part of the city's historic black district. Consists primarily of small 1- and 2-story frame residences and apartments. Private. N.R. 1992.

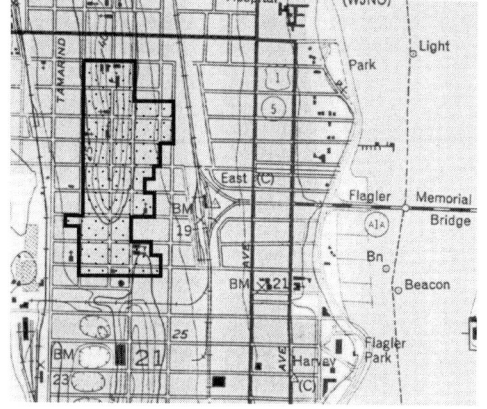
Northwest Historic District

West Palm Beach. NORTON HOUSE. 253 Barcelona Rd. 1925. Monterey style. Marion Sims Wyeth, architect. Originally built in 1925, it was extensively altered by Wyeth in 1935 and 1937. Norton, a Chicago steel executive, was an avid art collector. Now used as an art museum. Private. N.R. 1990.

West Palm Beach. OLD NORTHWOOD HISTORIC DISTRICT. early 20th century. 335 buildings, 320 of historical interest. Frame Vernacular and Revival styles predominate. The district consists mainly of 1- and 2-story single-family residences. Once one of West Palm Beach's more expensive neighborhoods. Private. N.R. 1994.

West Palm Beach. OLD PALM BEACH JUNIOR COLLEGE BUILDING. 813 Gardenia Ave. 1927. Mediterranean Revival. William Manly King, architect. Corner pavilions with parapets and cast-concrete detail. Stucco walls. Originally served as a science/manual training building for Old Palm Beach High School. Presently vacant. Public. N.R. 1991.

West Palm Beach. OLD WEST PALM BEACH NATIONAL GUARD ARMORY. 1703 S. Lake Ave. 1939, Art Moderne. William Manly King, architect. Constructed with Work Progress Administration (WPA) funds. Presently an art gallery. Public. N.R. 1993.

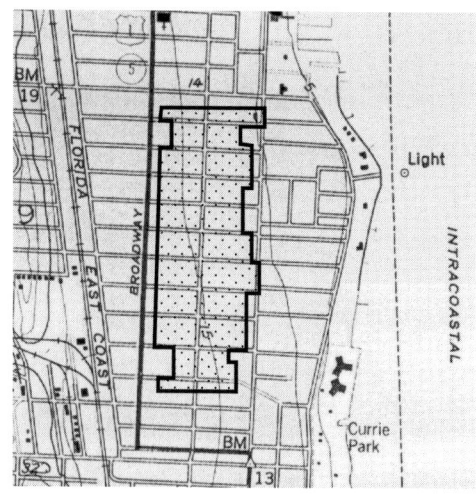
Old Northwood Historic District

West Palm Beach. PALM BEACH MERCANTILE COMPANY. 206 Clematis St. c. 1902, 1916, 1923. Vernacular. The building began as a single-story, 2-room structure. Second floor added in 1902. 3 additional floors added in 1916 and the partial sixth floor in 1923. Presently vacant. Private. N.R. 1994.

West Palm Beach. SEABOARD COAST LINE RAILWAY PASSEN-GER STATION. Tamarind Ave. at Datura St. 1925. Mediterranean Revival. L. Philips Clarke, architect. 2 stories with tower on north facade, 1 story on south facade, masonry, stuccoed, arched main entrance with engaged Corinthian columns, elaborate Spanish Baroque decorations. The railroad company diverged from its standard architectural form for this station because of the importance of many of the passengers who used it. Private. N.R. 1973.

PINELLAS COUNTY

Bay Pines. BAY PINES SITE. Veterans' Administration Medical Center. 500 B.C.–A.D. 1000. Deptford period to Weeden Island period. 2 midden mounds representative of the 2 archaeological periods of Deptford and Weeden Island. Private. N.R. 1983.

Belleair. BELLEVIEW-BILTMORE HOTEL. 25 Belleview Blvd. 1896+. Eclectic with Shingle-style elements. Michael J. Miller and Francis J. Kinnard, architects. 4¹/₂ stories, frame, 3 principal sections, each 400 feet long, broad verandas. Largest wood-frame building in Florida. Hotel constructed for Henry B. Plant, who developed the railway system on the Florida west coast during the 1890s and sought to increase traffic by building tourist facilities. Private. N.R. 1979.

Belleview-Biltmore Hotel, 1987

Belleair. OLD BELLEAIR GARDEN CLUB. 903 Ponce de Leon Blvd. 1931. Masonry Vernacular. Roy Wakeling, architect. 1 story. Originally the town hall, but in 1965 became the garden club. Private. N.R. 1994.

Clearwater. CLEVELAND STREET POST OFFICE. 650 Cleveland St. 1932. Mediterranean Revival. Theodore H. Skinner, architect. 2 stories, masonry, main facade faced with Florida limestone, barrel-tile roof. A good example of the use of regional architectural style for a small government facility. Public. N.R. 1980.

Clearwater. LOUIS DUCROS HOUSE. 1324 S. Fort Harrison Ave. 1897. Frame Vernacular. 2 stories, frame, gabled roof, veranda with turned posts. Louis Ducros, French immigrant, was an early settler of Clearwater who operated a photo studio. Home initially was a workers' cottage during the construction of the nearby Belleview-Biltmore Hotel. Private. N.R. 1979.

Clearwater. HARBOR OAKS RESIDENTIAL DISTRICT. 1914–1937. 109 buildings, 87 of historical interest. Revival, Vernacular, and contemporary styles predominate. Neighborhood established by a New York real estate developer and featured innovative land use controls and infrastructure development unusual for the period. Private. N.R. 1988.

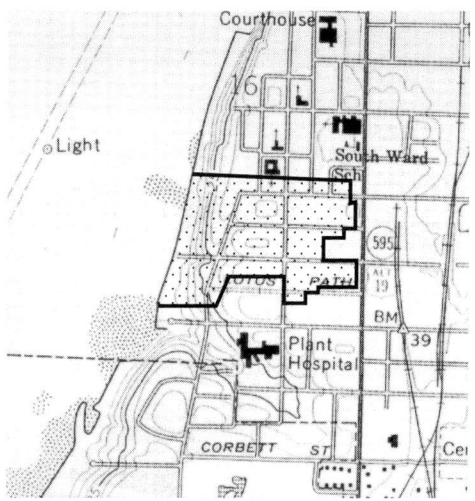

Harbor Oaks Residential District

Donald Roebling Estate, c. 1935

Clearwater. OLD PINELLAS COUNTY COURTHOUSE. 315 Court St. 1917, 1924, 1926. Classical Revival. Francis J. Kennard, architect. 2 stories. 2 wings added in 1924 and 1926. Interior restoration in 1984–85. The first permanent building erected as the seat of county government in Pinellas County. Still in use. Public. N.R. 1992.

Clearwater. DONALD ROEBLING ESTATE (Spotswood). 700 Orange Ave. 1929+. Tudor Revival. Roy W. Wakeling, architect. 2½-story main house, red brick, bay windows on entrance and garden facade, semi-octagonal elevator tower added in 1939. Home of Donald Roebling, inventor. Among other things he invented an amphibious vehicle here that was the prototype of one used extensively in World War II. Private. Estate subdivided. N.R. 1979.

Clearwater. SOUTH WARD SCHOOL. 610 S. Fort Harrison Ave. 1906 (oldest of 3 in complex). Eclectic. 2 stories, rusticated concrete block. Site of the first public elementary school and high school in Pinellas County. Oldest school building in the county. Public. N.R. 1979.

J.O. Douglas House

Dunedin. ANDREWS MEMORIAL CHAPEL. Buena Vista and San Mateo. 1888 (moved in 1971). Gothic Revival. 1½ stories, frame. An early Presbyterian Church in Dunedin. First located on the corner of Scotland and Highland Sts., the church was moved several times. House museum. Public. N.R. 1972.

Dunedin. J.O. DOUGLAS HOUSE. 209 Scotland St. 1880 +. Frame Vernacular. 2 stories, 1-story hipped-roof porch with jigsaw tracery, and sawn balustrade at main entrance. The oldest house in Dunedin; home of an early city merchant who emigrated from Scotland. Little alteration has been made to the house. Private. N.R. 1979.

Safety Harbor. INGLESIDE. 333 S. Bayshore Blvd. 1889. Frame Vernacular with Classical Revival elements. 2 stories. One of the few buildings remaining from the town's earliest period. Still used as a residence. Originally the home of William Leech, a wealthy grove owner who came from Virginia. Private. N.R. 1992.

Ingleside

Vicinity of Safety Harbor. SAFETY HARBOR SITE. Philippe Park, 2355 Bayshore Dr. A.D. 1500–A.D. 1700. Safety Harbor period. Site consists of a large flat-topped shell mound about 150 feet in diameter and 20 feet high. A late prehistoric site occupied into the early Spanish period. Type site for the Safety Harbor phase. It is generally believed that the village was visited by Pedro Menéndez de Avilés in 1567. Public-Private. N.R. 1966.

St. Petersburg. ALEXANDER HOTEL. 535 Central Ave. 1919. Classical Revival. A. Neel Reid, architect. 4 stories, buff-colored brick, 3-tier veranda on each of 2 main wings, intricate bas-relief detail on verandas, wrought-iron rails. One of the first modern hotels in St. Petersburg. Built by Peter A. Demens, Russian immigrant who became a Florida lumberman and then a developer. Now used for offices. Private. N.R. 1984.

St. Petersburg. BOONE HOUSE. 601 5th Ave. N. 1910–1920. Colonial Revival. 2 stories, masonry, stuccoed, pedimented portico, 4 Ionic columns support the pedimented roof. Built by Benjamin T. Boone, North Carolinian, who became a leading early St. Petersburg developer. One of the city's oldest masonry residences. Restored as private offices in 1985. Private . N.R . 1986.

St. Petersburg. CASA COE DA SOL. 510 Park St. 1931. Mediterranean Revival. Addison Mizner, architect. 2 stories, stuccoed, wide variety of window designs, interior is lavishly decorated with wrought-iron railings, cast-stone columns. Each room is unique. The last building designed by Mizner and the only one on Florida's Gulf coast. Mizner Industries products can be seen throughout the house. Private. N.R. 1980.

St. Petersburg. CASA DE MUCHAS FLORES. 1446 Park St. N. 1926+. Mediterranean Revival. Henry H. DuPont, architect. 2 to 3 stories, masonry, stuccoed, barrel-tile roof. Interior is highlighted by wrought iron and decorative tiles, marble floors, and beam ceiling. Built for Thomas W. Miller, Ohio rubber tire manufacturer, who was not socially acceptable to Palm Beach society and consequently built on the Gulf coast. Private. N.R. 1985.

Alexander Hotel

Casa de Muchas Flores

St. Petersburg. CENTRAL HIGH SCHOOL. 2501 5th Ave. N. 1926+. Mediterranean Revival. William B. Ittner, architect. 2 stories, brick, arcade along the 1st floor of the main facade, red clay tile roof. Architecturally considered the most significant educational building in the city. Until 1953 the only public high school in St. Petersburg. Public. N.R. 1984.

St. Petersburg. DENNIS HOTEL. 326 1st Ave. N. 1925. Eclectic with Classical and Mediterranean elements. Henry Cunningham, architect. 8 stories, masonry, main facade clad in cast stone, brick facing, decorative tile and granite, Corinthian columns at entrance. One of 10 large hotels built during the land boom period by Nick Dennis. It attracted many national celebrities. Private. N.R. 1986.

St. Petersburg. FIRST METHODIST CHURCH OF ST. PETERSBURG. 212 3rd St. 1924–1926. Gothic Revival. James J. Baldwin, architect. 4 stories. 144-foot belltower. In 1950–51 a Gothic Revival chapel built on west side and physically linked to main structure. Considered one of the finest examples of Gothic Revival architecture in St. Petersburg. Private. N.R. 1990.

St. Petersburg. POTTER HOUSE. 557 2nd St. S. 1905. Frame Vernacular. $2^1/_2$ stories, 1-story rear kitchen building, 1-story entrance porch. Built by prominent civic and business leader Cramer B. Potter. Little altered. Private. N.R. 1986.

Central High School, 1987

St. Petersburg. ST. PETERSBURG LAWN BOWLING CLUB. 500 4th Ave. N. 1926. Masonry Vernacular clubhouse. Clubhouse complex and 2 bowling courts, one with 19 rinks, the other with 6 rinks. Oldest formally organized lawn bowling club in Florida and tenth in the nation. Begun by Al Mercer, from Toronto, Canada. Public. N.R. 1980.

St. Petersburg. ST. PETERSBURG PUBLIC LIBRARY. 300 5th St. N. 1915. Beaux Arts. W.C. Henry and Henry Whitefield, architects. 1 story, masonry, stuccoed, cast-concrete ornamentation, roof has continuous parapet. First permanent home of the St. Petersburg public library. Built with a donation from the Carnegie Foundation. Public. N.R. 1986.

St. Petersburg. ST. PETERSBURG WOMAN'S CLUB. 40 Snell Isle Blvd. 1929. Mediterranean Revival. Frank F. Jonsberg and Ray W. Wakeling, architects. 2 stories. Building is flanked by 2 wings. Barrel-tile roof. Has played a major cultural and civic role in St. Petersburg since 1929. Continues in its original function. Private. N.R. 1994.

St. Petersburg. SNELL ARCADE. 405 Central Ave. 1928. Mediterranean Revival. Richard Kiehnel and M. Leo Elliott, architects. 9 stories, masonry, full use of the site to 4th floor, a tower rises from the 4th to the 9th floor, copper canopy shades 1st floor. Structure notable for its lavish use of ornamental terra-cotta on the facade and interior wall ornamentation. Private. N.R. 1982.

Snell Arcade

St. Petersburg. STUDEBAKER BUILDING. 600 4th St. S. 1925. Tudor Revival elements. 2 stories, red brick, flat roof. 1st and 2nd floors visually separated by a band of concrete that has been stuccoed. Unusual example of the application of Tudor Revival elements to a commercial structure, an auto showroom. The stucco panels support Studebaker Automobile Co. logo. Private. N.R. 1985.

St. Petersburg. U.S. POST OFFICE. 76 4th St. N. 1916. Classical Revival with Spanish Colonial elements. George W. Stewart, architect. 2 stories, granite, terra-cotta and marble trim, full-width front and side loggia. An original building designed for the local environment. Open on 3 sides with no stairs to permit patrons to enter with ease at any hour. Public. N.R. 1975.

United States Post Office

St. Petersburg. VEILLARD HOUSE. 262 4th Ave. N. 1901 (moved in 1979). Queen Anne and Chalet elements. Theodore Anderson and Henry DuPont, architects. 2 stories, rusticated block, large open front porch, mock half-timbering. Home of Ralph Veillard, prominent city merchant and civic leader. Private. N.R. 1982.

Don Ce Sar Hotel, 1987

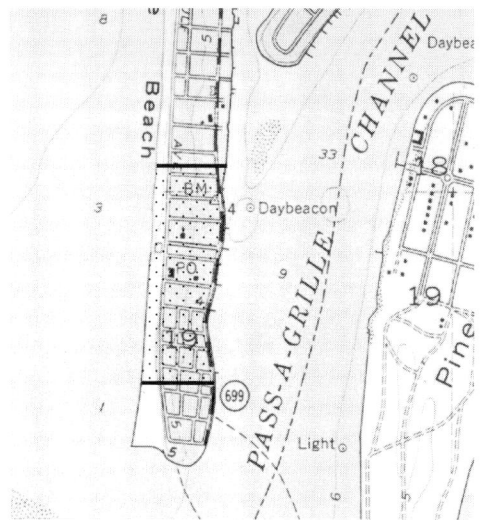

Pass-A-Grille Historic District

St. Petersburg. VINOY PARK HOTEL. 501 Beach Dr. NE. 1925. Mediterranean Revival. Henry L. Taylor, architect. 7-story central block with 3 5-story wings and 2 2-story wings. Interior public areas with much ceiling and wall ornamentation. One of the earliest and largest of St. Petersburg's resort hotels built during the Florida land boom. Designed to appeal to a wealthy clientele. Private. N.R. 1978.

St. Petersburg. WEEDEN ISLAND SITE. Weedon Island Rd. A.D. 500–A.D. 1000. Weeden Island period. A village complex of refuge piles, domiciliary mounds, and a sand burial mound. The artifact assemblage in the burial mound forms the basis for defining the Weeden Island cultural phase. Private. N.R. 1972.

St. Petersburg. JOHN C. WILLIAMS HOUSE. 444 5th Ave. S. 1891–1892. Queen Anne. $2^1/_2$ stories, gabled roof sections, veranda. The builder, John C. Williams, is credited with the founding of St. Petersburg. In 1906, with additions, building converted to a hotel. Private. N.R. 1975.

Vicinity of St. Petersburg. FORT DE SOTO BATTERIES. Mullet Key. 1898–1945. 2 gun batteries on the west shore of Mullet Key. The major feature is the massive earth-covered concrete structure of Battery Laidley. Excellent example of military coastal defense construction. Some original armament still in place. Public. N.R. 1977.

St. Petersburg Beach. DON CE SAR HOTEL. 3400 Gulf Blvd. 1928. Mediterranean Revival elements. Henry DuPont, architect. 5 to 10 stories, pink concrete, stuccoed, 4 corner towers, each with belfry arches. Popular 325-room luxury resort hotel built at height of state's land boom. Attracted many famous guests, including F. Scott Fitzgerald, Clarence Darrow, Babe Ruth, and Lou Gehrig. Private. N.R. 1975.

St. Petersburg Beach. PASS-A-GRILLE HISTORIC DISTRICT. 1890–1920. 115 buildings, 97 of historical interest. Frame and Masonry Vernacular predominate. The 1- and 2-story residences and commercial buildings reflect the construction techniques and building types of the late 19th and early 20th centuries. Public and Private. N.R. 1989.

Vinoy Park Hotel

Tarpon Springs. ARCADE HOTEL. 210 Pinellas Ave. 1926. Spanish Mission. Wolpert and Brown, architects. 2 stories, masonry, stuccoed, arcaded loggia on main facade with a gallery above, tile roof. The major example of Mediterranean Revival commercial architecture in Tarpon Springs to survive from the 1920s. The city's major hotel before World War II. Commercial arcade restored in 1985. Private. N.R. 1984.

Tarpon Springs. E.R. MERES SPONGE PACKING HOUSE. 106 Read St. c. 1905. Frame Vernacular. 2 stories. Corrugated metal siding. Building retains all of its original features except the sponge drying platform. It is still used for its original function. Private. N.R. 1991.

Tarpon Springs. OLD TARPON SPRINGS CITY HALL. 101 S. Pinellas Ave. 1915, 1947. Classical Revival. Ernest D. Ivey, architect. 2 stories. Gabled and hipped roof. 1-story north wing constructed in 1947. The major public building in Tarpon Springs from 1915 to 1987. Now a local museum. Public. N.R. 1990.

Tarpon Springs. OLD TARPON SPRINGS HIGH SCHOOL. 324 E. Pine St. 1925. Mediterranean Revival elements. Emmitt Hull, architect. 2 stories. Beaux-Arts-style central entrance. The school is a reflection of the importance placed by a prosperous, optimistic community on education. Presently the Tarpon Springs City Hall. Public. N.R. 1990.

Tarpon Springs. SAFFORD HOUSE. Parkin Ct. 1883 (moved). Frame Vernacular with Victorian details. 2½ stories, frame, wide veranda on 2 facades. The original owner, Anson P.K. Safford, is credited with founding the Arizona school system. Safford and Hamilton Disston of the famous Disston land development project selected Tarpon Springs as the site of a winter resort for wealthy Northerners. Private. N.R. 1974.

Tarpon Springs. SPONGE DIVING BOATS. Tarpon Springs Sponge Docks, Dodecanese Blvd. 1927–1941. The 5 remaining sailing ships of a large fleet built locally between 1907 and 1940 to gather sponges in the Gulf. Some used today to demonstrate traditional sponge gathering techniques. St. Nicholas III (1939), St. Nicholas VI (1927), Duchess (1940), N.K. Symi (1935), George N. Cretekos (1941). Private. N.R. 1990.

Tarpon Springs. TARPON SPRINGS HISTORIC DISTRICT. 1881–1935. 218 buildings, 145 of historical interest. Frame and Masonry Vernacular with a few Classical Revival. Includes residences and commercial buildings. Reflects the atmosphere of early Tarpon Springs. Arcade Hotel is a notable building of period. St. Nicholas Greek Orthodox Cathedral built in 1943. Public and Private. N.R. 1990.

Jar found in fragments and restored, Weeden Island Site

Tarpon Springs Historic District

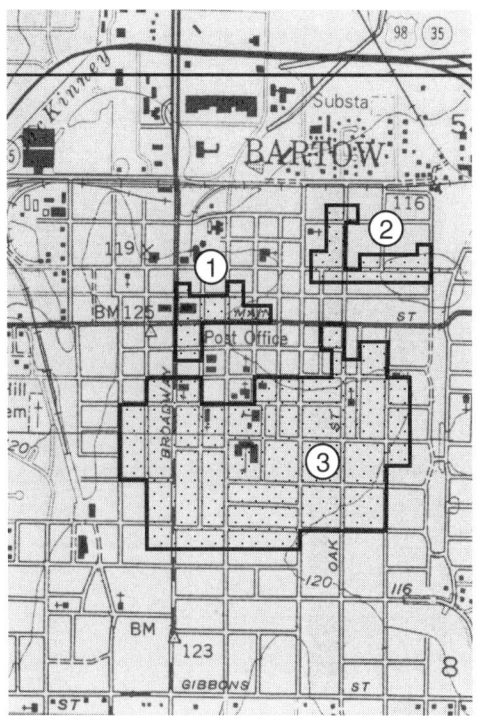

① **Bartow Downtown Commercial District**
② **Northeast Bartow Residential District**
③ **South Bartow Historic District**

Old Polk County Courthouse

South Florida Military College, c. 1900

POLK COUNTY

Bartow. BARTOW DOWNTOWN COMMERCIAL DISTRICT. 1887–1935. 27 buildings, 22 of historical interest. Masonry Vernacular and Classical Revival predominate. The oldest building in the district is the J.N. Smith House at 310 E. Davidson St. built in 1885. 6 buildings in the downtown commercial district survive from the 19th century. Public and Private. N.R. 1993.

Bartow. BENJAMIN FRANKLIN HOLLAND HOUSE. 590 E. Stanford St. 1895. Frame Vernacular with Shingle-style elements. E.R. Wharton, architect. $2^1/_2$ stories, frame, gabled roof sections, 1-story wraparound screened entrance porch. One of the finest examples of Shingle style in Florida. Boyhood home of the late U.S. Senator Spessard L. Holland. Private. N.R. 1975.

Bartow. NORTHEAST BARTOW RESIDENTIAL DISTRICT. 1886–1925. 29 buildings, 27 of historical interest. Frame and Masonry Vernacular and various Revival styles. A concentration of old buildings east of Bartow's commercial center. Most buildings date from between 1905 and 1915. Most are little altered. Private. N.R. 1993.

Bartow. OLD POLK COUNTY COURTHOUSE. 100 E. Main St. 1908, 1926. Classical Revival. E.C. Hosford and Francis J. Kennard, architects. 3 stories. Projected Corinthian porticos and a Baroque dome. East and west wings, designed by Kennard, added in 1926. Located on the same site of two earlier courthouses. The major public building in Polk County from 1908 to 1987. Presently a local museum. Public. N.R. 1989.

Bartow. SOUTH BARTOW HISTORIC DISTRICT. 1885–1941. 242 buildings, 176 of historical interest. Frame and Masonry Vernacular, Classical Revival, Prairie School. Bungalow styles are common. District includes residences, churches, schools and clubhouses. Little changed from when the area was developed. An affluent area. Many buildings were designed by professional architects. Public and Private. N.R. 1993.

Bartow. SOUTH FLORIDA MILITARY COLLEGE. 1101 S. Broadway. 1895 (main structure). Frame Vernacular. 2 stories, at each end a 2-story octagonal tower. The college was founded in 1894 and was important in the early development of higher education in Florida. Closed in 1905. Private. N.R. 1972.

Bartow. JOHN J. SWEARINGEN HOUSE. 690 E. Church St. 1923+ . Colonial Revival. B. Clayton Bonfoey, architect. 2 stories, brick, monumental Ionic portico, 1-story gallery across the entire 1st-floor entrance facade. John J. Swearingen was a leading Florida attorney and a member of the state senate. One of the finest examples of Colonial Revival style in Polk County. Private. N.R. 1982.

Fort Meade. CHRIST CHURCH (Episcopal). 526 N. Oak. 1889. Frame Vernacular with Gothic Revival elements. J. H. Weddell, architect. 1 story, gabled tin roof, off-center side-entrance porch, 2-story corner tower, stick-work belfry. Probably the oldest religious structure in the county. Considered an unusual example of Carpenter Gothic in its use of horizontal drop siding. Private. N.R. 1974.

St. Mark's Episcopal Church

Haines City. DOWNTOWN HAINES CITY COMMERCIAL DISTRICT. 1913–1937. 25 buildings, 20 of historical interest. Masonry Vernacular, Mediterranean Revival, and other Revival styles predominate. The historic commercial area of downtown. Retains some of the city's commercial functions today, although much diminished from before World War II. Private. N.R. 1994.

Haines City. OLD CENTRAL GRAMMAR SCHOOL. 801 Ledwith Ave. 1925. Mission Revival. E.C. Hosford, architect. 2 stories. 5 main bays on front facade. It was the first modern educational facility erected in the city. Presently used as a cultural arts center. Public. N.R. 1994.

Haines City. OLD HAINES CITY NATIONAL GUARD ARMORY. 226 S. 6th St. 1932. Colonial Revival. 2 stories. Parapet-gable roof and pilasters that vertically divide the building. The only historic facility in the community that is related to the state militia and U.S. National Guard. Public. N.R. 1994.

Downtown Haines City Commercial District

Haines City. POLK HOTEL. 800–810 Hinson Ave. 1926. Italian Renaissance Revival. Frederick Wallick, architect. 9 stories. First skyscraper built in city and still one of the largest buildings. A reminder of economic development in the community during the land boom. Private. N.R. 1994.

Haines City. ST. MARK'S EPISCOPAL CHURCH. 102 N. 9th St. 1890. Late Gothic Revival. 1 story. Steeply pitched cross-gable roof. Oldest standing structure in the town. Private. N.R. 1994.

Lakeland. BEACON HILL/ALTA VISTA RESIDENTIAL DISTRICT. 1923–1940. 102 buildings, 77 of historical interest. Frame Vernacular, Bungalow and Colonial Revival are the predominate styles. The area contains single-family dwellings of 1 to 2 stories. Most are modest in scale. The majority were constructed in 1920s. Private. N.R. 1993.

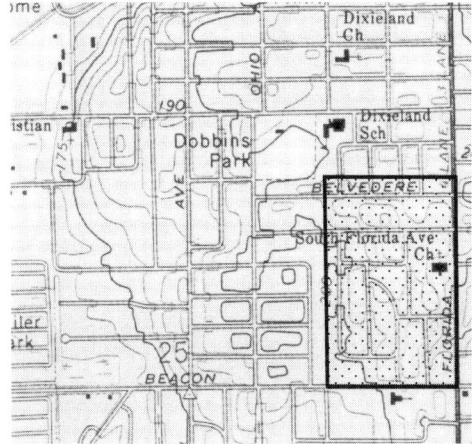

Beacon Hill/Alta Vista Residential District

East Lake Morton Residential Area

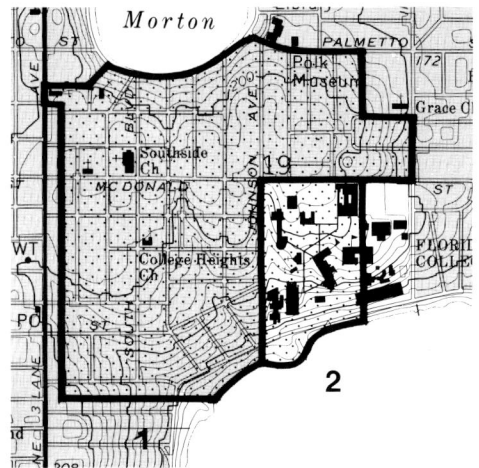

South Lake Morton Historic District (1) and Florida Southern College Architectural District (2)

Annie Pfeiffer Chapel, Florida Southern College Architectural District

Lakeland. EAST LAKE MORTON RESIDENTIAL AREA. 1900–1940. 296 buildings, 215 of historical interest. Frame Vernacular, Bungalow, Mediterranean Revival styles predominate. Most of the buildings were built as residences, although there are schools and social clubs in the district. An early middle-class neighborhood. Public and Private. N.R. 1993.

Lakeland. FLORIDA SOUTHERN COLLEGE ARCHITECTURAL DISTRICT. 1937–1955. 13 buildings. 7 structures designed by the famous architect Frank Lloyd Wright and 2 by a student (Nils Schweizer), 1 Classical Revival structure. The 7 structures by Frank Lloyd Wright were designed during his organic period. These 7 Wright buildings are significantly different from his other works. In addition the site plan which Wright developed for the campus reflects the only tangible expression of his planning concepts as idealized by his "Broadacres City" plan. Private. N.R. 1975.

Lakeland. LAKE MIRROR PROMENADE. Lemon St. and Lake Mirror Dr. 1926–1928. Eclectic Classicism. Charles W. Leavitt, architect. Finely detailed, reinforced concrete seawall extending 2300 yards around lake, 540-foot concrete retaining wall, vaulted arched loggia, and numerous other structures. The promenade is a prominent example of the City Beautiful Movement in Florida. It has become an integral part of the city's comprehensive plan for civic improvement. Public. N.R. 1983.

Lakeland. OLD LAKELAND HIGH SCHOOL COMPLEX. 400 N. Florida Ave. Collegiate Gothic Revival. W.B. Talley and E.C. Hosford, architects. 4 buildings. The original main building, designed by Talley, was built in 1902 but burned in 1925. Replaced by a building designed by Hosford in 1926. Auditorium was constructed in 1924, gymnasium in 1926. Public. N.R. 1993.

Lakeland. POLK THEATRE AND OFFICE BUILDING. 121 S. Florida Ave. 1927. Italian Renaissance. James E. Casale, architect. 4 stories. Typical of large theaters constructed in the 1920s. The interior conveys a Mediterranean atmosphere. Still in use. Private. N.R. 1993.

Lakeland. SOUTH LAKE MORTON HISTORIC DISTRICT. 1900–1942. 760 buildings within approximately 50 blocks. Almost without exception, the buildings are residential and of frame construction with wood siding or stucco, with 1- or 2-story front porches. Craftsman Bungalow style is common. The area is significant because of the large share of Bungalow-style structures (60 percent) followed by Frame Vernacular (25 percent). N.R. 1985.

Lake Wales. ATLANTIC COAST LINE RAILROAD DEPOT. 325 S. Scenic Highway. 1928. Mediterranean Revival. 1 story. Barrel-tile roof. The only transportation building left from the town's early period. It is now a local transportation museum. Public. N.R. 1990.

Lake Wales. CHALET SUZANNE. 20 buildings, 15 of historical interest. Eclectic styles. A complex of distinctly eclectic buildings clustered around a collection of natural and man-made landscape features. The restaurant was opened in 1925 and long has had a national reputation. The Chalet is one of Central Florida's oldest and most important tourist attractions. Private. N.R. 1990.

Lake Wales. CHURCH OF THE HOLY SPIRIT. 1099 Hesperides Rd. 1927. Spanish Mission. P.C. Samuell, architect. 1 story. Considered a superb example of its style. Sold to the city of Lake Wales by the Catholic Diocese in 1989. It now is a local museum. Public. N.R. 1990.

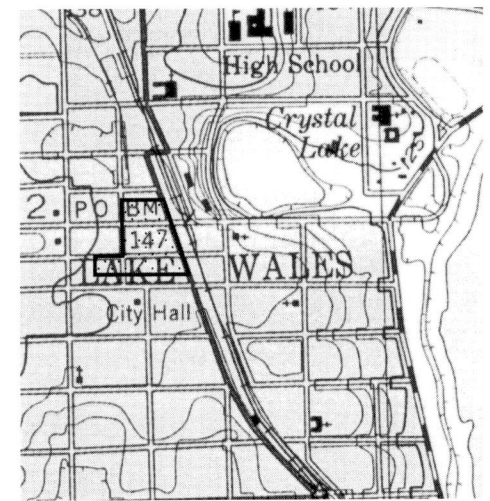

Lake Wales Commercial Historic District

Lake Wales. DIXIE WALESBILT HOTEL (Grand Hotel). 115 N. 1st St. 1926. Masonry Vernacular with Mediterranean Revival elements. Fred A. Bishop, architect. 10 stories. One of the few historic skyscrapers in Florida. Hotel completed at the end of the Florida land boom and never realized its hopes. Still in use. Private. N.R. 1990.

Lake Wales. FIRST BAPTIST CHURCH. 338 E. Central Ave. 1923. Classical Revival. 2 stories. Considered an excellent example of its style. Monumental portico with colossal Ionic columns and pilasters. Private. N.R. 1990.

Lake Wales. LAKE WALES CITY HALL. 152 E. Central Ave. 1928. Masonry Vernacular with Mediterranean Revival elements. George Jacobs, architect. 2 stories. Low, pitched hip roof with barrel tiles. The first building in the town to serve the local government. Completed at the end of the community's boom period. Public. N.R. 1990.

Dixie Walesbilt Hotel

Lake Wales. LAKE WALES COMMERCIAL HISTORIC DISTRICT. 1913–1928. 21 buildings, 16 of historical interest. Masonry Vernacular and Revival styles predominate. The district is almost entirely composed of buildings associated with the early commercial development of the community between 1913 and 1928. Public and Private. N.R. 1990.

Lake Wales. LAKE WALES MULTIPLE PROPERTY LISTING. Lakeshore Blvd and Sessoms Ave. 1914–1916. Colonial Revival. 2 stories. 3 highly representative examples of Colonial Revival. Bullard House (1914), 644 S. Lakeshore Blvd; Johnson House (1914), 315 E. Sessoms Ave; Tillman House (1916), 301 E. Sessoms Ave. Residences of some of the most important early residents of the town. Private. N.R. 1990.

Mountain Lake Colony House

Lake Wales. MOUNTAIN LAKE COLONY HOUSE. 1916, 1921, 1925. Mediterranean Revival. Frederick Law Olmsted Jr. and Charles R. Wait, architects. 3 stories. Pergolas, loggias, balconets, and a barrel-tile roof. Original architect Olmsted was the son of one of the nation's most famous landscape architects. In its day one of Central Florida's most fashionable resort hotels. Still in use. Private. N.R. 1991.

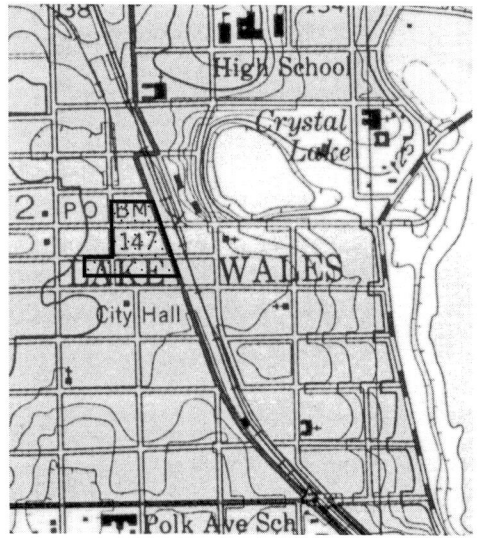
Mountain Lake Estates Historic District

Lake Wales. MOUNTAIN LAKE ESTATES HISTORIC DISTRICT. 1920s+.101 buildings, 65 of historical interest. Classical Revival and other Revivals predominate. An exclusive residential area initially developed in the 1920s. Designed by Olmsted Brothers of Brookline, Massachusetts, near the highest point in Central Florida. Within the district are an 18-hole golf course and 2 properties earlier added to the National Register (El Retiro and the Colony House). Private. N.R. 1993.

Vicinity of Lake Wales. BOK MOUNTAIN LAKE SANCTUARY AND SINGING TOWER. 2 mi. N of Lake Wales. 1922. Gothic motif. Milton B. Medary, architect. 205-foot tower, steel frame, coquina stone, and marble facing, sculpted pinnacles, balcony, pointed arched entrance, elaborate carved screens, friezes and ornamentation depicting fables and natural and human scenes, large imported carillon. Conceived by Edward W. Bok, editor of *Ladies Home Journal*. The sanctuary consists of approximately 130 acres and was designed by Frederick Law Olmsted, Jr. Private. N.R. 1972.

Vicinity of Lake Wales. CASA DE JOSEFINA. U.S. 27A, 2 mi. SE of Lake Wales. 1923. Eclectic with Italian, Spanish, Gothic, and other elements. Edward B. Stratton, architect. 1 and 2 stories, flat roof, with crenelated parapets, 2-story central pavilion with arcaded wings, decorative balconies with wrought-iron detail. Built as a residence for Polk County banker and realtor Irwin Arthur Yarnell. Private. N.R. 1975.

Vicinity of Lake Wales. EL RETIRO. U.S. 27A, at Mountain Lake. 1930–1932. Mediterranean Revival. Charles Wait, architect. 2 stories, masonry, stuccoed, windows and entrance cast stone, wrought-iron balconies. One of the last Mediterranean-Revival-style estates built in area before the Great Depression. The community in which the building is situated was designed to attract the nation's business elite. Private. N.R. 1985.

PUTNAM COUNTY

Crescent City. HUBBARD HOUSE (San Sui). 600 N. Park St. c. 1879. Frame Vernacular with Queen Anne and Shingle-style elements. 2½ stories, frame, clapboarding, shingle siding, front and side porches. Built by Henry G. Hubbard, who introduced the camphor tree and Japanese persimmon to Florida. Elaborate botanical garden used for plant acclimatization once surrounded the house. Private. N.R. 1973.

Melrose. MELROSE WOMAN'S CLUB (Literary and Debating Society). Pine St. 1893. Frame Vernacular. E.L. Judd, architect. 1 story, front porch. The Woman's Club supported many civic and social functions in the community, including the library. Most of the early members were from New England, a fact reflected in the style of the building. Private. N.R. 1978.

Bok Singing Tower

Palatka. BRONSON-MULHOLLAND HOUSE. Madison St. between 1st and 2nd Sts. 1845. Greek Revival. 2¹/₂ stories, frame, full-width, 2-tier portico recessed beneath the roof. Home of Judge Issac Hopkins Bronson, from Rutland, New York, who moved to Palatka where he was appointed a judge and became very active in the civic and social life of the town. Public. N.R. 1972.

Palatka. PALATKA NORTH HISTORIC DISTRICT. 1840–1931. 71 buildings of historical interest in 11 blocks. Predominant styles: Classical Revival, Victorian, and Frame Vernacular. Notable structure: the Bronson-Mulholland House, Greek Revival (1845). The earliest settled portion of the city, where a number of important citizens built their homes. N.R. 1983.

Palatka. PALATKA SOUTH HISTORIC DISTRICT. 1852–1930. 210 buildings, of which 169 are of historical interest, within 23 blocks. Predominant styles are Frame Vernacular, Colonial Revival, Bungalow, and Victorian. Notable building: the Conant House, 603 Emmett St. (1886), richly decorated Queen Anne style. Most fashionable 19th-century residential area in Palatka. It contains several antebellum homes. N.R. 1983.

Palatka. ST. MARK'S EPISCOPAL CHURCH. 2nd and Main Sts. 1854. Gothic Revival. 1 story, board-and-batten siding, corner tower with pyramidal roof. One of the oldest churches in Palatka. Private. N.R. 1973.

Palatka. UNION DEPOT. Main St. and 12th St. 1908. Richardson Romanesque. 1 story. Typical Richardson pattern of random window openings and many hexagonal dormered bays. Built by the Atlantic Coast Line. Since 1970 the depot has been handling freight of the Seaboard Coast Line Railroad. Private. N.R. 1988.

Vicinity of Welaka. MOUNT ROYAL. 3 mi. S of Welaka. A.D. 1200–A.D. 1600. Middle Mississippian period. Burial mound and associated midden areas. The burial mound has produced significant data pertinent to the expansion of Mississippian culture in Florida. Private. N.R. 1973.

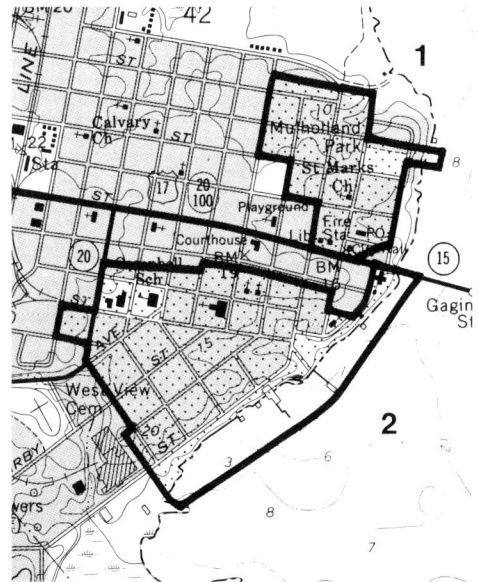

Palatka North Historic District (1) and Palatka South Historic District (2)

St. Mark's Episcopal Church

ST. JOHNS COUNTY

Ponte Vedra Beach. SHELL BLUFF LANDING. Guana River State Park. 3000 B.C.–A.D. 1300. Middle Archaic, Deptford, and St. Johns periods. An oyster-shell midden, which extends approximately 450 meters N/S on the bluff above the river, and from 150 to 250 meters E/W. Site was occupied for over 5000 years and includes artifacts from the colonial period as well as from Pre-Columbian periods. Public. N.R. 1991.

St. Augustine. ABBOTT TRACT HISTORIC DISTRICT. 1838–1930. 124 historic buildings within 17 blocks. Predominant style: Frame Vernacular with open or screened porches, gabled roofs. Some Revival structures as well as others with Victorian elements. Notable structure: Castle Warden (1887), Moorish Revival style. The district has the highest percentage of pre-1930 buildings in the city. First real estate development outside the colonial city. N.R. 1983.

St. Augustine. ALCAZAR HOTEL. 79 King St. 1887–1889. Spanish Renaissance and Moorish. John M. Carrere and Thomas Hastings, architects. 4 stories, central courtyard, main entrance flanked by 2 tall towers. The hotel was built by Henry M. Flagler as part of a complex of 3 buildings in his quest to create a "Riviera" of the city and its surroundings. The architects were young graduates of L'Ecole des Beaux-Arts of Paris sent by Flagler to Spain to study Spanish and Moorish architecture. Hotel is now the Lightner Museum and City Hall. Private-Public. N.R. 1971.

St. Augustine. AVERO HOUSE. 39 St. George St. Early 18th century. Spanish colonial elements. 2 stories, stuccoed, 1st-floor windows have rejas (bars). 4 vigas (roof beams) on front facade. Among the oldest houses in the district, once used as a private oratory by Catholic Minorcans and as a place of worship for Greeks who migrated from the failed New Smyrna colony. Private. N.R. 1972.

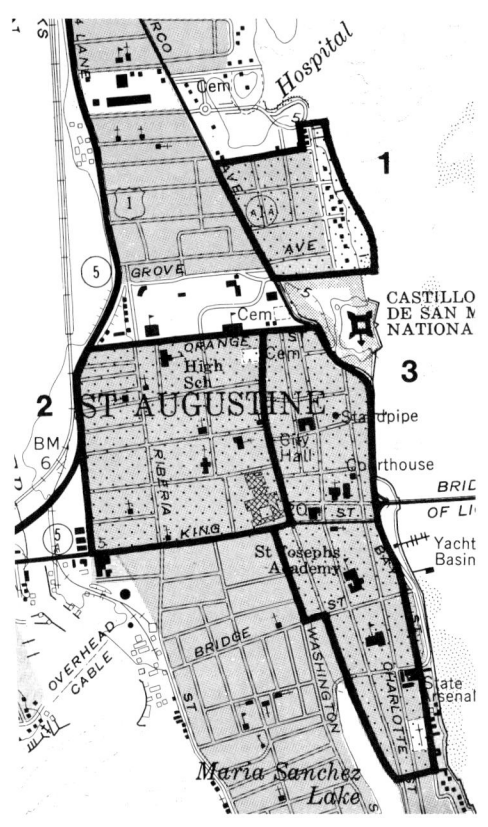

① **Abbott Tract Historic District**
② **Model Land Company Historic District**
③ **St. Augustine Historic District**

St. Augustine. BRIDGE OF LIONS. King St. 1926. J.E. Greiner, architect. 1583 feet long, designed to complement the Mediterranean-Revival-style architecture of downtown St. Augustine. 4 towers with tile roofs flank the drawspan of the bridge. 2 marble lions on the city side. Public. N.R. 1982.

St. Augustine. CASTILLO DE SAN MARCOS NATIONAL MONUMENT. 1 Castillo Dr. 1672–1696. Built on the site of several earlier wooden forts. Present stone fort, moat, and outworks built to protect Spanish territory in Florida as well as Spanish shipping along the coast. Oldest masonry fortification in continental U.S. Between 1680 and 1759 it was the hub of turmoil in the Southeast between the Spanish and English. Served as military prison in 19th century. Museum. Public. N.R. 1966.

Castillo de San Marcos National Monument

St. Augustine. CATHEDRAL OF ST. AUGUSTINE. Cathedral St. 1797, restored 1887–1888, remodeled 1965–66. Spanish Colonial and Renaissance Revival. 1 story, coquina, concrete, twin Doric columns at main entrance. The parish of St. Augustine, established in 1594, is the oldest in the U.S. An early 18th-century church on site was largely destroyed in 1887. Restored structure retains only the facade and portions of side walls from the older one. Private. N.R. 1970.

Gonzales-Alvarez House

St. Augustine. GONZALES-ALVAREZ HOUSE (Oldest House). 14 St. Francis St. c. 1723, 1775–1786, 1790. Stone Vernacular. Originally 2 stories, with frame porch, frame 2nd floor added later. Oldest house in city, an excellent example of the area's 18th-century vernacular architectural evolution. Greatly altered over time. Private. N.R. 1970.

St. Augustine. GRACE UNITED METHODIST CHURCH. 8 Carrera St. 1887. Spanish Renaissance Revival with Moorish elements. John M. Carrere and Thomas Hastings, architects. 2 stories, masonry with salmon-colored brick, square turret, with conical roof, terra-cotta trim, and ornamentation. Built by Henry M. Flagler and is an excellent example of early use of poured concrete in construction. Private. N.R. 1979.

St. Augustine. HOTEL PONCE DE LEON. King and Cordova Sts. 1887–1888. Spanish Renaissance Revival with Moorish Revival elements. John M. Carrere and Thomas Hastings, architects. 3$^{1}/_{2}$ to 4$^{1}/_{2}$ stories, modified U-shaped, central dome flanked by square towers. Interior decorated with Tiffany glass, murals, and mosaic tiles. The premier of 3 Flagler hotels in the city. Considered one of the finest examples of its architectural style in the U.S. and the first large building to be made of poured concrete. Now Flagler College. Private. N.R. 1975.

Interior, Hotel Ponce de Leon, 1891

St. Augustine. LINCOLNVILLE HISTORIC DISTRICT. 1870–1930. 688 buildings, 548 of historical interest. Wood Vernacular, Mediterranean Revival, and Bungalow styles predominate. All contributing structures built before 1930. District grew from a small black settlement founded there after the Civil War. Coquina used for foundations, wood for the buildings. Black builders designed and built many of the buildings. Public and Private. N.R. 1991.

St. Augustine. LINDSLEY HOUSE. 214 St. George St. 18th century. Spanish Colonial elements. 2$^{1}/_{2}$ stories, masonry, stuccoed, 2 narrow, wood-covered balconies on south and east facades, stepped gable ends. Used today for receptions. Private. N.R. 1971.

St. Augustine. LLAMBIAS HOUSE. 31 St. Francis St. Late 18th century. Spanish and English Colonial elements. 2 stories, hipped roof, 2nd-floor balcony, rear 2-story veranda. The house is an excellent example of local architectural style. Numerous alterations, but restored in 1952. Public. N.R. 1974.

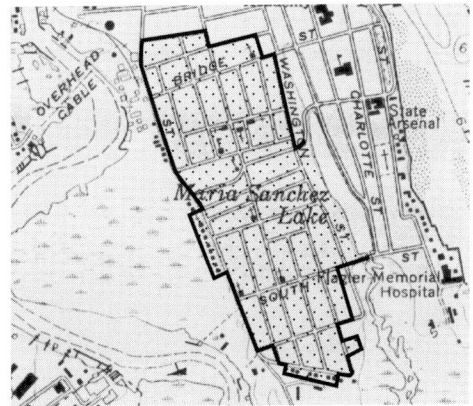

Lincolnville Historic District

O'Reilly House

Old St. Johns County Jail

St. Augustine. MARKLAND (Andrew Anderson House). 102 King St. 1893, 1899, 1901. Classical Revival. 2¹/₂ stories, coquina block, 2-story gallery on the south and east facades. Veranda features large Ionic columns. Built by Dr. Andrew Anderson, Sr., from New York, a leader in the community. He and his son influenced Henry Flagler in his decision to make the city a winter resort. Presently part of Flagler College. Private. N.R. 1978.

St. Augustine. MODEL LAND COMPANY HISTORIC DISTRICT. 1839–1930. 20 blocks. Predominant styles: Frame Vernacular and various Revival styles. Hotel Ponce de Leon and Grace United Methodist Church are notable structures. Residential neighborhood developed mainly during the Flagler era and in which many of Flagler's administrators lived. The city's most outstanding examples of late 19th century buildings found within it. N.R. 1983.

St. Augustine. OLD ST. JOHNS COUNTY JAIL (Authentic Old Jail). 167 San Marcos Ave. c. 1891. Romanesque Revival. 2¹/₂ stories, masonry. Built by P.J. Pauly and Brothers Jail Building and Manufacturing Company for the city with money advanced by Henry F. Flagler, the city's leading developer. Now a tourist attraction. Private. N.R. 1987.

St. Augustine. O'REILLY HOUSE. 32 Aviles St. c. 1763. Spanish and American Colonial elements. 2¹/₂ stories, coquina stone, stuccoed, 2nd-story balcony. One of the 10 oldest structures in the city. Used as a convent for a time. Private. N.R. 1974.

St. Augustine. RODRIQUES-AVERO-SANCHEZ HOUSE. 52 St. George St. 18th and 19th centuries. Spanish and Colonial American elements. 2¹/₂ stories, coquina, frame, clapboarding, gable roof. Illustrates the evolution of a Spanish residence from a small 1-room dwelling into the extant 2¹/₂-story structure. Frame upper story is 19th century. Private. N.R. 1971.

St. Augustine. ST. AUGUSTINE HISTORIC DISTRICT. 1600–1900. 31 known houses in the district pre-date 1821. Stone and tabby vernacular buildings with Spanish and Colonial American elements predominate. Founded in 1565, St. Augustine is the oldest European settlement within the United States. Typical Spanish colonial town, with a number of reconstructed buildings, a central marketplace, and narrow streets. N.R. 1986.

St. Augustine. ST. AUGUSTINE LIGHTHOUSE AND KEEPER'S QUARTERS. Old Beach Rd. 1871–1874. Conical tower. Brick, 165 feet tall. Keeper's quarters: 2 stories, Vernacular, red brick, partially destroyed by fire in 1970. The oldest surviving brick structure in St. Augustine, it is near the site of a wooden watchtower built by Spanish in the 16th century and a later stone tower converted to a lighthouse in 1824. Rebuilt between 1871 and 1874. Public. N.R. 1981.

St. Augustine Historic District

St. Augustine. ST. AUGUSTINE OSTRICH AND ALLIGATOR FARM. 999 Anastasia Blvd. 1921, 1937. Vernacular. 30-acre complex of buildings that form one of Florida's oldest continuously operating tourist attractions. The building complex dates from 1937. One of the 2 buildings, the 3-story tower, is an excellent example of Mission style. Private. N.R. 1992.

St. Augustine. SANCHEZ POWDER HOUSE SITE. Marine St. 18th and 19th centuries. Site of powder magazine constructed by Spanish between 1797 and 1800. Originally built of coquina with a tile roof. Used by U.S. Government until 1860. Public. N.R. 1972.

St. Augustine. SOLLA-CARCABA CIGAR FACTORY (Pamies and Arango Cigar Factory). 88 Riberia St. 1909. Masonry Vernacular with Mediterranean Revival elements. Fred A. Henderich, architect. 4 stories. Barrel-tile roof. Oldest surviving industrial building in St. Augustine. Presently a warehouse. Private. N.R. 1993.

Solla-Carcaba Cigar Factory

St. Augustine. VILLA ZORAYDA (Zorayda Castle). 83 King St. 1883. Moorish Revival. Franklin W. Smith, architect. 2 stories. Liberal use of ornamentation and unusual window shapes. Irregular shape, built of reinforced concrete. The earliest Moorish Revival style residence in Florida. Served as winter residence of Bostonian Smith, an amateur architect who traveled widely in Spain. Now a museum. Private. N.R. 1993.

St. Augustine. XAVIER LOPEZ HOUSE. 93½ King St. 1903. Queen Anne Revival. 2 stories. House has a gable roof, tiered veranda, conical roofed tower. Lopez was a prominent merchant and town public servant. Private. N.R. 1993.

St. Augustine. XIMENEZ-FATIO HOUSE. 20 Aviles St. 1797–1802. Spanish and American Colonial elements. 2½ stories, frame with plastering, wooden-frame balconies, roof with gabled dormers. Built for Andres Ximenez, Spanish merchant, the building has served as a store, public billiard parlor, and boardinghouse. Museum. Private. N.R. 1973.

Xavier Lopez House

Vicinity of St. Augustine. FISH ISLAND SITE. Matanzas River S of St. Augustine. 18th and 19th centuries. Site of one of Florida's earliest groves. Established by Jesse Fisher, from New York, who acquired the property in 1763. Plantation produced oranges, figs, peaches, pomegranates and limes. Plantation declined in the early territorial period. Private. N.R. 1972.

Vicinity of St. Augustine. FORT MATANZAS NATIONAL MONUMENT. 14 mi. S of St. Augustine on Fl. A1A. 16th to 19th century. Stone tower built as part of the defense system of St. Augustine. Site of much fighting among French, Spanish, and British for area supremacy. On this site, in 1565, the Spaniard Pedro Menéndez de Avilés had executed over 300 captured members of a French Huguenot military expedition sent to colonize Florida. First watchtower built by Spanish to warn the town of approaching ships (late 16th century). Fort abandoned when U.S. acquired Florida. Public. N.R. 1966.

St. Augustine Beach. SPANISH COQUINA QUARRIES. Fl. A1A on Anastasia Island. 17th and 18th centuries. Quarries on island opened in late 17th century. Coquina stone consists of ground shells held loosely together by a calcareous cement formed by the reaction of water, sand, and calcium. Coquina hardens when dried. Stone transported to St. Augustine, where it was used in the construction of many buildings including Castillo de San Marcos. Public. N.R. 1972.

Cresthaven

ST. LUCIE COUNTY

Ft. Pierce. CASA CAPRONA. 2605 St. Lucie Blvd. 1926. Mediterranean Revival. Arthur Beck, architect. 2 stories, frame, stuccoed, tile roof. Envisioned as the centerpiece of the proposed winter community of San Lucie Plaza, which failed after the collapse of the Florida land boom. Private. N.R. 1984.

Ft. Pierce. CRESTHAVEN (Boston House). 239 S. Indian River Dr. 1909. Classical Revival. $2^1/_2$ stories, red brick, front portico has 3 boxed columns. Presently private offices. Private. N.R. 1985.

Ft. Pierce. FORT PIERCE SITE. South Indian River. 1838. Location of a palmetto log blockhouse and houses which included officers' and company quarters. One of a chain of forts built during the Second Seminole War. Abandoned in 1842. Private-Public. N.R. 1974.

Captain Hammond House

Ft. Pierce. ZORA NEALE HURSTON HOUSE. 1734 School Ct. 1957. Frame Vernacular. 1 story. Hurston (1901?–1960) was a black writer, folklorist, and anthropologist whose work has attained great respect since her death. She lived for the last few years of her life in the house. Private. N.R. 1991.

Ft. Pierce. ST. LUCIE HIGH SCHOOL (Ft. Pierce Elementary School). 1100 Delaware Ave. 1915, 1924, 1926. Mission Revival. W.B. Camp, architect. 2 stories, 3-story center section, brick bell tower. Oldest school in the county. Public. N.R. 1984.

St. Lucie Village. ST. LUCIE VILLAGE HISTORIC DISTRICT. 1850–1928. 50 buildings, 35 of historical interest. Frame Vernacular and Classical Revival. A linear district located along N. Indian River Drive on the Indian River Lagoon. Residential buildings range from modest Frame Vernacular to 3-story late Victorian. Site of Fort Capron, dating from the 3rd Seminole War (1850–1859) is on the property of 3015 N. Indian River Dr. Private. N.R. 1989.

White City. CAPTAIN HAMMOND HOUSE. 5775 Citrus Ave. 1902. Frame Vernacular. 2 stories. Board-and-batten exterior. The building design was influenced by Danish architectural styles. The town was settled by Danes. Captain Hammond was a retired New England sea captain. Private. N.R. 1990.

St. Lucie Village Historic District

SANTA ROSA COUNTY

Bagdad. BAGDAD VILLAGE HISTORIC DISTRICT. 1840–1930. 222 buildings, 144 of historical interest. Frame Vernacular, many with both Creole and Gulf Coast elements. Site of one of West Florida's largest lumber mills. Like other mill towns, Bagdad declined when the mill closed. The town has a number of 2-story commercial buildings built from plans purchased from Stearns and Culver of Chicago. Public and Private. N.R. 1987.

Vicinity of Chumuckla. THOMAS CREEK ARCHAEOLOGICAL DISTRICT. East of Chumuckla. 8000 B.C.–early 19th century. Archaic to Historic period. Several sites in area show evidence of human occupation for approximately 10,000 years. Public. N.R. 1985.

Milton. BETHUNE BLACKWATER SCHOONER. Well-preserved coastal schooner submerged in harbor. Located on the edge of a small slough that connects with Blackwater River. Little is known about its origin. Site has been studied intensely by underwater archaeologists. Public. N.R. 1991.

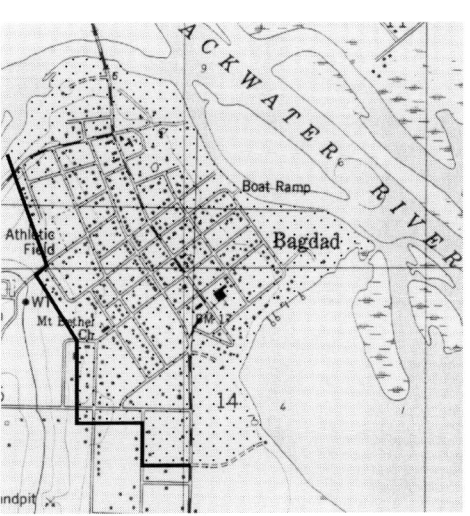

Bagdad Village Historic District

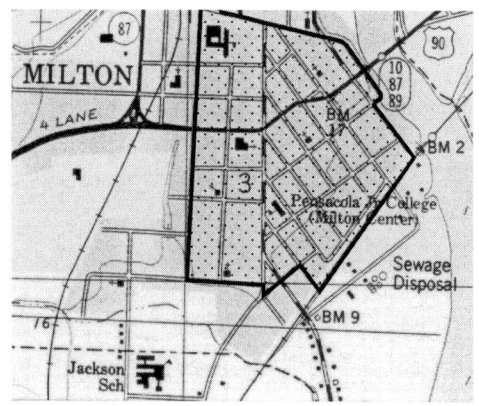

Milton Historic District

Ollinger-Cobb House

Milton. FLORIDA STATE ROAD NO. 1. E of Milton, parallel to U.S. 90. 1921. 6-mile brick highway completed in 1921. Most presently not in use. The first section of a paved highway that was to run from Jacksonville to the Pacific coast. It was to be named the Old Spanish Trail. Public and Private. N.R. 1991.

Milton. LOUISVILLE AND NASHVILLE DEPOT. 206 Henry St. 1909. Frame Vernacular. 1 story. Building follows standard plan of L and N Railroad Co. stations. Little altered from when it was built. Private. N.R. 1982.

Milton. MILTON HISTORIC DISTRICT. 1840–1930. 162 buildings, 117 or historical interest. Frame Vernacular, Colonial Revival, Bungalow styles predominate. Town was of great importance as a lumber center. Located at the upper navigable limits of the Blackwater River. In its early days 3-masted schooners sailed up the river to pick up cotton and lumber. Public and Private. N.R. 1987.

Milton. MT. PILGRIM AFRICAN BAPTIST CHURCH. Corner of Alice and Clara Sts. 1916. Gothic Revival. Wallace A. Rayfield, architect. 1 story. Red brick exterior, windows are Gothic arched. Designer was one of the nation's leading black architects. Constructed by members of the congregation who were primarily descendants of the original members of the church. Private. N.R. 1992.

Milton. OLLINGER-COBB HOUSE. 302 Pine St. c. 1870. Gothic elements. 1¹/₂ stories, frame, originally a simple cottage, but altered to include a large pyramidal roof tower and other elements, mainly Gothic. Home of Joseph Ollinger, ship's carpenter who immigrated from Luxembourg and later owned a shipyard. Shipyard burned during retreat of Confederates in the Civil War, but rebuilt later. Private. N.R. 1983.

Milton. ST. MARY'S EPISCOPAL CHURCH AND RECTORY. 300 and 301 Oak St. 1872+. Gothic Revival (church), Greek Revival (rectory). Church: 1 story, frame, board-and-batten, with gabled roof. Rectory: 1¹/₂ stories, frame, full-width porch. Church and rectory erected by Dr. Charles E. McDougall, rector of the church as well as a physician. Private-Public. N.R. 1982.

Vicinity of Milton. ARCADIA MILL SITE. 1 mi. SW of Milton. 1817–1855. One of the earliest industrial complexes in territorial Florida. Composed of a saw mill, a cotton textile mill, a mule-powered railroad, a rock quarry, a bucket factory, and workers' living quarters. The site is expected to yield important information about industrial technology and society in the Antebellum South. Private. 1987.

SARASOTA COUNTY

Miakka School House, 1985

Englewood. LEMON BAY WOMAN'S CLUB. 51 N. Maple St. 1926. Prairie School. Thomas Reed Martin and Clare C. Hosmer, architects. 1 story. Club was organized in 1918 as the Lemon Bay Mother's Club. The club became a leading force in the civic life of Englewood. Still used as a clubhouse. Private. N.R. 1988.

Miakka. MIAKKA SCHOOLHOUSE. Miakka and Wilson Rds. 1914. Frame Vernacular. 1 story, pyramidal-roofed bell tower. Only example in the county of a simple rural schoolhouse. The only educational facility in area for 30 years, and first school in the county built under a bond issue. Public. N.R. 1986.

Osprey School

Vicinity of North Port Charlotte. LITTLE SALT SPRINGS. Off U.S. 41N. 5000 B.C. and earlier. Archaic period. Limestone sinkhole 250 feet wide surrounded by dense subtropical vegetation. Numerous skeletal remains and artifacts found within sinkhole. Private. N.R. 1979.

Osprey. OSPREY SCHOOL. 1926. Masonry Vernacular. M. Leo Elliott, architect. 1 story. The school features an ornate entrance bay flanked by symmetrical classroom wings. Presently vacant. Public. N.R. 1994.

Vicinity of Osprey. OSPREY ARCHAEOLOGICAL AND HISTORIC SITE. North of Osprey on Little Sarasota Bay. 2150 B.C.–A.D. 1900. Weeden Island, Englewood, and Safety Harbor periods. Coastal hardwood hammock. Site consists of 3 extensive shell middens and a burial mound as well as several 19th-century structures. Private. N.R. 1975.

Sarasota. BACHELLER-BREWER MODEL HOME ESTATE. 1926. 1903 Lincoln Dr. 6 buildings, 4 of historical interest. The district contains a 2-story main house in Mediterranean Revival style, servants quarters, fishing pier, seawall and boat landing. Private. N.R. 1992.

Sarasota. BAY HAVEN SCHOOL. 2901 W. Tamiami Cr. 1926. Mediterranean Revival. M. Leo Elliott, architect. 2 stories, masonry, stuccoed, central courtyard, exterior open corridors, 3-bay open loggia at entrance. One of several local schools designed by Tampa architect M. Leo Elliott. Public. N.R. 1984.

Sarasota. KARL BICKEL HOUSE. 101 N. Tamiami Trail. 1925. Mediterranean Revival. Dwight James Baum, architect. 2 stories. 2-story center structure with 2 1-story wings. Originally built as the office of a realty company. Converted into a private residence in 1933 for Karl Bickel, then owner of United Press. Private. N.R. 1994.

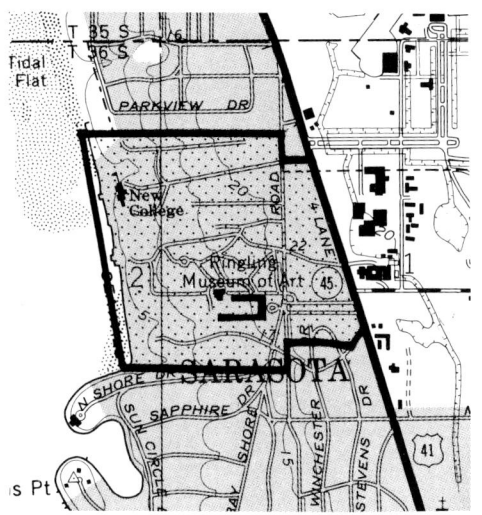

Caples'-Ringlings' Estates Historic District

John Ringling Residence Ca'd'Zan',
Caples'-Ringlings' Estates Historic District

Corrigan House

Sarasota. BURNS COURT HISTORIC DISTRICT. 1924–1925. 15 buildings within 1 block. Homes of Mediterranean Revival style with Spanish Colonial Revival and Mission Revival motifs. 15 1-story, stuccoed bungalows, all in the same style, designed by Thomas Reed Martin. Built as Sarasota's first "cooperative home subdivision," the 15 bungalows with garages are remarkably intact. N.R. 1984.

Sarasota. CAPLES'-RINGLINGS' ESTATES HISTORIC DISTRICT. 1920s. 3 large estates and a museum on approximately 150 acres. Mediterranean Revival. The John Ringling residence Ca'd'Zan, Dwight James Baum, architect, is a notable structure. Said to have been inspired by the Doges Palace in Venice, Italy. District composed of the contiguous, former estates of John and Charles Ringling, two of the five brothers who owned the famous circus, and Ralph Caples, Sarasota developer who was their friend. Private. N.R. 1982.

Sarasota. CITY WATER WORKS. 1015 N. Orange Ave. 1926. Mediterranean Revival. 2 stories, red brick, barrel-tile hipped roof. Public. N.R. 1984.

Sarasota. CORRIGAN HOUSE (Nagirroc). 463 Sapphire Dr. 1926. Mission Revival. Stuccoed hollow-clay-tile exterior. The house was designed and constructed to comply to rigid guidelines of the subdivision. Corrigan retired to Sarasota from New York. The house name is his name spelled backward. Private. N.R. 1994.

Sarasota. F.A. DECANIZARES HOUSE. 1215 N. Palm Ave. 1925 and earlier. Mediterranean Revival. 2 stories, wood frame, later covered with stucco facade. Original wood-frame house moved to the site and later a stucco facade applied in the Mediterranean Revival style. Private. N.R. 1984.

Sarasota. DEMARCAY HOTEL. S. Palm Ave. 1922. Mission Style. 2 stories, masonry, stuccoed, 5 bays, ogee-arch windows above 1st and 5th bay on 2nd floor. Part of a complex which included the Mira Mar Hotel and Apartment complex. Private. N.R. 1984.

Sarasota. EARLE HOUSE. 1924. Classical Revival. Alfred C. Clas, architect. 2 stories. Owner was a winter resident from New York who eventually retired to Sarasota. Private. N.R. 1993.

Sarasota. EDWARDS THEATER. 57 N. Pineapple Ave. 1926. Mediterranean Revival. Roy A. Benjamin, architect. 4$\frac{1}{2}$ stories, steel frame, masonry, stuccoed. Auditorium has plaster and beamed ceiling, ornamental plaster cartouches. Building included shops and apartments, but the 1500-seat auditorium was its most famous component. Called "The Temple of Silent Art and Make Believe." Private. N.R. 1984.

Sarasota. EL PATIO. 500 N. Audubon Place. 1926. Mediterranean Revival. Lillias Piper, architect. 2 stories. U-shaped building with stuccoed exterior. Built during land boom, it was restored in 1991. Private. N.R. 1993.

Sarasota. EL VERNONA–BROADWAY APARTMENTS. 1133 4th St. 1926. Mediterranean Revival. Dwight James Baum, architect. 3 stories, masonry, stuccoed, oval octagonal tower, barrel-tile polygonal roof. Significant for architectural design and association with nationally renowned architect Baum. Private. N.R. 1984.

Sarasota. FIELD ESTATE. Field Rd. and Camino Real. 1925–1927. Mediterranean Revival. David Adler, architect. 2 stories, masonry, stuccoed, tile roof (main building). A 16-acre estate with 4 historic buildings: the main house, the bathhouse, a gatehouse, and an art studio. It was the home of the philanthropic Field and Palmer families who contributed much to making the city a winter resort. Private. N.R. 1986.

El Vernona-Broadway Apartments, 1983

Sarasota. FRANCES-CARLTON APARTMENTS. 1221–1227 N. Palm Ave. 1924. Mediterranean Revival. Alex Browning and Francis James, architects. 3 stories, masonry, stuccoed, 4 blocks, 1 wedge-shaped, the others rectangular; domed observatory and a mirador. Early apartment house notable for its design that took advantage of Sarasota Bay's views and winds. Private. N.R. 1984.

Sarasota. DR. JOSEPH D. HALTON HOUSE. 308 Cocoanut Ave. 1910. Transitional Queen Anne. Joseph S. Maus, architect. 2 stories, artificial stone facade. Home of one of Sarasota's early physicians. House illustrates an early local use of pressed or artificial stone in construction. Private. N.R. 1984.

Frances-Carlton Apartments, 1983

Sarasota. EDSON KEITH ESTATE. 5500 S. Tamiami Trail. 1916. 7 buildings, 4 of historical interest. 60-acre estate. 2-story main house is Italian Renaissance designed by Otis and Clark. Contains middens with artifacts from 500 B.C. to A.D 800. Since 1987 the property has been a public park. Public. N.R. 1991.

Dr. Joseph D. Halton House, 1983

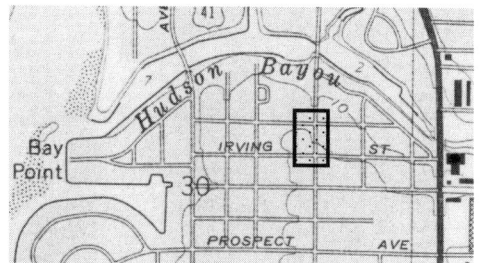

Rigby's "La Plaza" Historic District

Sarasota. DR. WALTER KENNEDY HOUSE. 1876 Oak St. 1926. Mediterranean Revival. Dwight James Baum, architect. 2 stories. Barrel-tile roof, detached garage and servants' quarters. Kennedy was a local optometrist. Private. N.R. 1994.

Sarasota. S.H. KRESS BUILDING. 1442 Main St. 1932. Art Deco style. 3 stories, concrete, Art Deco front facade, buff tile, and polychrome terracotta with extensive ornamentation. Important local example of the Art Deco style. Private-Public. N.R. 1984.

Sarasota. L.D. REAGIN HOUSE. 1213 N. Palm Ave. 1926. Mediterranean Revival. Thomas Reed Martin, architect. 1¹/₂ stories, masonry, stuccoed, 3 contiguous 1-story blocks with a 2-story rear elevation. L.D. Reagin was an early editor of the *Sarasota Times*. Private. N.R. 1984.

Sarasota. RIGBY'S "LA PLAZA" HISTORIC DISTRICT. 1926. 9 buildings, 8 of historic interest. Mediterranean Revival. 5 of the 8 buildings of historic interest are 1 story, the other 3 are 2 story. All are concrete block. Designed by T. Miller Bryan, the area was developed by Harry Rigby during the land boom as a rental complex. Private. N.R. 1994.

Roth Cigar Factory, 1983

Sarasota. ROTH CIGAR FACTORY. 30 Mira Mar Ct. 1923. Mission Revival. Thomas Reed Martin, architect. 2 stories, masonry, stuccoed, roof parapet topped by scrolled and foliated cartouche, metal grille on balcony. Designed to integrate architecturally with the nearby Mira Mar Hotel and Apartment complex. Factory produced cigars for local consumption. Private. N.R. 1984.

Sarasota County Courthouse

118

Sarasota. SARASOTA COUNTY COURTHOUSE. 2000 Main St. 1927. Mediterranean Revival. Dwight James Baum, architect. 2 story, masonry, stuccoed, 2 wings with central multistory campanile, barrel-tile roof. A notable example of Baum's work. Design is a synthesis of Spanish Colonial Revival, Spanish Renaissance, with Baroque and Roccoco elements. Public. N.R. 1984.

Sarasota. SARASOTA HERALD BUILDING. 539 S. Orange Ave. 1925. Mediterranean Revival with Spanish Mission overtone. 1 story, masonry, stuccoed, barrel-tile roof, rejas (window grilles). An early use of Mediterranean Revival for an industrial structure. Private. N.R. 1984.

Sarasota. SARASOTA HIGH SCHOOL. 1001 S. Tamiami Trail. 1926. Collegiate Gothic. M. Leo Elliott, architect. 3 stories with $4^1/_2$-story entrance, red brick, glazed terra-cotta detail, Gothic Revival colonettes. One of 3 educational buildings in Sarasota designed by Elliott. Public. N.R. 1984.

Sarasota. SARASOTA MULTIPLE RESOURCE AREA. 1884–1935. Approximately 70 buildings scattered throughout city. Predominant styles are Frame Vernacular, Mediterranean Revival, Classical Revival, Bungalow, Queen Anne, and Mission Revival. Works of Dwight James Baum, M. Leo Elliott, and Thomas Reed Martin found in area. The properties reflect the historical and architectural development of the city. N.R. 1984.

Sarasota. SARASOTA TIMES BUILDING. 1214–1216 1st St. 1926. Mediterranean Revival. Dwight James Baum, architect. 3 stories, masonry, stuccoed, cast-stone facade. An outstanding example of the architect's application of Mediterranean Revival to an industrial structure. Private. N.R. 1984.

Southside Elementary School, main entrance

Sarasota. SARASOTA WOMAN'S CLUB. (Florida State Theatre). 1241 N. Palm Ave. 1915. Jacobethan Revival. H.N. Hall, architect. $1^1/_2$ stories, wood frame, half-timbered and parget facade. Home until 1979 of the Woman's Club, which has been responsible for many civic improvements in the community. Private. N.R. 1985.

Sarasota. SOUTHSIDE SCHOOL. 1901 Webber St. 1926. Mediterranean Revival. M. Leo Elliot, architect. 2 stories, masonry, stuccoed and cast stone, central courtyard, entrance decorated with a cast-stone ornamentation, 3-bay loggia at main entrance. Public. N.R. 1984.

Sarasota. THOMAS HOUSE. 5030 Bay Shore Rd. 1926. Mission and Mediterranean Revival. Fred J. Orr, architect. 2 stories. Outstanding example of its architectural style. Private. N.R. 1994.

Thomas House

Sarasota. U.S. POST OFFICE–FEDERAL BUILDING. 111 S. Orange Ave. 1934. Classical Revival. George Albee Freeman and Louis A. Simon, architects. 2 stories, steel frame, bounded by a balustrated stone railing, central colonnade at main entrance with 8 Corinthian columns. Believed to be the last executed monumental design of nationally renowned architect Freeman. Public. N.R. 1984.

Sarasota. J.G. WHITFIELD ESTATE. 704 Bayshore Rd. 1925. Mediterranean Revival. Dwight James Baum, architect. 2 stories, masonry, stuccoed, built around interior patio, barrel-tile roof, metal window grilles and balcony rails, Sullivanesque cornice frieze. The house is significant in design, craftsmanship, and association with a prominent local architect. Private. N.R. 1984.

Sarasota. H.B. WILLIAMS HOUSE. 1509 S. Orange Ave. 1926. Mediterranean Revival. Thomas Reed Martin, architect. 2 stories, masonry, stuccoed, built around interior patio, barrel-tile roof, metal window grilles and balcony rails, Sullivanesque cornice frieze. The house is significant in design, craftsmanship, and association with a prominent local architect. Private. N.R. 1984.

Sarasota. DR. C.B. WILSON HOUSE. 235 S. Orange Ave. c. 1906, addition 1913. Shingle Vernacular. 2 stories, pressed stone, gabled and dormered ends clad in wood shingles. Residence of early Sarasota families. Later the home of C.B. Wilson, prominent local physician. Private. N.R. 1984.

Senator Copeland House, Venice Multiple Property Group

Venice. ARMADA ROAD MULTI-FAMILY DISTRICT. 1925–1928. 20 buildings, 12 of historical interest. Mediterranean Revival. The district is comprised of 2-story apartment houses of similar style. The district was part of the original plan for Venice and was to be a buffer between the commercial center and a single-family residential neighborhood. Private. N.R. 1989.

Venice. EAGLE POINT HISTORIC DISTRICT. 1916. 31 buildings, 22 of historical interest. Frame Vernacular. Developed as a seasonal hunting resort for wealthy Northerners. Buildings were designed to create a rustic "close-to-nature" atmosphere. Presently vacant. Pre-Historic archaeological sites on the property. Private. N.R. 1991.

Venice. ENGLEWOOD HISTORIC DISTRICT. 1925–1928. 42 buildings, 36 of historical interest. Mediterranean and Colonial Revival. The only collection of small-sized Mediterranean-Revival-style residences in community. It was a successful attempt by the early city planners to develop a district of modest housing conforming to the city's architectural goals. Private. N.R. 1989.

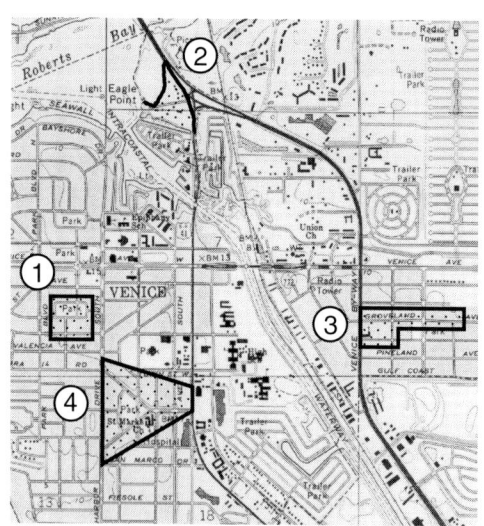

① Armada Road Multi-Family District
② Eagle Point Historic District
③ Englewood Historic District
④ Venezia Park Historic District

Venice. HOTEL VENICE. 200 N. Nassau St. 1927. Mediterranean Revival. Leon Gillette, architect. 3 stories, U-shaped, stuccoed, modillioned cornice, 2 4-story towers, lobby has 2 ranks of square columns. Served as the central focus of Venice, a planned community developed in its entirety by the Brotherhood of Locomotive Engineers. Private. N.R. 1984.

Venice. VENICE MULTIPLE PROPERTY GROUP. 1925–1927. Mediterranean Revival. 1 and 2 stories. 4 buildings, all the same style within a neighborhood designed for high-income families. Senator Copeland House (1925), 710 Armada Rd. S; Levillain-Letton House (1926), 229 S. Harbor Dr.; Blalock House (c. 1926), 241 S. Harbor Dr.; Venice Railroad Depot (1927), 303 E. Venice Ave. Private. N.R. 1989.

Venice. VENEZIA PARK HISTORIC DISTRICT. 1925–1928. 48 buildings, 37 of historical interest. Mediterranean Revival. Designed around a large trapezoidal-shaped park. Houses are 1- and 2-story hollow clay tile and stucco with barrel-tile roofs. Developed as part of the plan of early Venice. N.R. 1989.

Vicinity of Venice. WARM MINERAL SPRINGS. About 12 mi. SE of Venice on U.S. 41. c. 8000 B.C. Paleo-Indian, Archaic, Formative, and Historic periods. Large free-flowing mineral spring. A number of ledges around the basin contain shallow caves which were Indian burial sites when sea level was much lower. Private. N.R. 1977.

SEMINOLE COUNTY

Longwood. BRADLEE-McINTYRE HOUSE. 130 W. Warren Ave. c. 1885. Queen Anne. 2¹/₂ stories, frame, clapboard, polygonal, front corner tower, wraparound 1-story veranda. Winter home of the Bradlee family of Boston. Originally located in Altamonte Springs but moved to present location in 1973. Used as offices of the Central Florida Society for Historic Preservation. Private. N.R. 1991.

Longwood. LONGWOOD HISTORIC DISTRICT. c. 1880–1926. 53 buildings, 38 of historical interest. Frame Vernacular predominates. Most of the early development of the town took place west of the railroad. W. Church and W. Warren avenues formed the core of the town. The commercial section then and now was on E. Lake St. A prominent structure is the Longwood Hotel (1886) at 150 S. C.R. 427. Public and Private. N.R. 1990.

Longwood. LONGWOOD HOTEL (Longwood Village Inn). 150 E. Lake St. 1887+. Frame Vernacular. Joseph B. Clouser, architect. 3-story, frame, wraparound veranda. A rare surviving example of a small, wood-frame hotel built in many small communities throughout Florida at the end of the last century. Still one of the largest buildings in Longwood. Presently used for offices. Private. N.R. 1984.

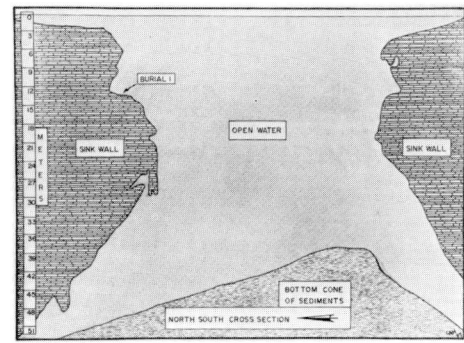

Cross Section of Warm Mineral Springs. The skeleton from burial 1, found in 1973, has been radiocarbon dated 10,240 years b.p. Burial 1 is one of the oldest intentional burials recovered in the Western Hemisphere.

Bradlee-McIntyre House

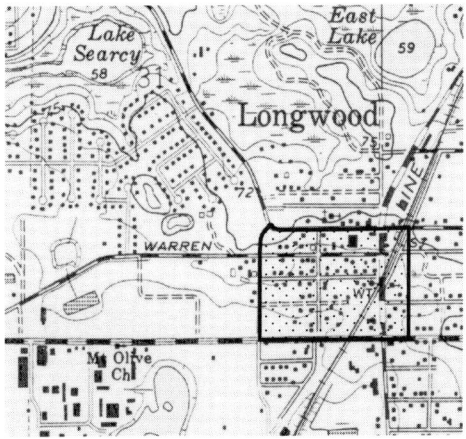

Longwood Historic District

121

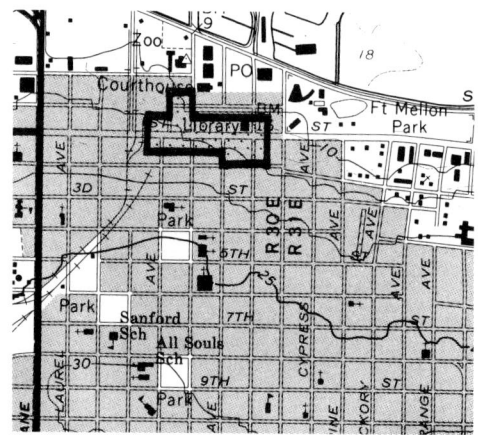

Sanford Commercial District

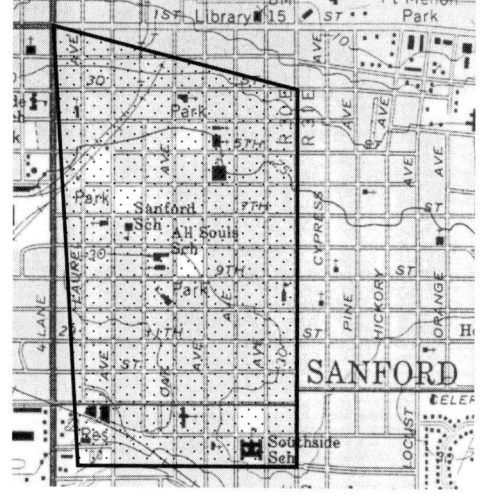

Sanford Residential Historic District

Sanford Grammar School

Sanford. FERNALD-LAUGHTON MEMORIAL HOSPITAL (Old), (Florida Hotel). 500 S. Oak Ave. c. 1910, 1919, 1927. Colonial Revival. 2-story, frame, 1st floor has a beige-brick veneer, 2nd story has woodshingle siding, French tile roof. The only hospital in the city from 1919 to 1955. Originally the home of George Fernald, local hardware store owner. After his death converted to hospital. Presently a rooming house. Private. N.R. 1987.

Sanford. ST. JAMES A.M.E. CHURCH. 1913. Gothic Revival. Prince W. Spears, architect. Pyramidal main roof and two towers. Red brick exterior. Closely associated with the religious and social life of the African-American community of Sanford. Designer was a local African-American builder. Private. N.R. 1992.

Sanford. SANFORD COMMERCIAL DISTRICT. 1886–1924. 26 historic structures within 11 city blocks. 1- to 2-story buildings, the majority with Italianate elements. Notable are those buildings built for Henry B. Plant's investment company. One of the best-preserved collections of 19th- and 20th-century commercial architecture in Florida. Ninety percent of the structures built between 1886 and 1910 within the district still are intact. N.R. 1976.

Sanford. SANFORD GRAMMAR SCHOOL. 301 W. 7th Ave. 1902. Romanesque Revival. Wilbur Talley, architect. 2 stories, red brick, massive 3-story bell tower. One of the oldest school buildings in Florida. Its most famous alumnus is Walter L. "Red" Barber, nationally known sports announcer. Teaching Museum. Public. N.R. 1984.

Sanford. SANFORD RESIDENTIAL HISTORIC DISTRICT. 1880–1930. 503 buildings, 434 of historical interest. Frame and Masonry Vernacular predominate, many with revival influence. District was developed over a period of 50 years from a pine forest. Early development consisted of small homes located between 3rd and 5th streets on Magnolia and Palmetto avenues. Churches and schools were built along Park and Oak avenues between 3rd and 5th streets. Between 1915 and 1927 district assumed its present form. Public and Private. N.R. 1989.

SUMTER COUNTY

Vicinity of Bushnell. DADE BATTLEFIELD HISTORIC MEMORIAL. 1 mi. SW of junction of U.S. 301 and Fl. 476. 1835. On December 28, 1835, Seminole Indians, resisting forced relocation to the West, ambushed a detachment of 108 Federal troops led by Major Francis L. Dade. Only 3 soldiers survived. This incident led to the 7-year Second Seminole War. Museum. Public. N.R. 1972.

SUWANNEE COUNTY

Live Oak. BISHOP B. BLACKWELL HOUSE. 110 Parshley St. 1886. Eclectic. 2 stories, brick, front portico, 1-story wing. Home of B.B. Blackwell, a politician, attorney, financier, and utilities company owner. It is one of the oldest houses in Live Oak and the only one of its time with a brick exterior. Private. N.R. 1985.

Old Live Oak City Hall

Live Oak. OLD LIVE OAK CITY HALL. 212 N. Ohio Ave. 1908–1909. Italian Villa. 2 stories, brick tower. Italian Villa style is rare in Florida. Building is a symbol of the prosperity and civic pride brought to a small agricultural community when railroad lines reached it. Public. N.R. 1986.

Live Oak. UNION DEPOT AND ATLANTIC COAST LINE FREIGHT STATION. 200 block of N. Ohio Ave. 1903 and 1909. Masonry Vernacular with Romanesque Revival elements. 1½ stories, brick. Structures are associated with growth brought about by railroad development. Public. N.R. 1986.

Vicinity of Live Oak. HULL-HAWKINS HOUSE. Fl. 49, 10 mi. S of Live Oak. c. 1866. Greek Revival. 2 stories, center pedimented, 2-tier portico with square Doric columns. The house was built for Noble A. Hull, who immigrated from Georgia to become a merchant and prominent in state politics. Private. N.R. 1973.

Hull-Hawkins House

TAYLOR COUNTY

Perry. OLD PERRY POST OFFICE. 201 E. Green St. 1935. Masonry Vernacular with Mediterranean Revival elements. 1 story. Only public building erected in the county by the Public Works Administration, a Depression Era effort to provide employment. George Snow Hill, prominent Florida painter, was given a government grant to execute a mural. Entitled Cypress Logging, it is now found in the new post office. Public. N.R. 1989.

Old Perry Post Office

Perry. OLD TAYLOR COUNTY JAIL. 400 block of N. Washington St. 1912. Masonry Vernacular. Benjamin Bosworth Smith, architect. 2 stories. T-shaped, with hipped roof. The oldest remaining public building in Taylor County. One of the few remaining jails with a sheriff's residence in Florida. Private. N.R. 1989.

Townsend Building

UNION COUNTY

Lake Butler. TOWNSEND BUILDING. 410 W. Main St. c. 1910. Masonry Vernacular with Italian Renaissance elements. The building, now vacant, was the town's most distinctive commercial building during the period when the town was in the center of a thriving agricultural district. Private. N.R. 1992.

VOLUSIA COUNTY

Southern Cassadaga Spiritualist Camp Meeting Association Historic District

Barberville. BARBERVILLE CENTRAL HIGH SCHOOL. 1776 Lightfoot Lane. 1920. Frame Vernacular with Colonial Revival and Craftsman elements. Francis Miller, architect. 1 story. 2 separate buildings joined by a breezeway. Building served the educational needs of northwestern Volusia County for many decades. Now a museum complex that illustrates the history of the county in late 19th and early 20th centuries. Public. N.R. 1993.

Cassadaga. SOUTHERN CASSADAGA SPIRITUALIST CAMP MEETING ASSOCIATION HISTORIC DISTRICT. 1895–1938. 80 buildings, 67 of historical interest. Mostly Frame Vernacular residences, but several commercial, religious, and apartment buildings. Cassadaga was founded in 1895 as a religious community. It came to be the group's second largest center after its New York headquarters. Still a Spiritualist center. Private. N.R. 1991.

Daytona Beach. THE ABBEY (Thompson's General Store, Rhodes House). 426 S. Peach St. c. 1875, 1904. Frame Vernacular with Colonial Revival elements. 2 stories, weatherboard siding, flat-roofed portico over main entrance. Originally used as a store by Lawrence Thompson. Converted to house in 1904 when acquired by Adelaide Rhodes from Ohio. One of oldest structures in city. Private. N.R. 1987.

Daytona Beach. MARY McLEOD BETHUNE HOUSE. Bethune-Cookman College campus. 1920s. Frame Vernacular. $2^{1}/_{2}$ stories, front entrance with partially enclosed hipped porch. Home of the founder of Bethune-Cookman College and leading spokesperson for the concerns of black Americans. Private. N.R. 1974.

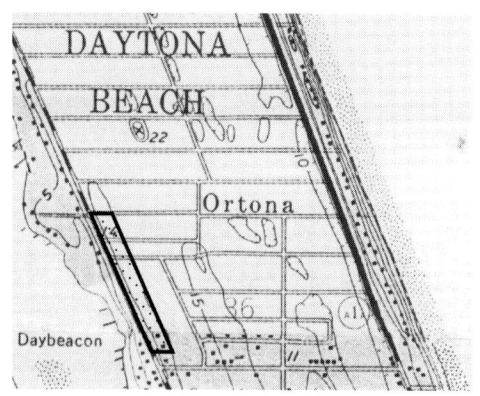
El Pino Parque Historic District

Daytona Beach. EL PINO PARQUE HISTORIC DISTRICT. 1923–1936. 14 buildings, 11 of historical interest. Mainly Revival styles. A distinctive collection of residential architecture constructed between 1924 and 1936. Developed as one of the most exclusive subdivisions on Daytona Beach during its land boom in the middle 1920s. Private. N.R. 1993.

Daytona Beach. AMOS KLING HOUSE. 220–222 Magnolia Ave. 1907. Frame Vernacular. $2^1/_2$ stories. Irregular-shaped building with weatherboard siding and wood shingle roof. Winter home of Kling, a prominent Ohio businessman and father-in-law of Warren G. Harding, president of the United States. Private. N.R. 1993.

Daytona Beach. S.H. KRESS AND COMPANY BUILDING. 140 S. Beach St. 1932. Art Deco. Edward F. Sibbert, architect. 3 stories, buff brick, parapet walls with terra-cotta copings, terra-cotta ornamentation on 2 facades. An outstanding example of Art Deco style in the city. The design is typical of many Kress Company buildings constructed during the period. Private. N.R. 1983.

Daytona Beach. MERCHANTS BANK BUILDING. 252 S. Beach St. 1910 and 1926. Beaux Arts. W.B. Talley, architect. 2 stories, Ionic columns, large arched windows, triangular pediment. Representative of commercial and economic life of Daytona Beach through 2 world wars. The facade of the building has become a landmark of the cityscape. Private. N.R. 1986.

Merchants Bank Building

Daytona Beach. OLDS HALL (Arroyo Garden Hotel). 340 S. Ridgewood Ave. 1923. Mediterranean Revival. Jacob Espedahal, architect. 4 stories. U-shaped building with a central block and north and south wings. Exterior is stucco. Virtually all apartments retain original art glass. An old hotel that in 1942 became a retirement home for ministers and missionaries. Private. N.R. 1993.

Daytona Beach. ROGERS HOUSE. 436 N. Beach St. 1878 (moved in 1919). Frame Vernacular. 2 stories, walls of weatherboard on 1st floor and decorative shingle on 2nd. Built by David D. Rogers, a founder of the city. Private. N.R. 1986.

Olds Hall

Daytona Beach. SOUTH BEACH STREET HISTORIC DISTRICT. 1876–1938. 196 buildings, 157 or historical significance. Frame Vernacular, Bungalow, Art Deco predominate. Runs parallel to the Halifax River and reflects the development of the city from the 1870s to the 1930s. The northern 2 blocks consist of a commercial district with many Masonry Vernacular buildings. Public and Private. N.R. 1988.

Daytona Beach. HOWARD THURMAN HOUSE. 614 Whitehall St. c. 1888. Frame Vernacular. 2 stories. Shed roof, front porch, breezeway at the rear leads to a reconstructed detached kitchen. Thurman, raised in Daytona Beach, was the first African-American to hold the post of dean at a predominately white university (Boston University). Thurman was also the first black in Florida to finish the 8th grade. Now a museum. Private. N.R. 1990.

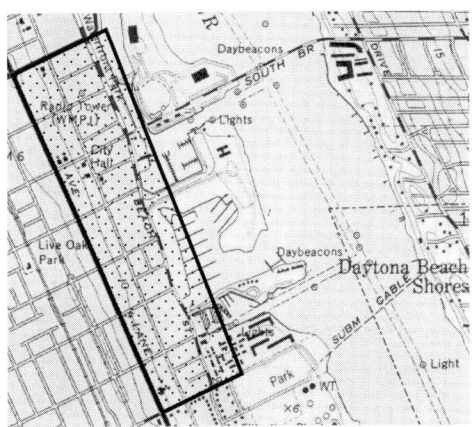
South Beach Street Historic District

Daytona Beach. U.S. POST OFFICE. 220 N. Beach St. 1932. Mediterranean Revival. Harry M. Griffin, architect. 2 stories. The front portico is faced with stone from the Florida Keys. A series of 5 arches frame the windows of the first floor. 4 cast iron light standards on limestone bases are situated on either side of the 2 front entrances. Built as a work project in the Depression. Public. N.R. 1988.

Daytona Beach. WHITE HALL. 640 2nd St. 1916. Elements of Colonial and Georgian Revival. 2 stories. Masonry building associated with Bethune-Cookman College, a private, historically African-American educational institution. Oldest building on campus. Private. N.R. 1992.

Daytona Beach. S. CORNELIA YOUNG MEMORIAL LIBRARY. 302 Vermont Ave. 1916, 1930. Mission and Mediterranean Revival. D.F. Fuquay and Harry M. Griffin, architects. 2 stories. Gabled roofs and a smooth stucco exterior. Original design by Fuquay, the 1930 addition by Griffin. Oldest library in the city. Built in response to the influx of seasonal visitors and retirees. Public. N.R. 1992.

DeBary. DeBARY HALL DeBary Mansion State Park. 1871. Eclectic. 2 stories, frame, 2-tier veranda around 3 sides. Built as the plantation house of Baron Frederick DeBary, wine importer, who wintered here until his death in 1898. Public. N.R. 1972.

DeBary Hall

DeLand. DeLAND HALL. Stetson University Campus. 1884+. Stick style. 2$^1/_2$ stories, projected bell tower. The oldest building in Florida continuously associated with higher education. Built by Henry A. DeLand, a New Yorker, who founded DeLand. He deeded the building to the university. Private. N.R. 1983.

DeLand. DOWNTOWN DELAND HISTORIC DISTRICT. 1886–1929. 86 buildings, 68 of historical interest. Masonry Vernacular predominate. The physical development of the district began in the late 1870s, but the early buildings that survive today were built after 1886. The district has lost some physical integrity resulting largely from poor maintenance, and the alteration or destruction of some structures. Sufficient numbers remain to convey a sense of the historic period. Public and Private. N.R. 1987.

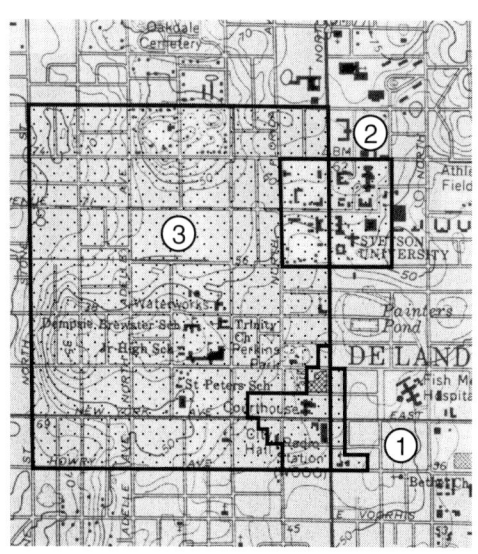

① Downtown Deland Historic District.
② Stetson University Campus Historic District.
③ West Deland Residential District.

DeLand. OLD DELAND MEMORIAL HOSPITAL. Stone St. 1920, 1926. Italian Renaissance and Masonry Vernacular. J.T. Cairns, F.M. Miller, and Gouveneur M. Peek, architects. 2$^1/_2$ stories. The 1920 building (2$^1/_2$ stories, designed by Cairns and Miller); the addition (1 story) designed by Peek. The addition was built for black patients. Although vacant, they still represent early health facilities in the area. Public. N.R. 1989.

DeLand. JOHN B. STETSON HOUSE. 1031 Camphor Lane. 1886. Frame Vernacular. George T. Pearson, architect. 3 stories, shingle siding. The winter home of the famous Philadelphia hat manufacturer whose name is associated with Stetson University. Private. N.R. 1978.

DeLand. STETSON UNIVERSITY CAMPUS HISTORIC DISTRICT. 1884–1934. 14 buildings, 11 of historical interest. Second Empire, Colonial and Mediterranean Revival predominate. Frame and masonry buildings associated with one of Florida's oldest institutions of higher education. DeLand Hall, built in 1884, is the earliest building. Private. N.R. 1991.

DeLand. WEST DELAND RESIDENTIAL DISTRICT. 1884–1942. 472 buildings, 375 of historical interest. Frame Vernacular, Bungalow, and various Revival styles. District is mainly single-family residences dating from the late 19th century. District contains schools, churches, and other noncommercial buildings. Public and Private. N.R. 1992.

Enterprise. ALL SAINTS' EPISCOPAL CHURCH. DeBary Ave. NE and Clark St. 1883. Gothic Revival. 1 story, frame, board-and-batten siding. One of the oldest of the original Episcopal mission churches in Central Florida. Private. N.R. 1974.

Holly Hill. HOLLY HILL MUNICIPAL BUILDING. 1065 Ridgewood Ave. 1942. Masonry Vernacular. Alan J. MacDonough, architect. 1 story. Constructed of local coquina. Begun as a public works project during the Depression, it was completed in 1942. It served as the city hall, police and fire station. Public. N.R. 1993.

Lake Helen. LAKE HELEN HISTORIC DISTRICT. 1885–1940. 79 buildings, 71 of historical interest. Several Revival styles, early 20th century American styles. The majority of buildings were constructed as residences. 3 churches, commercial buildings, a library and school in the district. Many buildings reflect Revival style popular during the period district developed. Public and Private. N.R. 1993.

Lake Helen. ANNA STEVENS HOUSE. 201 E. Kicklighter Rd. 1895. Frame Vernacular. 2¹/₂ stories. One of the oldest and largest examples of Frame Vernacular construction in Lake Helen. Winter residence of Stevens, a wealthy and influential widow from Michigan who had ties with the nearby Spiritualist community of Cassadaga. Private. N.R. 1993.

New Smyrna Beach. EL REAL RETIRO (Handley House). 636 N. Riverside Drive. 1923, 1937. Mediterranean Revival. 2 stories. A large residential complex on the Indian River. Built by Handley, a Long Island, New York, financier and stockbroker. Private. N.R. 1987.

Holly Hill Municipal Building

Lake Helen Historic District

Anna Stevens House

127

New Smyrna Beach. NEW SMYRNA BEACH HISTORIC DISTRICT. 1885–1935. 413 buildings, 314 of historical interest. Frame and Masonry Vernacular and some Revival styles predominate. Majority of the structures are Vernacular. Coquina use on porch piers, pedestals and copings. Residences, commercial, educational and government buildings represented. Public and Private. N.R. 1990.

New Smyrna Beach. WOMAN'S CLUB OF NEW SMYRNA. 403 Magnolia St. 1924, 1934. Masonry Vernacular with Mediterranean Revival elements. Philip H. Reed and Harry M. Griffin, architects. 1 story. Large fireplace in the interior made of coquina. Although built in 1924, its interior was not completed until 1934. Continues as social center for the community. Private. N.R. 1989.

Vicinity of New Smyrna Beach. NEW SMYRNA SUGAR MILL RUINS. 1 mi. W of New Smyrna Beach off Fl. 44. 1830. In 1830 a steam sugar and saw mill were erected; 5 years later the mills and other buildings were destroyed by Indians. Site further altered by soldiers who were garrisoned there during the Seminole Wars. Public. N.R. 1970.

Vicinity of New Smyrna Beach. TURTLE MOUND. 9 mi. S of New Smyrna Beach on Fl. A1A. A.D. 800–A.D. 1400. St. Johns period. One of the largest prehistoric shell middens along this section of the East Coast. Mound is roughly 30 feet high. Within it have been found shells, animal bones, and pottery fragments. Public. N.R. 1970.

Vicinity of Oak Hill. ROSS HAMMOCK SITE. Inland from Intracoastal Waterway within the Canaveral National Seashore. A.D. 1–A.D. 1400, A.D. 1860+ St. Johns period and Historic period. A village midden and 2 burial mounds and a Confederate saltworks. Public. N.R. 1981.

Ormond Beach. ANDERSON-PRICE MEMORIAL LIBRARY BUILDING 42 N. Beach St. 1916. Classical Revival. Ogden Codman, Jr., architect. 1 story, masonry, stuccoed, portico with 4 columns. Headquarters of the Ormond Beach Village Improvement Association, later renamed the Ormond Beach Woman's Club (1957). Improvement Association was the driving civic force in the village for years. Private. N.R. 1984.

Ormond Beach. CASEMENT ANNEX. 127 Riverside Dr. 1904. Monterey style. 2 stories. Considered an early example of the Monterey style. Built for Junius T. Smith. In 1918 it was sold to John D. Rockefeller, who owned the Casements nearby. Used as an annex for his business staff. Private. N.R. 1988.

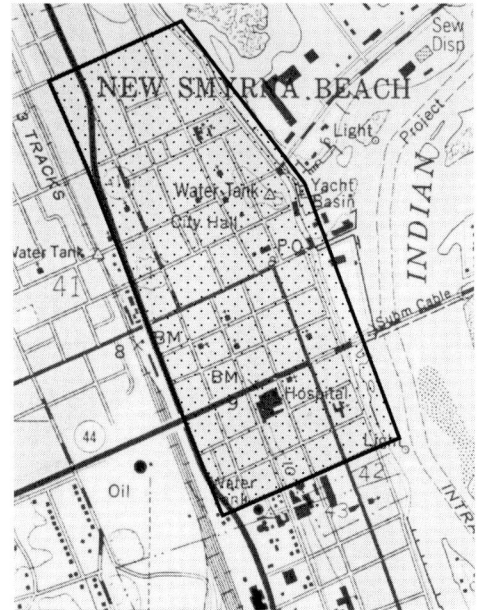

New Smyrna Beach Historic District

Turtle Mound

Ormond Beach. THE CASEMENTS. 25 Riverside Drive. Early 1890s. Shingle style. 2 stories, enclosed porch. Purchased by John D. Rockefeller in 1918 and used as his winter home until his death in 1937. The name "Casements" is believed derived from the many casement windows in the living room. Presently used as municipal cultural center. Public. N.R. 1972.

Ormond Beach. DIX HOUSE. 178 N. Beach St. 1878–1880. Frame Vernacular. 2^1/$_2$ stories. Side-gabled L-shaped house, 2-story veranda. One of only 2 houses in the town surviving from the 1870s. The Dix sisters came from Connecticut and built the home there as their winter residence. Later operated as a boarding house. Private. N.R. 1989.

Ormond Beach. THE HAMMOCKS. 311 John Anderson Highway. 1904. Shingle style. 2^1/$_2$ stories. Porch at NW corner, and porte cochere on N side. Owner, Joseph D. Price, was one of the principal founders and promoters of the community. Private. N.R. 1989.

Ormond Beach. HISTORIC WINTER RESIDENCES OF ORMOND BEACH. 1878–1925. 7 buildings, all of historical interest. Frame Vernacular. Multiple property group of 7 residences, all built before 1900. One house, the John Anderson Lodge at 71 Orchard Lane, was built for the developer of Ormond Beach. Anderson came from Portland, Oregon. Private. N.R. 1989.

Ormond Beach. LIPPINCOTT MANSION. 150 S. Beach St. 1895. Eclectic, Queen Anne elements. 3 stories, shingle siding, 3-story round tower. Built by wealthy northern family. Outstanding example of an affluent Ormond Beach family home of the period. Presently an office and residence. Private. N.R. 1985.

The Casements

Ormond Beach. ORMOND HOTEL. 15 E. Granada Blvd. 1888, 1902, 1905, 1909. Frame Vernacular. George Penfield, architect. A complex which includes a 4-story, central block and 3 wings of 4 and 5 stories. A huge sprawling frame structure, the last of Henry Flagler's frame luxury hotels. After World War I, with the rise of tourism farther down the coast, patronage declined. Private. N.R. 1980.

Ormond Beach. THE PORCHES. 176 S. Beach St. 1883. Frame Vernacular. 2^1/$_2$ stories. L-shaped plan. 2-story veranda. One of the few winter residences of the town to survive the 19th century. Private. N.R. 1988.

Ormond Beach. ROWALLAN. 235 John Anderson Hwy. 1913. Classical Revival. 2^1/$_2$ stories. 28-room wood frame residence. Large central block and symmetrical wings. Constructed as a winter residence for a retired merchandise executive from Rochester, New York. Private. N.R. 1988.

Ormond Hotel, c. 1915

Ormond Beach. TALAHLOKA. 19 Orchard Lane. 1886, 1911. Frame Vernacular. 2 stories. A hunting lodge constructed of palmetto logs. 2-story veranda surrounds the structure. Built in the style of lodges of the Adirondack Mts. A 19th-century residence made from unusual local materials. John Anderson, a local developer from Portland, Maine, had it built. Private. N.R. 1989.

Vicinity of Ormond Beach. NOCOROCO (Tomoka State Park). 2 mi. N of Ormond Beach. A.D. 1500–A.D. 1600. St. Johns period. The site of a Timucuan village first described by Alvaro Mexia in 1605. Excavations were conducted on the site in the 1940s and revealed that European acculturation had just begun at the time of Mexia's visit. Museum. Public. N.R. 1973.

Ponce Inlet. PONCE DE LEON INLET LIGHTHOUSE. S. Peninsula Dr. 1887. Conical. Brick, 168-foot tall, part of a complex that includes 3 brick 1-story buildings. The 3rd lighthouse built in the area, the 1st having been established by the British. Navigation along the coast here is especially treacherous. Museum. Public. N.R. 1972.

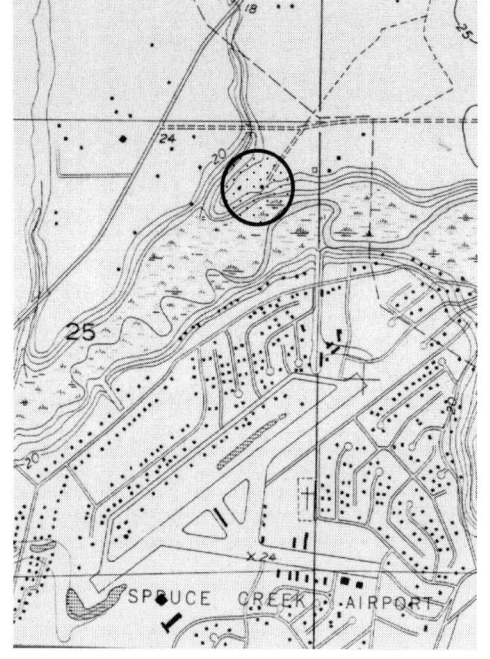

Gamble Place Historic District

Port Orange. GAMBLE PLACE HISTORIC DISTRICT. 1907–1938. 27 buildings, 25 of historical interest. Frame Vernacular predominate. Winter retreat of James N. Gamble, one of the owners of Proctor and Gamble, manufacturer of home products. Many distinguished people visited here, including President Howard Taft and John D. Rockefeller. Includes a chalet called Snow White's Cottage erected in 1938 as a playhouse. Also a Witch's Hut built in same year. Private. N.R. 1993.

Vicinity of Port Orange. DUNLAWTON PLANTATION–SUGAR MILL RUINS. Old Sugarmill Rd. 0.4 mi. E of Fl. 5A. c. 1830. Ruins of mill structures and machinery. Part of Dunlawton Plantation, 1 of 16 plantations destroyed by Seminoles (1835) ending sugar production in the area. Public. N.R. 1973.

Vicinity of Port Orange. SPRUCE CREEK MOUND COMPLEX. SW bank of Spruce Creek. A.D. 800–A.D. 1565. St. Johns II period. A large pyramidal sand mound and a smaller sand mound. First discovered in 1874. When excavated in that year a number of skeletons found. Many artifacts from the Colonial period have been discovered in the mound. Public. N.R. 1990.

Machinery, Dunlawton Sugar Mill Ruins

130

WAKULLA COUNTY

St. Marks Lighthouse

Crawfordville. OLD WAKULLA COUNTY COURTHOUSE. Church St. 1892–1893 (moved in 1948). Frame Vernacular. 2¹/₂ stories, central louvered cupola with octagonal pavilion roof. A rare example of the very functional and simple public buildings built in rural Florida during the late 19th century. Public. N.R. 1976.

St. Marks. FORT SAN MARCOS DE APALACHE. 18 mi. S of Tallahassee off Fl. 363. 1660+ . Stonework remains of Spanish fort. Since 1660 the site of three forts occupied by Spanish, French, British, and Americans. Converted to trading post in British period. Captured and occupied in 1818 by U.S. troops led by Andrew Jackson who was campaigning against the Seminole Indians. Confederates refortified the site during Civil War. Museum. Public. N.R. 1966.

Vicinity of St. Marks. ST. MARKS LIGHTHOUSE. .5 mi. W of St. Marks. St. Marks Wildlife Refuge. 1829, 1841. Conical. Stone and brick, stuccoed, 80-feet tall. Originally built too close to sea, light was relocated farther inland in 1841. Played a major role in Confederate coastal defense. Public. N.R. 1972.

Old Sopchoppy High School Gymnasium

Sopchoppy. OLD SOPCHOPPY HIGH SCHOOL GYMNASIUM. Corner of 2nd Ave. and Summer St. c. 1940. Masonry Vernacular. James A. Stripling, architect. 1 story. Built of native limestone it is a fine expression of local workmanship. A Depression-era government work project. Public. N.R. 1990.

Vicinity of Wakulla Beach. BIRD HAMMOCK. 2 mi. N of Wakulla Beach. A.D. 100–A.D. 800. Early Swift Creek period to Weeden Island period. Ceremonial and habitation site; includes 3 mounds, 2 of which are burial mounds and several midden deposits. Private. N.R. 1972.

Wakulla Springs. WAKULLA SPRINGS ARCHAEOLOGICAL AND HISTORIC DISTRICT. Prehistoric–1930s. 77 buildings, 62 of historical interest. Mediterranean Revival, Frame and Masonry Vernacular. Located in the 2902-acre Edward Ball Wakulla Springs State Park. The most significant building is Wakulla Lodge, built in the 1930s in the Mediterranean Revival style. Presently a hotel and conference center. Numerous archaeological sites within the district. Public. N.R. 1993.

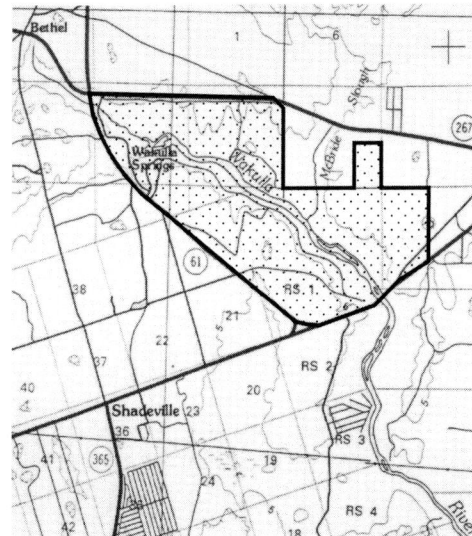

Wakulla Springs Archaeological and Historic District

DeFuniak Springs. PERRY L. BIDDLE HOUSE. 203 Scribner Ave. 1887. Frame Vernacular. 2 stories. Cross-gable roof with a simple frieze encircling the building. One of the best examples of houses constructed in an early period of the town's history. Biddle was born in Pennsylvania, but became an early West Florida developer. Private. N.R. 1992.

DeFuniak Springs. CHAUTAUQUA AUDITORIUM. Circle Dr. 1910. Classical Revival. 2 stories, frame, central dome, center and end pedimented porticos with 1st- and 2nd-floor Doric columns. Patterned after the original Chautauqua building in upstate New York, center of an adult educational and cultural organization. Played a major role in the cultural life of the region for about 25 years. Public. N.R. 1972.

DeFuniak Springs. DEFUNIAK SPRINGS HISTORIC DISTRICT. 1884–1940. 245 buildings, 166 of historical interest. Frame Vernacular and various Revival styles predominate. District contains a large share of the community's historic buildings. Most historic buildings continue to serve their original functions. Besides homes there are commercial, transportation, government, educational, religious, and medical buildings in the district. Area retains the landscape design of W.J. Van Kirk, who drew up the town plan of the city. Public and Private. N.R. 1992.

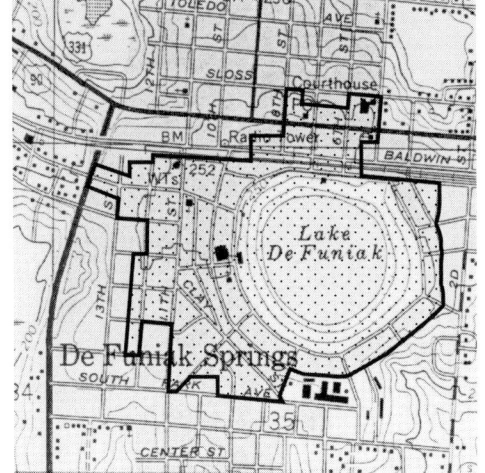

DeFuniak Springs Historic District

Chautauqua Auditorium

DeFuniak Springs. SUN BRIGHT (Sidney Catts House). 606 Live Oak Ave. 1890+. Queen Anne. 2^1/$_2$ stories, 2-story galleries on east and west facades, 3^1/$_2$-story octagonal tower. The home of Sidney Johnston Catts, Governor of Florida (1917-1921). Built during the period the Lake DeFuniak Land Co. was developing the town as a Chautauqua retreat. Private. N.R. 1970.

WASHINGTON COUNTY

Chipley. SOUTH 3RD STREET HISTORIC DISTRICT. 1887–1938. 21 buildings, 16 of historical interest. Frame Vernacular. An old, affluent neighborhood that emerged about 10 years after town was founded. Most of the town leaders lived within the district. Curiously, those who built here chose Vernacular styles instead of the then-popular Revival styles found in most other communities of the day. Private. N.R. 1989.

South 3rd Street Historic District

Vicinity of Vernon. MOSS HILL CHURCH. Jct. of Vernon and Greenhead Rds. 1857. Frame Vernacular. 1 story. The church is the oldest unaltered building in Washington County and is credited as the second building in the county with glass windows. An excellent example of unaltered frontier construction. Private. N.R. 1983.

Moss Hill Church

APPENDIX

Properties Categorized by Function and Listed Chronologically.

Agricultural

Fish Island Site. St. Johns. 18th century, 112.
Kingsley Plantation. Duval. early 19th century, 42.
Bulow Plantation Ruins. Flagler. 1826, 47.
Dunlawton Plantation–Sugar Mill Ruins. Volusia.
    c. 1830, 130.
New Smyrna Sugar Mill Ruins. Volusia. 1830, 128.
Lyndhurst Plantation. Jefferson. 1850–1855, 65.
Red Bank Plantation. Duval. 1854–1857, 39.
Yulee Sugar Mill Ruin. Citrus. c. 1860, 15.
Moseley Homestead. Hillsborough. 1886, 54.
The Kampong. Dade. c. 1890, 21.
Carlton Albert Estate. Hardee. 1903, 51.

Arts and Entertainment

Gallie's Hall and Buildings. Leon. 1873, 71.
Villa Zorayda. St. Johns. 1883, 111.
Baird Theater (Simmonson Opera House). Alachua.
    1887, 1.
Pensacola Athletic Club (Rafford Hall). Escambia.
    1889, 45.
Perkins Opera House. Jefferson. 1890, 64.
Marjorie Kinnan Rawlings House. Alachua. c. 1890, 1.
Ernest Hemingway House. Monroe. late 19th century,
    82.
Henry John Klutho House. Duval. 1908, 38.
Chautauqua Auditorium. Walton. 1910, 132.
African Queen. Monroe. 1912, 81.
Lyric Theater. Dade. c. 1914, 28.
Vizcaya. Dade. 1914–1916, 32.
Ferran Park and the Alice McClelland Memorial
    Bandshell. Lake. 1918, 65.
St. Augustine Ostrich and Alligator Farm. St. Johns.
    1921, 111.
Bok Mountain Lake Sanctuary and Singing Tower.
    Polk. 1922, 106.
Rock Gate (Coral Castle). Dade. 1923, 24.
Aladdin Theatre Building. Brevard. 1924, 8.
Florida Theatre. Indian River. 1924, 61.
Saenger Theater. Escambia. 1924–1925, 46.
Venetian Pool. Dade. 1924, 23.
Hialeah Race Track. Dade. 1925, 23.
Norton House. Palm Beach. 1925, 94.
Olympia Theater and Office Building. Dade. 1925, 29.
Tampa Theater and Office Building. Hillsborough.
    1925, 59.

Edwards Theater. Sarasota. 1926, 116.
Florida Theatre. Duval. 1926–1927, 37.
Lake Mirror Promenade. Polk. 1926, 104.
Lyric Theatre. Martin. 1926, 80.
Paramount Theatre Building. Palm Beach. 1926, 93.
St. Petersburg Lawn Bowling Club. Pinellas. 1926, 99.
Polk Theatre and Office Building. Polk. 1927, 104.
Old WRUF Radio Station. Alachua. 1928, 3.
Hervey Allen Study (The Glades Estate). Dade. 1934,
    34.
Maitland Art Center. Orange. 1937, 87.
Marine Studios (Marineland). Flagler. 1937, 48.
Little Theatre. Duval. 1938, 38.
Zora Neale Hurston House. St. Lucie. 1957, 113.

Associations, Clubs and Societies

Quincy Woman's Club. Gadsden. 1852, 50.
El Pasaje (Cherokee Club). Hillsborough. 1886, 56.
Pensacola Athletic Club. Escambia. 1889–1890, 45.
Melrose Woman's Club. Putnam. 1893, 106.
St. Michael's Creole Benevolent Association Hall.
    Escambia. 1895–1896, 46.
Morocco Temple. Duval. 1910–1911, 38.
El Centro Español of West Tampa. Hillsborough. 1912,
    56.
Masonic Temple. Duval. 1912–1916, 38.
Lake Weir Yacht Club. Marion. 1913, 78.
Centro Asturiano. Hillsborough. 1914, 55.
Young Men's Hebrew Association. Duval. 1914, 42.
Sarasota Woman's Club (Florida State Theatre).
    Sarasota. 1915, 119.
Anderson-Price Memorial Library Building. Volusia.
    1916, 128.
Circulo Cubano de Tampa (Cuban Club).
    Hillsborough. 1918, 56.
Woman's Club of Coconut Grove. Dade. 1921. 21.
Clermont Woman's Club. Lake. 1923, 1927, 65.
Woman's Club of New Smyrna. Volusia. 1924, 1934,
    128.
Boynton Woman's Club. Palm Beach. 1925, 91.
Punta Gorda Woman's Club. Charlotte. 1925, 15.
Lemon Bay Woman's Club. Sarasota. 1926, 115.
Miami Woman's Club. Dade. 1926, 29.
St. Petersburg Lawn Bowling Club. Pinellas. 1926, 99.
Woman's Club of Jacksonville. Duval. 1927, 42.
Masonic Temple of Tampa, Number 25. Hillsborough.
    1928, 58.
St. Petersburg Woman's Club. Pinellas. 1929, 99.
Woman's Club of Palmetto. Manatee. 1930, 77.
Old Belleair Garden Club. Pinellas. 1931, 95.

Woman's Club of Eustis. Lake. 1931, 66.
Keewaydin Club. Collier. 1935, 18.
Old Vero Beach Community Center. Indian River.
 1935, 62.
Coral Gables Woman's Club. Dade. 1936, 22.

Educational

Quincy Library (Quincy Academy). Gadsden.
 1850–1851, 50.
Old School House. Hillsborough. 1858, 58.
DeLand Hall. Volusia. 1884+, 126.
Epworth Hall. Alachua. 1884, 2.
Rochelle School. Alachua. c. 1885, 6.
Melrose Woman's Club (Literary and Debating
 Society). Putnam. 1893, 106.
First Coconut Grove School House. Dade. 1894, 20.
Buckingham School. Lee. 1895, 67.
Ransom School (Pagoda). Dade. 1895, 1902, 21.
South Florida Military College. Polk. 1895, 102.
Old Lakeland High School Complex. Polk. 1902, 1924,
 1926, 104.
Sanford Grammar School. Seminole. 1902, 122.
Old Jacksonville Free Public Library. Duval.
 1903–1905, 38.
David S. Walker Library. Leon. 1903, 73.
Silver Palm School. Dade. 1904, 23.
South Ward School. Pinellas. 1906, 96.
Carnegie Library. Leon. 1908, 70.
Chautauqua Auditorium. Walton. 1910, 132.
Boynton School. Palm Beach. 1913, 91.
Delray Beach Schools. Palm Beach. 1913, 91.
Neva King Cooper Elementary School. Dade. 1913, 24.
Miakka School House. Sarasota. 1914, 115.
George Miller House. Hillsborough. 1914, 55.
Plant City High School. Hillsborough. 1914, 55.
Southside School. Dade. 1914, 1922, 1925, 31.
Old Tampa Free Public Library. Hillsborough. 1915, 59.
St. Lucie High School (Ft. Pierce Elementary School).
 St. Lucie. 1915, 1924, 1926, 113.
St. Petersburg Public Library. Pinellas. 1915, 99.
Anderson-Price Memorial Library Building. Volusia.
 1916, 128.
Centennial Hall–Edward Waters College. Duval. 1916,
 36.
White Hall. Volusia. 1916, 126.
S. Cornelia Young Memorial Library. Volusia. 1916,
 1930, 126.
Edwin M. Stanton School. Duval. 1917, 41.
Bradenton Carnegie Library. Manatee. 1918, 76.
Davie School. Broward. 1918, 11.
Barberville Central High School. Volusia. 1920, 124.
Oakland Park Elementary School. Broward. 1920, 13.
Mary McLeod Bethune House. Volusia. c. 1920s, 124.
Columbia County High School. Columbia. 1921, 1926,
 20.
Coral Gables Elementary School. Dade. 1923, 22.

Old Dillard High School. Broward. 1924, 12.
Old Central Grammar School. Polk. 1925, 103.
Old Tarpon Springs High School. Pinellas. 1925, 101.
Bay Haven School. Sarasota. 1926, 115.
Central High School. Pinellas. 1926+, 98.
Charlotte High School. Charlotte. 1926, 14.
Oakland Park Elementary School. Broward. 1926, 13.
Old Fort Braden School. Leon. 1926, 73.
Osprey School. Sarasota. 1926, 115.
Sarasota High School. Sarasota. 1926, 119
Southside School. Sarasota. 1926, 119.
Deerfield School. Broward. 1927, 11.
Paul Lawrence Dunbar School. Lee. 1927, 68.
Miami Senior High School. Dade. 1927, 28.
Old Palm Beach Junior College Building. Palm Beach.
 1927, 94.
Miami Edison Senior High School. Dade. 1928–1931,
 28.
Old P.K. Yonge Laboratory School. Alachua. 1934, 3.
Keewaydin Club. Collier. 1935, 18.
Old Vero Beach Community Center. Indian River.
 1935, 62.
Leon High School. Leon. 1936, 72.
Old Sopchoppy High School Gymnasium. Wakulla. c.
 1940, 131.

Engineering

Boulware Spring Waterworks. Alachua. 1895–1908, 1.
I. and E. Greenwald Steam Engine No. 1058. Dade.
 1906, 27.
Lock No. 1, North New River Canal. Broward. 1911,
 13.
Old City Waterworks. Leon. 1923, 73.
City Water Works. Sarasota. 1926, 116.

Government

Cascades Park. Leon. 1820–1840, 70.
Plaza Ferdinand II. Escambia. 1821, 46.
Florida State Capitol (Old Capitol). Leon. 1839, 71.
Manatee County Courthouse (Original). Manatee.
 1859–1860, 77.
House of Refuge at Gilbert's Bar. Martin. 1876, 80.
Osceola County Courthouse. Osceola. 1886-1890, 90.
Old Post Office and Customhouse. Monroe. 1889, 1891,
 82.
Clay County Courthouse. Clay. 1890, 16.
Little White House (Quarters A). Monroe. 1890, 82.
St. Johns County Jail. St. Johns, c. 1891, 110.
Old Wakulla County Courthouse. Wakulla. 1892, 131.
Old Hamilton County Jail. Hamilton. 1893, 51.
City of Miami Cemetery. Dade. 1897, 25.
Catherine Street Fire Station. Duval. 1902, 36.
Federal Building, U.S. Courthouse, Postal Station.
 Hillsborough. 1902, 56.
Old Bradford County Courthouse. Bradford. 1902, 7.

Old Jacksonville Free Public Library. Duval. 1903, 38.
Old Calhoun County Courthouse. Calhoun. 1904+, 13.
Old Baker County Courthouse. Baker. 1908, 6.
Old Live Oak City Hall. Suwannee. 1908–1909, 123.
Old Polk County Courthouse. Polk. 1908, 1926, 102.
U.S. Post Office. Alachua. 1909, 4.
Old Citrus County Courthouse. Citrus. 1912, 16.
Old Taylor County Jail. Taylor. 1912, 123.
Old U.S. Post Office and Courthouse. Dade. 1912, 29.
Lee County Courthouse. Lee. 1915, 68.
Old Tarpon Springs City Hall. Pinellas. 1915, 1947, 101.
Tampa City Hall. Hillsborough. 1915, 59.
St. Petersburg Public Library. Pinellas. 1915, 99.
United States Post Office. Pinellas. 1916, 99.
Old Pinellas County Courthouse. Pinellas. 1917, 1924, 1926, 96.
Bradenton Carnegie Library. Manatee. 1918, 76.
Fire Station No. 4. Dade. 1922, 26.
Windermere Town Hall. Orange. 1922, 89.
Administration Buildings. Palm Beach. 1925, 90.
Dade County Courthouse. Dade. 1925, 25.
Boca Raton Old City Hall. Palm Beach. 1926, 90.
Fire Station No. 2. Dade. 1926, 26.
Highlands County Courthouse. Highlands. 1926, 53.
Central Station. Highlands. 1927, 52.
Coral Gables City Hall. Dade. 1927–1928, 21.
Kelsey City City Hall. Palm Beach. 1927, 92.
Old Hendry Courthouse. Hendry. 1927, 52.
Sarasota County Courthouse. Sarasota. 1927, 119.
Lake Wales City Hall. Polk. 1928, 105.
Old Lake Worth City Hall. Palm Beach. 1929, 92.
Cleveland Street Post Office. Pinellas. 1932, 95.
U. S. Post Office. Volusia. 1932, 126.
U.S. Post Office and Courthouse. Dade. 1933, 31.
U.S. Post Office–Federal Building. Sarasota. 1934, 120.
Old Perry Post Office. Taylor. 1935, 123.
U.S. Post Office. Palm Beach. 1937, 93.
Coral Gables Police and Fire Station. Dade. 1939, 22.
Holly Hill Municipal Building. Volusia. 1942, 127.
Cape Canaveral Air Force Launch Pads Nos. 5,6,13,14,19,26,34, and Control. Brevard. 1950+, 8.
Launch Complex 39. Brevard. 1968, 11.

Hotels and Apartments

Island Hotel. Levy. 1861, 75.
Lakeside Inn. Lake. 1883+, 66.
El Modelo Block. Duval. 1886–1889, 36.
Alcazar Hotel. St. Johns. 1887, 1889, 108.
Hotel Ponce de Leon. St. Johns. 1887, 109.
Longwood Hotel (Longwood Village Inn). 1887, 121.
Ormond Hotel. Volusia. 1888, 1902, 129.
Tampa Bay Hotel. Hillsborough. 1888, 59.
Belleview-Biltmore Hotel. Pinellas. 1896+, 95.
Bishop Andrews Hotel. Madison. 1902, 76.
Hotel Blanche. Columbia. 1902, 20.

Stranahan House (The Pioneer House). Broward. 1902, 12.
Plaza Hotel. Duval. 1903, 39.
New River Inn (City Hall Annex). Broward. 1905, 12.
Gulfview Hotel. Okaloosa. 1906, 86.
Hotel Thomas. Alachua. 1906–1910, 1928, 2.
San Carlos Hotel. Escambia. 1909+, 47.
Mountain Lake Colony House. Polk. 1916, 1921, 1925, 105.
Kentucky Home. Dade. 1918, 28.
Alexander Hotel. Pinellas. 1919, 97.
Old Palmetto Hotel. Indian River. 1921, 61.
Demarcay Hotel. Sarasota. 1922, 116.
Martina Apartments. Dade. 1922, 28.
Gulf Stream Hotel (El Nuevo Hotel). Palm Beach. 1923, 92.
Olds Hall. Volusia. 1923, 125.
310 W. Church Street Apartments (Ambassador Hotel). Duval. 1923, 41.
Via Mizner. Palm Beach. 1923, 93.
Algonquin Apartments. Dade. 1924, 24.
Frances-Carlton Apartments. Sarasota. 1924, 117.
Breakers Hotel Complex. Palm Beach. 1925, 92.
Casa Marina Hotel. Duval. 1925, 43.
Chalet Suzanne. Polk. 1925, 105.
Dennis Hotel. Pinellas. 1925, 98.
Priscilla Apartments. Dade. 1925, 30.
Ritz Apartments. Marion. 1925, 79.
Vinoy Park Hotel. Pinellas. 1925, 100.
Arcade Hotel. Pinellas. 1926, 101.
Carling Hotel. Duval. 1926, 36.
Clewiston Inn. Hendry. 1926, 52.
Dixie Court Hotel. Palm Beach. 1926, 93.
Dixie Hotel (Seagle Building). Alachua. 1926+, 2.
Dixie Walesbilt Hotel. Polk. 1926, 105.
El Vernona-Broadway Apartments. Sarasota. 1926, 117.
Grand Concourse Apartments. Dade. 1926, 33.
Hibiscus Apartments. Palm Beach. 1926, 94.
Le Claire Apartments. Hillsborough. 1926, 57.
Miami-Biltmore Hotel. Dade. 1926, 23.
Old Palmetto Hotel. Indian River. 1926, 61.
Polk Hotel. Polk. 1926, 103.
Vineta Hotel. Palm Beach. 1926, 93.
John Edmunds Apartment House (Mirador). Escambia. 1927, 44.
Harder Hall. Sebring. 1927, 53.
Hotel Venice. Sarasota. 1927, 121.
Marion Hotel. Marion. 1927, 78.
Don Ce Sar Hotel. Pinellas. 1928, 100.
Driftwood Inn and Restaurant. Indian River. 1937, 61.

Indian Settlements

Torreya State Park. Liberty. Prehistoric–19th century, 75.
Arch Creek Historic and Archaeological Site. Dade. Prehistoric–19th century, 33.

Warm Mineral Springs. Sarasota. c. 8000 B.C., 121.
Little Salt Springs. Sarasota. c. 5000 B.C., 115.
Windover Archaeological Site. Brevard. c. 5000 B.C., 11.
Indian Fields. Brevard. 4000 B.C.–2000 B.C.,
    500 B.C.–A.D. 800, A.D. 800–A.D. 1565, 10.
Moccasin Island. Brevard. 4000 B.C., 9.
Persimmons Mound. Brevard. 4000 B.C–2000 B.C.,
    500 B.C.–A.D. 800, A.D. 800–A.D. 1565, 9.
Turtle Mound (Duda Ranch Mound). Brevard.
    4000 B.C.–2000 B.C., 500 B.C.–A.D. 800,
    A.D. 800–A.D. 1565, 10.
Kimball Island Midden Archaeological Site. Lake.
    c. 3000 B.C., 65.
Shell Bluff Landing. St. Johns. 3000 B.C.–A.D. 1300, 108.
Osprey Archaeological and Historic Site. Sarasota.
    c. 2150 B.C.–A.D. 1900, 115.
Bowers Bluff Middens Archaeological District. Lake.
    c. 2000 B.C., 65.
Twin Mounds Archaeological District. Orange.
    2000 B.C., 89.
Madira Bickel Mound. Manatee. c. 1000 B.C.–A.D. 1600,
    78.
Upper Tampa Archaeological District. Hillsborough.
    c. 1000 B.C., 60.
Princess Mound. Clay. 800 B.C.–A.D. 1300, 16.
Bay Pines Site. Pinellas. 500 B.C.–A.D. 1000, 95.
Bubba Midden. Clay. 500 B.C.–A.D. 800, 17.
Garden Patch Archaeological Site. Dixie. 500 B.C.–
    A.D. 400, 35.
Jupiter Inlet Historic and Archaeological Site. Palm
    Beach. c. 500 B.C., 91.
Pierce Site. Franklin. c. 500 B.C.–A.D. 1400, 48.
The Plaza Site. Collier. c. 500 B.C.–A.D. 1700, 18.
Yent Mound. Franklin. c. 500 B.C.–A.D. 500, 49.
Big Mound City. Palm Beach. c. 300 B.C.–A.D. 1660, 91.
Fort Walton Mound. Okaloosa. c. A.D. 0–A.D. 50 , 86.
Yon Mound and Village Site. Liberty. c. A.D. 0–A.D. 350
    and A.D. 800–A.D. 1500 , 75.
Ross Hammock Site. Volusia. c. A.D. 1–A.D. 1400, A.D.
    1860+ , 128.
Bird Hammock. Wakulla. c. A.D. 100–A.D. 800, 131.
Otis Hare Archeological Site. Liberty. c. A.D. 100–
    A.D. 700, 75.
Rock Mound Archaeological Site. Monroe. c. A.D. 100–
    A.D. 1300, 81.
Hinson Mounds. Collier. c. A.D. 400–A.D. 90 , 18.
Platt Island. Collier. c. A.D. 400–A.D. 900, 18.
Turner River Site. Collier. c. A.D. 400–A.D. 1400, 19.
Burns Lake Site. Collier. c. A.D. 500-A.D. 140 , 19.
Grand Site. Duval. c. A.D. 500–A.D. 1600, 42.
Mullet Key. Citrus. c. A.D. 500–A.D. 1500, 15.
Porter's Bar Site. Franklin. c. A.D. 500, 48.
Weeden Island Site. Pinellas. c. A.D. 500–A.D. 1000, 100.
Cockroach Key. Hillsborough. c. A.D. 700–A.D. 1500, 55.
Demere Key. Lee. c. A.D. 800–A.D. 1700, 69.
Halfway Creek Site. Collier. c. A.D. 800–A.D. 1400, 18.
C.J. Ostl Site. Collier. c. 800 A.D.–A.D. 1200, 18.

Spruce Creek Mound Complex. Volusia. A.D. 800–
    A.D. 1565, 130.
Turtle Mound. Volusia. c. A.D. 800–A.D. 1400 , 128.
Cayson Mound and Village Site. Calhoun. c. A.D. 900–
    A.D. 1500, 13.
Crystal River Indian Mounds. Citrus. c. A.D. 1000–
    A.D. 1500 , 15.
Sugar Pot Site. Collier. c. A.D. 1000–A.D. 1400 , 19.
Mount Royal. Putnam. c. A.D. 1200–A.D. 1600 , 107.
Waddells Mill Pond Site. Jackson. c. A.D. 1200–
    A.D. 1500 , 63.
Josslyn Island Site. Lee. c. A.D. 1300–A.D. 1600 , 69.
Lake Jackson Mounds. Leon. c. A.D. 1300 , 72.
Pineland Site. Lee. c. A.D. 1300 , 69.
Mound Key. Lee. c. A.D. 1500 , 67.
Nocoroco (Tomoka State Park) c. A.D. 1500–A.D. 1600,
    130.
Safety Harbor Site. Pinellas. c. A.D. 1500–A.D. 1700 , 96.
Mission of San Juan del Puerto Archaeological Site.
    Duval. c. 1578–1763, 42.
San José de Ocuya. Jefferson. A.D. 1600–1703, 64.
San Miguél de Asile Mission Site. Jefferson. A.D. 1607 ,
    63.
San Luis de Apalache. Leon. A.D. 1633–1663, 73.
San Juan de Aspalaga Site. Jefferson. A.D. 1640–1704 ,
    65.
San Pedro y San Pablo de Patale. Leon. mid-17th
    century, 74.
Escambe (San Cosmo y San Damias de Escambe).
    Leon. mid-17th century, 74.

Manufacturing and Minerals

Spanish Coquina Quarries. St. Johns. late 17th century,
    112.
Arcadia Mill Site, Santa Rosa. 1817–1855, 114.
El Modelo Block. Duval. 1886-1889, 36.
Ybor Factory Building. Hillsborough. 1886, 60.
Solla-Carcaba Cigar Factory. St. Johns. 1909, 111.
Roth Cigar Factory. Sarasota. 1923, 118.
Ryan and Company Lumberyard. Orange. 1924, 87.
Florida Power and Light Company Ice Plant. Brevard.
    1927, 8.
Coca-Cola Bottling Plant. Marion. 1939, 78.

Medical

Old St. Luke's Hospital. Duval. 1878, 39.
Brewster Hospital. Duval. 1885, 35.
Dr. James M. Jackson Office. Dade. 1905, 28.
Fernald-Laughton Memorial Hospital. Seminole.
    c. 1910, 1919, 1927, 122.
Pensacola Hospital. Escambia. 1915, 46.
Miami City Hospital. Dade. 1918, 28.
Old Deland Memorial Hospital. Volusia. 1920, 1926,
    126.
Carroll Building. Orange. 1932, 86.

Military

De Soto National Memorial. Manatee. 1539–1543, 77.
Fort Caroline National Memorial. Duval. 1564, 42.
Fort Matanzas National Monument. St. Johns. 1565, 112.
Fort San Marcos de Apalache. Wakulla. 1660+, 131.
Castillo de San Marcos National Monument. St. Johns. 1672–1696, 108.
Fort George Site. Escambia. 1778, 44.
Sanchez Powder House Site. St. Johns. late 18th century, 111.
Fort Gadsden Historical Memorial (Negro Fort). Franklin. 1814–1818, 49.
Indian Key. Monroe. 1825–1845, 83.
Fort Pickens. Escambia. 1834, 47.
Dade Battlefield Historical Memorial. Sumter. 1835, 122.
Fort Cooper. Citrus. 1836, 16.
Fort Foster (Camp Foster, Fort Alabama) Hillsborough. 1836, 60.
Burnsed Blockhouse. Baker. 1837, 7.
Okeechobee Battlefield. Okeechobee. 1837, 86.
Fort Pierce Site. St. Lucie. 1838, 112.
Old West Palm Beach National Guard Armory. Palm Beach. 1939, 94.
U.S. Arsenal–Officers' Quarters. Gadsden. 1839, 49.
Egmont Key. Hillsborough. 1840–1945, 60.
Fort Zachary Taylor. Monroe. 1845–1866, 82.
U.S. Naval Station. Monroe. 1845–1942, 83.
Fort Jefferson National Monument. Monroe. 1846+, 80.
Fort Clinch. Nassau. 1847+, 85.
Payne's Creek Massacre–Fort Chokonikla Site. Hardee. 1849-51, 51.
U.S. Coast Guard Headquarters, Key West Station. Monroe. 1856-1861, 83.
West Martello Tower. Monroe. 1861–1866, 83.
Yellow Bluff Fort. Duval. 1862, 43.
Martello Gallery–Key West Art and History Museum. Monroe. 1862, 82.
Olustee Battlefield (Battle of Ocean Pond). Baker. 1864, 7.
Natural Bridge Battlefield. Leon. 1865, 74.
Fort de Soto Batteries. Pinellas. 1898-1945, 100.
The Armory. Monroe. c. 1900, 81.
Old Haines City National Guard Armory. Polk. 1932, 103.

Offices and Financial Institutions

Union Bank. Leon. 1841, 73.
Rogers Building (English Club). Orange. 1886+, 89.
Dyal-Upchurch Building. Duval. 1901–1902, 36.
Thiesen Building. Escambia. 1901+, 47.
Palm Beach Mercantile Company. Palm Beach. c. 1902, 1916, 1923, 94.

American National Bank Building. Escambia. 1908+, 43.
Merchants Bank Building. Volusia. 1910, 1926, 125.
Townsend Building. Union. c. 1910, 124.
St. James Building. Duval. 1911–1912, 40.
Old First National Bank of Punta Gorda. Charlotte. 1912, 14.
Hillsboro State Bank Building. Hillsborough. 1914, 54.
Old Bunnell State Bank. Flagler. 1917, 47.
Hähn Building. Dade. 1921, 27.
Florida Baptist Convention Building (Rogers Building). Duval. 1924–1925, 37.
Administration Buildings. Palm Beach. 1925, 90.
Buckman and Ulmer Building. Duval. 1925, 35.
City National Bank Building. Dade. 1925, 25.
Congress Building. Dade. 1925, 25.
Freedom Tower. Dade. 1925, 26.
Groover-Stewart Drug Company Building. Duval. 1925, 37.
Huntington Building. Dade. 1925, 27.
J. & S. Building. Dade. 1925, 27.
Meyer-Kiser Building. Dade. 1925–1926, 28.
Palm Beach Daily News Building. Palm Beach. 1925, 92.
Sarasota Herald Building. Sarasota. 1925, 119.
Shoreland Arcade. Dade. 1925, 30.
South Atlantic Investment Corporation Building. Duval. 1925, 41.
Tinker Building. Orange. 1925+, 89.
Dixie Hotel (Seagle Building). Alachua. 1926, 1.
Ingraham Building. Dade. 1926, 27.
Sarasota Times Building. Sarasota. 1926, 119.
Security Building. Dade. 1926, 30.
H.W. Smith Building. Charlotte. 1926, 15.
Exchange Bank Building. Leon. 1927, 71.
Snell Arcade. Pinellas. 1928, 99.
S.H. Kress and Company Building. Hillsborough. 1929, 57.
Title and Trust Company. Duval. 1929, 41.
S.H. Kress and Company Building. Sarasota. 1932, 118.
S.H. Kress and Company Building. Volusia. 1932, 125.
Alfred I. du Pont Building. Dade. 1937, 26.

Religious

Old Spanish Monastery. Dade. 1141, 33.
Mission of San Juan del Puerto Archaeological Site. Duval. c. 1578–1763, 42.
San Miguél de Asile Mission Site. Jefferson. 1607–1704, 63.
San Luis de Apalache. Leon. 1633, 73.
San Luis de Aspalaga Site. Jefferson. 1640–1704, 65.
Escambe (San Cosmo y San Damias de Escambe). Leon. mid-17th century, 74.
San José de Ocuya Site. Jefferson. mid-17th century, 64.
San Pedro y San Pablo de Patale. Leon. mid-17th century, 74.

Cathedral of St. Augustine. St. Johns. 1797, 109.
Old Christ Church. Escambia. 1830–1832, 45.
First Presbyterian Church. Leon. 1835–1838, 71.
Trinity Episcopal Church. Franklin. 1839, 48.
Methodist-Episcopal Church at Black Creek. Clay. 1847, 17.
Orange Springs Methodist Episcopal Church and Cemetery. Marion. c. 1852, 1867, 80.
St. Mark's Episcopal Church. Putnam. 1854, 107.
Moss Hill Church. Washington. 1857, 133.
St. Joseph's Church Buildings. Escambia. 1857, 1892, 1920, 46.
Pisgah United Methodist Church. Leon. 1858–1859, 74.
Old Philadelphia Presbyterian Church. Gadsden. 1859, 50.
St. Mary's Episcopal Church and Rectory. Santa Rosa. 1872+, 114.
St. Margaret's Episcopal Church. Clay. 1875, 16.
St. Mary's Church. Clay. 1878, 16.
United Methodist Church. Hamilton. 1878, 51.
St. John's Episcopal Church. Leon. 1881, 73.
All Saints' Episcopal Church. Volusia. 1883, 127.
Grace United Methodist Church. St. Johns. 1887, 109.
St. Andrew's Episcopal Church. Duval. 1887, 40.
St. Gabriel's Episcopal Church. Brevard. 1887. 10.
Andrews Memorial Chapel. Pinellas. 1888, 96.
Holy Trinity Episcopal Church. Lake. 1888, 66.
Old St. Luke's Episcopal Church and Cemetery. Brevard. 1888, 8.
Christ Church (Episcopal). Polk. 1889, 103.
St. Mark's Episcopal Church. Polk. 1890, 103.
Mount Zion A.M.E. Church. Marion. 1891, 79.
Community Chapel of Melbourne Beach. Brevard. 1892, 1942, 8.
City of Miami Cemetery. Dade. 1897-1920, 25.
First Baptist Church. Madison. 1898+, 76.
Bethel Baptist Institutional Church. Duval. 1904, 35.
Mount Zion A.M.E. Church. Duval. 1905, 38.
Church of the Immaculate Conception. Duval. 1907, 36.
Old Holy Redeemer Catholic Church. Osceola. 1912, 90.
First Christian Church. Escambia. 1913, 44.
St. James A.M.E. Church. Seminole. 1913, 122.
St. Joseph's Catholic Church. Brevard. 1914, 9.
Mt. Pilgrim African Baptist Church. Santa Rosa. 1916, 114.
Plymouth Congregational Church. Dade. 1917, 21.
Brickell Mausoleum. Dade. 1921, 24.
Gesu Church. Dade. 1922, 26.
Episcopal House of Prayer. Hillsborough. 1923, 56.
First Baptist Church. Polk. 1923, 105.
Trinity Episcopal Cathedral. Dade. 1923, 31.
Coral Gables Congregational Church. Dade. 1924, 22.
First Methodist Church of St. Petersburg. Pinellas. 1924-1926, 98.
Riverside Baptist Church. Duval. 1924, 39.

Central Baptist Church. Dade. 1926, 25.
First Church of Christ Scientist (St. George Orthodox Church). Orange. 1926, 87.
Church of the Holy Spirit. Polk. 1927, 105.
Greater Bethel AME Church. Dade. 1927, 27.
Beth Jacob Social Hall and Congregation. Dade. 1928, 1936, 32.
Mount Zion Baptist Church. Dade. 1928, 29.
St. John's Baptist Church. Dade. 1940, 30.

Residential, Rural

Bellevue (Murat House). Leon. early 19th century, 74.
Kingsley Plantation. Duval. early 19th century, 42.
Joshua Davis House. Gadsden. 1827, 49.
Torreya State Park (Gregory House). Liberty. c. 1830, 75.
Burnsed Blockhouse. Baker. 1837, 7.
Erwin House. Jackson. c. 1840, 62.
Asa May House. Jefferson. c. 1840, 63.
Willoughby Gregory House (Krausland). Gadsden. c. 1843, 49.
Lafitte Log House. Jefferson. c. 1844, 63.
Robert Gamble House. Manatee. 1845–1850, 77.
Kanapaha (Haile Plantation). Alachua. c. 1850, 5.
Lyndhurst Plantation. Jefferson. 1850, 65.
Red Bank Plantation. Duval. 1854–1857, 39.
Turnbull-Ritter House. Jefferson. 1856, 63.
Great Oaks (Bryan Mansion). Jackson. 1857-1861, 62.
Dennis-Coxetter House. Jefferson. c. 1859, 63.
Lloyd-Bond House. Jefferson. c. 1864, 63.
Hull-Hawkins House. Suwannee. c. 1866, 123.
Palmer House. Jefferson. c. 1867, 64.
DeBary Hall. Volusia. 1871, 126.
Alfred Ayer House. Marion. 1885, 79.
T.R. Ayer House. Marion. 1885, 79.
General Robert Bullock House. Marion. 1885, 79.
Coles-Buzzett Farm House. Leon. 1885, 70.
Moseley Homestead. Hillsborough. 1886, 54.
Talahlaka. Volusia. 1886, 1911, 130.
Dr. George E. Hill House. Brevard. 1890, 8.
Marjorie Kinnan Rawlings House. Alachua. c. 1890, 1.
James Riley Josselyn House. Marion. c. 1895, 78.
Carlton Albert Estate. Hardee. 1903, 51.
Florida Pioneer Museum. Dade. 1904, 23.
Casa de Josefina. Polk. 1923, 106.
El Retiro. Polk. 1930, 106.
Hervey Allen Study (The Glades Estate). Dade. 1934, 34.

Residential, Urban

Avero House. St. Johns. early 18th century, 108.
Lindsley House. St. Johns. early 18th century, 109.
Rodriques-Avero-Sanchez House. St. Johns. early 18th century, 110.

Gonzales-Alvarez House (Oldest House). St. Johns.
c. 1723, 1775–1786, 109.

O'Reilly House. St. Johns. c. 1763, 110.

Llambias House. St. Johns. late 18th century, 109.

Ximenez-Fatio House. St. Johns. 1797–1802, 111.

Lavalle House. Escambia. c. 1803–1815, 45.

The Grove. Leon. c. 1825, 71.

The Columns. Leon. c. 1830, 70.

Wirick-Simmons House. Jefferson. 1830s, 65.

Palmer-Perkins House. Jefferson. c. 1836, 64.

Dr. Joseph Y. Porter House. Monroe. 1838, 83.

Ely-Criglar House. Jackson. c. 1840, 62.

David G. Raney House. Franklin. c. 1840, 48.

Theophilus West House. Jackson. c. 1840, 63.

Judge P.W. White House. Gadsden. c. 1843, 50.

Goodwood (Old Croom Mansion). Leon. 1844, 71.

Bronson-Mulholland House. Putnam. 1845, 107.

Stockton-Curry House. Gadsden. c. 1845, 50.

Clark-Chalker House. Clay. c. 1850s, 17.

John S. Sammis House. Duval. 1850s, 40.

Brokaw-McDougall House (Peres-Brokaw House).
Leon. c. 1850, 69.

E.C. Love House. Gadsden. c. 1850, 49.

Johnson-Caldwell House. Leon. c. 1852, 72.

Maj. James B. Bailey House (Bailey Retirement Center).
Alachua. 1854, 1.

Wardlaw-Smith House. Madison. c. 1860, 76.

Merrick-Simmons House. Nassau. 1861, 85.

Hull-Hawkins House. Suwannee. 1866, 123.

Matheson House. Alachua. 1867, 3.

Charles William Jones House. Escambia. 1869+, 44.

Ollinger-Cobb House. Santa Rosa. c. 1870, 114.

Clara Barkley Dorr House. Escambia. 1871, 43.

King-Hooton. Escambia. 1871, 44.

Denham-Lacy House. Jefferson. 1874, 64.

William Kimbrough Pendleton House (The Palms).
Lake. c. 1876, 66.

Napoleon Bonaparte Broward House. Duval. 1878, 35.

Comstock-Harris House (East Bank). Orange. 1878, 89.

Dix House. Volusia. 1878-1880, 129.

Rogers House. Volusia. 1878, 125.

Hubbard House (San Sui). Putnam. c. 1879, 106.

Dial-Goza House. Madison. c. 1880, 76.

J.O. Douglas House. Pinellas. 1880+, 96.

The Porches. Volusia. 1883, 129.

Safford House. Pinellas. 1883, 101.

Villa Zorayda. St. Johns. 1883

William H. Waterhouse House. Orange. 1884, 87.

Withers-Maguire House. Orange. c. 1884, 87.

Bradlee-McIntyre House. Seminole. 1885, 121.

Fairbanks House. Nassau. 1885, 84.

Johnson-Wolff House. Hillsborough. 1885, 57.

Tabby House (C.W. Lewis House). Nassau. 1885, 85.

Bishop B. Blackwell House. Suwannee. 1886, 123.

Thomas Edison Winter Estate. Lee. 1886+, 68.

John B. Stetson House. Volusia. 1886, 127.

Waite-Davis House. Orange. 1886, 87.

Perry L. Biddle House. Walton. 1887, 132.

Mitchell-Tibbets House. Orange. 1887, 86.

Howard Thurman House. Volusia. c. 1888, 125.

George Randolph Frisbee Jr. House. Clay. 1889, 17.

Ingleside. Pinellas. 1889, 96.

The Casements. Volusia. c. 1890, 129.

Eduardo H. Gato House. Monroe. c. 1890, 82.

Haskell-Long House. Clay, 1890, 17.

The Kampong. Dade. c. 1890, 21.

Neilson House. Alachua. 1890, 6.

Palm Cottage. Collier. 1890+, 19.

Sun Bright (Sidney Catts House). Walton. 1890+, 133.

The Ralph M. Munroe House (The Barnacle). Dade.
1891, 21.

John Denham Palmer House. Nassau. c. 1891, 85.

Pritchard House. Brevard. c. 1891, 10.

John C. Williams House. Pinellas. 1891, 100.

Mote-Morris House. Lake. 1892, 66.

John Gilmore Riley House. Leon. 1892, 73.

Judge George Robbins House. Brevard. c. 1892, 10.

Joseph W. Russ, Jr., House. Jackson. 1892-1896, 1910,
62.

Donnelly House. Lake. 1893, 66.

Markland (Andrew Anderson House). St. Johns. 1893,
1899, 1901, 110.

Dr. P. Phillips House. Orange. 1893, 88.

T.C. Taliaferro House. Hillsborough. 1893, 59.

T.G. Henderson House. Columbia. 1894, 20.

E.C. Smith Home. Marion. 1894, 79.

Bailey House. Nassau. 1895, 84.

Henry Ford Estate. Lee. c. 1895, 68.

Benjamin Franklin Holland House. Polk. 1895, 102.

Lippincott Mansion. Volusia. 1895, 129.

John Lee McFarlin House. Gadsden. c. 1895, 50.

Mary Phifer McKenzie House. Alachua. 1895+, 3.

Anna Stevens House. Volusia. 1895, 127.

Wager House. Brevard. c. 1895, 10.

Charles Deering Estate. Dade. 1896, 23.

Perry L. Biddle House. Walton. 1887, 132.

George A. Chalker House. Clay. 1897, 17.

Louis Ducros House. Pinellas. 1897, 95.

Palm Cottage. Dade. c. 1897, 30.

Anderson-Frank House. Hillsborough. 1898, 55.

Edward Hill Brewer House (The Palms). Orange.
1899+, 89.

Coral Gables House. Dade. 1899, 1906, 22.

Ernest Hemingway House. Monroe. Late nineteenth
century, 82.

Henry Morrison Flagler House (Whitehall). Palm
Beach. 1901, 92.

Murphy-Burroughs House. Leon. 1901, 68.

Veillard House. Pinellas. 1901, 99.

Captain Hammond House. St. Lucie. 1902, 113.

Thomas V. Porter House. Duval. 1902, 39.

John and Elizabeth Shaw Sunday House. Palm Beach.
1902 , 91

A.C. Freeman House. Charlotte. 1903, 14.

Xavier Lopez House. St. Johns. 1903, 111.
E.B. Shelfer House. Gadsden. 1903, 50.
Casements Annex. Volusia. 1904, 128.
The Hammocks. Volusia. 1904, 129.
William E. Curtis House. Hillsborough. 1905, 56.
Dr. James M. Jackson Office. Dade. 1905, 28.
Potter House. Pinellas. 1905, 98.
George Adderley House. Monroe. c. 1906, 84.
Dr. C.B. Wilson House. Sarasota. c. 1906, 80.
Horace Duncan House. Columbia. 1907, 20.
Amos Kling House. Volusia. 1907, 125.
Hutchinson House. Hillsborough. 1908, 57.
Henry John Klutho House. Duval. 1908, 38.
Cresthaven (Boston House). St. Lucie. 1909, 112.
Robert L. McKenzie House (Belle Booth House). Bay.
   1909, 7.
Stovall House. Hillsborough. 1909, 59.
Boone House. Pinellas. 1910-1920, 97.
Frosard W. Budington House. Clay. 1910, 17.
Clifford House. Lake. 1910, 65.
Dr. Joseph D. Halton House. Sarasota. 1910, 117.
Bamma Vickers Lawson House. Indian River. c. 1911,
   61.
Spell House. Brevard. c. 1911, 10.
Halissee Hall. Dade. 1912, 27.
James W. Townsend House. Marion. 1912, 80.
J.W. Warner House. Dade. 1912, 32.
Rowallan. Volusia. 1913, 129.
313 NW 7th Avenue. Alachua. c. 1913, 4.
D. A. Dorsey House. Dade. c. 1914, 25.
Journey's End. Lee. 1914, 67.
Vizcaya (James Deering Estate). Dade. 1914–1916, 32.
J.J. Bridges House. Orange. 1916, 87.
Colonial Estate. Osceola. 1916, 89.
Edson Keith Estate. Sarasota. 1916, 117.
Leiman House. Hillsborough. 1916, 58.
Porcher House. Brevard. 1916, 8.
Sample Estate (McDougald House). Broward. 1916, 13.
Mickens House. Palm Beach. 1917, 94.
El Jardin. Dade. 1918, 20.
Edward Hainz House. Highlands. 1919, 53.
Sebring H. Orvel House. Highland. 1919, 53.
Mary McLeod Bethune House. Volusia. 1920s, 124.
Bonnet House. Broward. 1920, 12.
Paul L. Vinson House. Highlands. 1920, 53.
William Gray Warden Residence. Palm Beach. 1922, 93.
El Real Retiro. Volusia. 1923, 127.
Freedman-Raulerson House. Okeechobee. 1923, 86.
Mar-A-Lago National Historic Landmark. Palm Beach.
   1923, 92.
John Swearingen House. Polk. 1923+, 103.
Via Mizner. Palm Beach. 1923, 93.
Earle House. Sarasota. 1924, 116.
Alderman House. Lee. 1925, 67.
Karl Bickel House. Sarasota. 1925, 115.
F.A. DeCanizares House. Sarasota. 1925, 116.
Field Estate. Sarasota. 1925, 117.

Norton House. Palm Beach. 1925, 94.
San Jose Estates Gatehouse. Duval. 1925, 40.
J.G. Whitfield Estate. Sarasota. 1925, 120.
Joseph Wesley Young House. Broward. 1925, 12.
Fred C. Aiken House. Palm Beach. 1926, 90.
Bacheller-Brewer Model Home Estate. Sarasota. 1926,
   115.
Casa Caprona. St. Lucie. 1926, 112.
Casa de Muchas Flores. Pinellas. 1926, 97.
Corrigan House. Sarasota. 1926, 116.
El Patio. Sarasota. 1926, 117.
Howey House. Lake. 1926, 66.
Jewett-Thompson House. Lee. 1926, 68.
Dr. Walter Kennedy House. Sarasota. 1926, 118.
L.D. Reagin House. Sarasota. 1926, 118.
Thomas House. Sarasota. 1926, 119.
Villa Bianca. Charlotte. 1926, 15.
H.B. Williams House. Sarasota. 1926, 120.
Covington House. Leon. 1927, 71.
Epping Forest. Duval. 1927, 36.
Lane-Towers House. Duval. 1927–1928, 38.
Tampania House. Hillsborough. 1927, 59.
Elizabeth Haines House. Highlands. 1928, 52.
Donald Roebling Estate (Spotswood). Pinellas. 1929,
   96.
Seagate (Powel Crosley, Jr. House). Manatee. 1929, 77.
Casa Coe da Sol. Pinellas. 1931, 97.
Governor John W. Martin House (Apalachee). Leon.
   1933-1934, 72.
John Huttig Estate. Orange. 1934, 88.
Judge Henry F. Gregory House. Indian River. 1937, 61.
Lewis House. Leon. 1954, 72.
Zora Neale Hurston House. St. Lucie. 1957, 113.

Retail and Wholesale

L.S. Pender General Store. Jackson. c. 1869, 62.
The Abbey (Thompson's General Store). Volusia.
   c. 1875, 124.
Evinston Community Store and Post Office. Alachua.
   1883–1884, 1.
Bradley's Country Store Complex. Leon. 1893-1970, 74.
Palm Beach Mercantile Company. Palm Beach. c. 1902,
   94.
Stranahan House (The Pioneer House). Broward. 1902,
   12.
Hatch's Department Store. Palm Beach. 1903, 93.
E. R. Meres Sponge Packing House. Pinellas. c. 1905,
   101.
Baird Hardware Company Warehouse. Alachua.
   c. 1910, 1.
Townsend Building. Union. c. 1910, 124.
St. James Building (Cohen Bros. Department Store).
   Duval. 1911, 40.
William Anderson General Merchandise Store. Dade.
   1912, 23.
Punta Gorda Ice Plant. Charlotte. 1913, 14.

Cox Furniture Warehouse. Alachua. 1914, 2.
Ted Smallwood Store. Collier. 1917, 18.
Thompson Fish House, Turtle Cannery and Kraals.
    Monroe. 1918–1944, 83.
Dormitories and Ice Houses Associated with the
    Fishing Industry. Lee. 1920–1945, 69.
West Coast Fishing Company Residential Cabin, Willis
    Fish Cabin and Icing Station. Charlotte. 1920–1930,
    14.
Via Mizner. Palm Beach. 1923, 1925, 93.
The Village Store. Duval. 1923–1938, 41.
Ryan and Company Lumber Yard. Orange. 1924, 87.
Buckman and Ulmer Building. Duval. 1925, 35.
J & S Building. Dade. 1925, 27.
Studebaker Building. Pinellas. 1925, 99.
Florida Power and Light Company Ice Plant. Brevard.
    1927, 8.
Sponge Diving Boats. Pinellas. 1927–1941, 101.
Cap's Place (Club Unique). Broward. 1928, 12.
S.H. Kress and Company Building. Hillsborough.
    1929, 57.
Star Garage. Alachua. 1931, 3.
Crystal Ice Company Building. Escambia. c. 1932, 43.
S.H. Kress Building. Sarasota. 1932, 118.
S.H. Kress and Company Building. Volusia. 1932, 125.
Walgreen Drug Store. Dade. 1936, 32.
Atlantic Gas Station. Dade. 1937, 24.
S & S Sandwich Shop. Dade. 1938, 30.

Science and the Environment

John Pennekamp Coral Reef State Park and Reserve.
    Monroe. A.D. 1700–A.D. 1900, 81.
Indian Key. Monroe. 1825, 83.
Pelican Island National Wildlife Refuge. Indian River.
    1903, 61.
Bat Tower. Monroe. 1929, 84.
Marine Studios (Marineland). Flagler. 1937, 48.
Cape Canaveral Air Force Station Launch Pads and
    Control. Brevard. 1950, 8.
Launch Complex 39. Brevard. 1968, 11.

Transportation

John Pennekamp Coral Reef State Park and Reserve.
    Monroe. c. 1700, 81.
Spanish Fleet Survivors and Salvors Camp Site. Indian
    River. 1715, 61.
San Jose Shipwreck Site. Monroe. 1733, 84.
San Felipe Shipwreck. Monroe. 1769, 81.
Cape Florida Lighthouse. Dade. 1825+, 25.
Indian Key. Monroe. 1825, 83.
St. Marks Lighthouse. Wakulla. 1829, 1841, 131.
Old Haulover Canal. Brevard. 1843, 9.
Cape St. George Lighthouse. Franklin. 1852, 49.
Carysfort Lighthouse. Monroe. 1852, 81.
Sand Key Lighthouse. Monroe. 1853, 83.

Jupiter Inlet Lighthouse. Palm Beach. 1854, 91.
Lloyd Railroad Depot. Jefferson. c. 1858, 64.
Old St. Johns Lighthouse. Duval. 1858, 43.
Pensacola Lighthouse and Keeper's Quarters.
    Escambia. 1859, 46.
St. Augustine Lighthouse and Keeper's Quarters. St.
    Johns. 1871, 111.
San Jose Estates Gatehouse. Duval. 1873, 40.
House of Refuge at Gilbert's Bar. Martin. 1876, 54.
Sanibel Lighthouse and Keeper's Quarters. Lee. 1884,
    69.
Ponce de Leon Inlet Lighthouse. Volusia. 1887, 130.
Melbourne Beach Pier. Brevard. 1888–1889, 9.
Old Orlando Railroad Depot. Orange. 1889, 88.
Boca Grande Lighthouse. Lee. 1890, 67.
Crooked River Lighthouse. Franklin. 1895, 48.
Jacksonville Terminal Complex. Duval. 1897, 1919, 37.
L and N Marine Terminal Building. Escambia. 1902+,
    44.
Union Depot and Atlantic Coast Line Freight Station.
    Suwannee. 1903, 1909, 123.
Vero Beach (FEC) Railroad Station. Indian River. 1903,
    62.
Florida Pioneer Museum. Dade. 1904, 23.
I. and E. Greenwald Steam Engine No. 1058. Dade.
    1906, 27.
Hillsboro Inlet Light Station. Broward. 1907, 13.
Plant City Union Depot. Hillsborough. 1908–1909, 55.
Union Depot. Putnam. 1908, 107.
Charlotte Harbor and Northern Railway Depot. Lee.
    1909, 67.
Louisville and Nashville Depot. Santa Rosa. 1909, 114.
African Queen. Monroe. c. 1912, 81.
L and N Passenger Station and Express Office.
    Escambia. 1912, 45.
Overseas Highway and Railway Bridges. Monroe.
    1912+, 81.
Union Railroad Station. Hillsborough. 1912, 60.
Old Mount Dora ACL Railroad Station. Lake. 1915, 66.
Apopka Seaboard Air Line Railway Depot. Orange.
    1918, 86.
Florida State Road No. 1. Santa Rosa. 1921, 114.
Florida East Coast Railway Locomotive No. 153. Dade.
    1922, 26.
Old Seaboard Air Line Depot. Highlands. 1924, 53.
Cape Florida Lighthouse. Dade. 1925, 25.
Douglas Entrance (La Puerta del Sol). Dade. 1925, 22.
Entrance to Central Miami. Dade. 1925, 26.
Seaboard Coast Line Railway Passenger Station. Palm
    Beach. 1925, 95.
Bridge of Lions. St. Johns. 1926, 108.
Lake Mirror Promenade. Polk. 1926, 104.
Los Robles Gate. Leon. 1926, 72.
Old Lake Placid ACL Railroad Depot. Highlands. 1926,
    52.
Old Seaboard Air Line Railroad Station. Broward. 1926,
    12.

Seaboard Coast Line Railroad Depot. Collier. 1926, 19.

Venetian Causeway. Dade. 1926, 32.

Seaboard Air Line Railway Station. Palm Beach. 1927, 91.

Atlantic Coast line Railroad Depot. Polk. 1928, 104.

Punta Gorda Atlantic Coast Line Depot. Charlotte. 1928, 14.

U.S. Car No. 1. Dade. 1928, 31.

Florida East Coast Railway Passenger Station. Palm Beach. 1930, 90.

Pan Arnerican Seaplane Base and Terminal Building. Dade. 1930–1938, 21.

Bethune Blackwater Schooner. Santa Rosa. date unknown, 113.

Districts and Areas

Thomas Creek Archaeological District. Santa Rosa. c. 8000 B.C.– early 19th century, 113.

Bowers Bluff Middens Archaeological District. Lake. 2000 B.C.–300 B.C., 65.

Twin Mounds Archaeological District. Orange. 2000 B.C.–A.D. 1565, 89.

Upper Tampa Archaeological District. Hillsborough. 1000 B.C.–A.D. 1400, 60.

Jupiter Inlet Historic and Archaeological Site. Palm Beach. 500 B.C.–19th century, 91.

Big Mound Key/Boggess Ridge Archaelogical District. Charlotte. A.D. 400, 14.

Wakulla Springs Archaeological and Historic District. Wakulla. Prehistoric–1930s, 131.

Offshore Reefs Archaeological District. Dade. Colonial Period to late 19th century, 24.

St. Augustine Historic District. St. Johns. 1600–1900, 110.

Fort Barrancas Historic District. Escambia. 17th–19th century, 44.

Pensacola Historic District. Escambia. 18th century–19th century, 45.

Micanopy Historic District. Alachua. 1776–1930, 6.

Calhoun Street Historic District. Leon. early 19th century, 70.

Park Avenue Historic District. Leon. early 19th century, 73.

Old Town Fernandina Historic Site. Nassau. 1811–1821, 85.

Key West Historic District. Monroe. 1822–1920, 82.

Newnansville Town Site. Alachua. 1824–1890, 1.

Pensacola Naval Air Station Historic District. Escambia. 1824–1899, 46.

Monticello Historic District. Jefferson. 1828–c. 1900, 64.

Perdido Key Historic District. Escambia. 1828–1940, 47.

Apalachicola Historic District. Franklin. 1835–c. 1900, 48.

Middleburg Historic District. Clay. 1835–1912, 17.

Abbott Tract Historic District. St. Johns. 1838–1930, 108.

Cedar Key Historic and Archaeological District. Levy. 1839–1920, 75.

Model Land Company Historic District. St. Johns. 1839–1930, 110.

Bagdad Village Historic District. Santa Rosa. 1840–1930, 113.

Fernandina Beach Historic District. Nassau. c. 1840 , 85.

Lloyd Historic District. Jefferson. c. 1840–1920, 64.

Milton Historic District. Santa Rosa. 1840–1930, 114.

Palatka North Historic District. Putnam. 1840–1931, 107.

Quincy Historic District. Gadsden. 1840s–1910, 50.

Braden Castle Park Historic District. Manatee. 1850, 1924–1929, 76.

St. Lucie Village Historic District. St. Lucie. 1850–1928, 113.

Palatka South Historic District. Putnam. 1852–1930, 107.

Call Street Historic District. Bradford. 1857, 7.

Lake Isabella Historic Residential District. Columbia. 1866–1940, 20.

Southeast Gainesville Residential District. Alachua. 1867–1934, 3.

Green Cove Springs Historic District. Clay. 1869–1938, 16.

Lincolnville Historic District. St. Johns. 1870–1930, 109.

North Hill Preservation District. Escambia. 1870–1930s, 45.

Riverside Historic District. Duval. 1871, 40.

Northeast Gainesville Residential District. Alachua. 1875–1920, 3.

Pleasant Street Historic District. Alachua. 1875–1935, 3.

South Beach Street Historic District. Volusia. 1876–1938, 125.

Melrose Historic District. Alachua. 1877–1929, 5.

Tuscawilla Park Historic District. Marion. 1877–1930, 79.

Historic Winter Residences of Ormond Beach. Volusia. 1878, 129.

Longwood Historic District. Seminole. c. 1880–1926, 121.

Ocala Historic District. Marion. 1880–1930, 79.

Punta Gorda Residential District. Charlotte. 1880–1910, 15.

Rockledge Drive Residential District. 1880–1926. Brevard, 9.

Sanford Residential Historic District. Seminole. 1880, 122.

Tarpon Springs Historic District. Pinellas. 1881, 101.

Springfield Historic District. Duval. 1882–1930, 41.

Springfield Multiple Property Listing. Duval. 1882–1930, 41.

Barton Avenue Residential District. Brevard. 1884–1926, 9.

DeFuniak Springs Historic District. Walton. 1884–1940, 132.

Sarasota Multiple Resource Area. Sarasota. 1884–1935, 119.

Stetson University Campus Historic District. Volusia. 1884, 127.

West DeLand Residential District. Volusia. 1884–1942, 127.

High Springs Historic District. Alachua. 1885–1940, 5.

Lake Helen Historic District. Volusia. 1885–1940, 127.

McIntosh Historic District. Marion. 1885–1930, 78.

New Smyrna Beach Historic District. Volusia. 1885–1935, 128.

South Bartow Historic District. Polk. 1885–1941, 102.

Arcadia Historic District. De Soto. 1886–1930, 34.

Downtown DeLand Historic District. Volusia. 1886–1929, 126.

Hyde Park Historic District. Hillsborough. 1886–1933, 57.

Northeast Bartow Residential District. Polk. 1886–1925, 102.

Sanford Commercial District. Seminole. 1886, 122.

Bartow Downtown Commercial District. Polk. 1887–1935, 102.

"Boomtown" Historic District. Marion. 1887–1920, 78.

Naples Historic District. Collier. 1887–1937, 19.

South 3rd Street Historic District. Washington. 1887–1938, 133.

Fort Myers Downtown Commercial District. Lee. 1888–1939, 68.

Ybor City Historic District. 1888–early 20th century, 60.

Lake Eola Heights Historic District. Orange. 1890–1940, 88.

Palmetto Historic District. Manatee. 1890–1930, 77.

Pass-A-Grille Historic District. Pinellas. 1890–1920, 100.

Titusville Commercial District. Brevard. 1890–1930, 10.

City of Newberry Historic District. Alachua. 1894–1938 6.

Koreshan Unity Settlement Historic District. Lee. 1894, 67.

Southern Cassadaga Spiritualist Camp Meeting Association Historic District. 1895–1938, 124.

Tall Timbers Plantation District. c. 1895, 69.

West Tampa Historic District. Hillsborough. 1895–1925, 60.

North Plant City Residential District. Hillsborough. 1898–1942, 55.

Magnolia Heights Historic District. Leon. 1899–1934, 72.

Old Northwood Historic District. Palm Beach. late 19th–early 20th centuries, 94.

The Alger-Sullivan Company Residential Historic District. Escambia. 1900–1934, 43.

East Lake Morton Residential Area. Polk. 1900, 104.

South Lake Morton Historic District. Polk. 1900–1942, 104.

Downtown Plant City Commercial District. Hillsborough. 1901–1925, 54.

University of Florida Campus Historic District. Alachua. 1905–1925, 4.

Gamble Place Historic District. Volusia. 1907, 130.

South River Drive Historic District. Dade. 1908–1914, 30.

Avondale Historic District. Duval. 1909–1936, 35.

Avon Park Historic District. Highlands. 1912–1935, 52.

Pigeon Key Historic District. Monroe. 1912, 84.

Downtown Haines City Commercial District. Polk. 1913, 103.

Lake Wales Commercial Historic District. Polk. 1913–1928, 105.

Harbor Oaks Residential District. Pinellas. 1914–1937, 95.

Lake Wales Multiple Property Group. Polk. 1914, 105.

Fort White Public School Historic District. Columbia. 1915–1940, 19.

Northwest Historic District. Palm Beach. 1915–1941, 94.

Eagle Point Historic District. Sarasota. 1916, 120.

Sebring Downtown Historic District. Highlands. 1916, 53.

Mountain Lake Estates Historic District. Polk. 1920s+, 106.

Springfield Multiple Property Listing. Duval. 1920s, 41.

Caples'-Ringlings' Estates Historic District. Sarasota. c. 1920, 116.

Miami Beach Architectural District. Dade. 1920–1940, 32.

Bay Shore Historic District. Dade. 1922–1941, 24.

Beacon Hill/Alta Vista Residential District. Polk. 1923, 103.

El Pino Parque Historic District. Volusia. 1923–1936, 124.

Burns Court Historic District. Sarasota. 1924–1925, 116.

Country Club Estates Thematic Resource Area. Dade. 1924, 33.

Valencia Subdivision Residential Area. Brevard, 1924–1926, 9.

Armada Road Multi-Family District. Sarasota. 1925–1928, 120.

Davis Island Multiple Property Listing. Hillsborough. 1925–1932, 56.

Englewood Historic District. Sarasota. 1925–1928, 120.

Miami Shores Thematic Resource Region. Dade. 1925, 33.

Opa-locka Thematic Resource Area. Dade. 1925–1928, 34.

San Jose Estates Thematic Resource Area. Duval. 1925–1926, 40.

Venezia Park Historic District. Sarasota. 1925–1928, 121.

Venice Multiple Property Group. Sarasota. 1925–1927, 121.

Whitfield Estates Broughton Street Historic District. Manatee. 1925–1943, 77.

Barton Avenue Residential District. Brevard. 1926, 9.

Rigby's "La Plaza" Historic District. Sarasota. 1926, 118.

MacFarlane Homestead Historic District. Dade. 1930–1940, 22.

Florida Southern College Architectural District. Polk. 1937–1955, 104.